Case Studies in e-Government

Edited by

Frank Bannister

Case Studies in e-government
Volume One
First published: March 2012

ISBN: 978-1-908272-33-1

Note to readers.
Some papers have been written by authors who use the American form of spelling and some use the British. These two different approaches have been left unchanged.

Published by: Academic Publishing International Limited, Reading, RG4 9AY, United Kingdom, info@academic-publishing.org
Printed by Good News Digital Books

Available from www.academic-bookshop.com

Contents

List of Contributors

Mohammed Arif, *School of Built Environment, University of Salford, Manchester, UK*
Mehdi Asgarkhani, *Faculty of Commerce, C.P.I.T., Christchurch, New Zealand*
Albert Boonstra, *University of Groningen, The Netherlands*
Akemi Takeoka Chatfield, *University of Wollongong, New south Wales, Australia*
Regina Connolly, *Dublin City University, Ireland*
Karin Furuli, *Sogn og Fjordane University College, Norway*
Gemma Gibert i Font, *Town Hall of Sant Andreu de Llavaneres, Catalonia, Spain*
David Griffin, *Leeds Metropolitan University, UK*
Kerstin Grundén, *University West, Trollhättan, Sweden*
Edward Halpin, *Leeds Metropolitan University, UK*
Paul Jaeger, *University of Maryland, USA*
Sigrun Kongsrud, *Norway.no, Leikanger, Norway*
Miriam Matteson, *University of Maryland, USA*
Janice C. Sipior, *Villanova University, USA*
Henk Sol, *University of Groningen, The Netherlands*
Philippa Trevorrow, *Leeds Metropolitan University, UK*
Jim Yonazi, *University of Groningen, The Netherlands*
Burke T. Ward, *Villanova University, USA*

About the editor

Dr Frank Bannister is an Associate Professor of Information Systems and Head of the Information Systems Department in Trinity College, Dublin. His main areas of specialization are electronic government, information systems value and privacy, risk and trust in on-line environments. He is one of the founders and remains the editor of the Electronic Journal of e-Government and was a founder, and for a time co-editor, of the Electronic Journal of Information Systems Evaluation. He is on the boards of a number of journals including Government Information Quarterly and Information Polity. He is a Fellow of the Institute of Management Consultants in Ireland, a Fellow of the Irish Computer Society, a Fellow of Trinity College, Dublin and a Chartered Engineer. He holds a MA, MusB, MSc, CDipAF and PhD.

Introduction to Case Studies in e-Government

Since my first experience, as a fairly mature doctoral student, of the ubiquitous PhD symposium, I have sat through quite a number of presentations by senior academics, often editors (or more grandly editors-in-chief), on how to get published in the best journals. The script is always pretty much the same and runs something like this. There is a pecking order of paper types. At the front of the queue is the new theoretical contribution supported by fresh empirical evidence. This is the acme of academic research. A paper which uses new findings to challenge, or better still demolish, an established theory (a rare special case which is not normally mentioned in these talks) would probably come next. Close behind is the purely theoretical contribution, though this form may be more valued in some fields than in others. This is followed by papers with new empirical evidence which is used to modify or confirm some existing theory. Next in line come papers which make some contribution to methodology or technique. If done well, a paper of any of the above types is almost certain to be published.

Other types of paper are harder to get into print, but one tried and tested approach is the meta paper, i.e. a paper about other papers or research. This commonly takes the form of a review or critique of the literature or some defined subset of it though there are other varieties of this species to be found. I will return to this subject below. In a similar category come papers which review the state of the world or the art in some sphere; for example a paper about the state-of-the-art in e-voting technology or a summary of interoperability standards. These are unlikely to be accepted unless they are both exceptionally good and comprehensive. Beyond these there are descriptive papers which provide an account of, for example, an implementation project or a system. Most editors will reject this type of paper unless it has an unusual angle that they think will interest their readers. At the bottom of the heap are papers which are little more than opinion pieces. These are almost never published except by invitation.

Literature reviews are a rather special case. While literature reviews are not highly regarded as research, they have the virtue of often being highly cited and all editors like to have highly cited articles in their journals as, inter alia, it increases a journal's impact factor. A good literature review is comprehensive and up to the minute. At least that is the ideal. Unfortunately, in the world of e-government, though literature reviews have proved to be a popular art form, the comprehensive literature review is a pleasure we still await. To be fair, given that the e-government field produces somewhere between 500 and 1,000 academic articles or papers alone each year, a comprehensive review is probably unreasonable to expect. On the other hand, partial reviews or analyses of the e-government literature abound. In the past decade studies of this nature have been published by Grönlund (twice), Norris & Moon, Scholl, Yildz and Heeks & Baildur amongst others. I must put my own hands up here and admit that I too have contributed to this list with a review in 2010 of papers presented in the first nine years of the European Conference on e-Government. Incidentally, and speaking from personal experience, whether or not this is 'real' research, preparing such papers is hard work!

So what has this to do with descriptive case studies?

To answer this question it is necessary to deconstruct the expression 'case study' just a little. The term case study covers a broad variety of academic activities, but it is useful to divide these into three categories. The first category is what might be called the research case study. This is where a formal case study methodology is used to develop or test theory in the textbook manner described by Yin and others. Such studies usually involve more than one case, though the single case study is not unknown. The second category of case study is the teaching case study in the Harvard Business School tradition. From time to time journals put out calls for such case studies and many lecturers find them a valuable contribution to pedagogy.

The third type of case study, the descriptive case study, falls somewhere in between these two. The purpose of such case studies may be neither to develop/apply theory nor to be used in the classroom (though they may be so employed). In the world of e-government research they typically describe an interesting application or project, though in some cases they may describe a government programme or even a national strategy. In a sense (and this is meant in the best possible way) they are the academic equivalent of high quality journalism. They describe in order to inform. They tell us that here is a novel application of technology or an innovative service that is technology enabled or a particular approach to a common problem or whatever. Some years ago when I was a member of a United Nations expert committee for the United Nations Public Administration Network (UNPAN) e-Government Readiness report, I urged UNPAN to go beyond just benchmarking and include in their biennial report a number of examples from around the world of successful applications or good practice in e-government. I felt, and still do, that these might contribute as much to developing e-government world-wide as any set of metrics.

Most of our most useful and practical learning in life is by copying what others do. In my 16 years as an international IT consultant I barely looked at an academic publication. When, after becoming an academic in the mid 1990s, I started to read the information systems 'literature' I was often underwhelmed, not to say surprised, to find that it mostly told me things that I already knew and in many cases things that I had known for well over a decade. In my previous life, while there was plenty of formal training, you learned most of what you knew on-the-job and/or from colleagues and clients not to mention from war stories, company lore and the school of hard knocks. You discussed your work with colleagues and vice versa around the water cooler or (preferably) the beer spigot. In this way knowledge grew and was spread around. The descriptive case study is in this tradition of knowledge management and dissemination. We learn from it by seeing how other people do things and do them well (or occasionally badly). How they solved a problem. How they managed a crisis. How they came up with a new idea. Of course all of this can be embedded in a theory or two if that is what it takes to get published, but often in such publications it is the case itself that is of greatest interest and it is the description of the case itself from which we learn most.

Which brings me full circle back to the aforementioned literature reviews. Most of the reviews referred to above note that the descriptive case study is by far the commonest type of e-government publication. While some authors are happy simply to observe this fact and move on, other authors (no names, but you can look up the originals if you wish) complain that the descriptive case study is a lower form of research life; indeed, in the view of some academics, unless a paper contributes something to theory it is not really research at all. Theory is, of course, important and central to the academy, but it is not the be-all and end-all of research. If every journal and conference were to refuse to publish anything that did not contain a worthwhile contribution to theory, the number of both would shrink rapidly and drastically. There is only so much new theory out there and there is even less of it that is worth knowing. Research that investigates and describes practice in a rigorous and informative manner will always be of value in its own right and, being blunt, is often more useful to both academics and practitioners than abstruse and hard to operationalise theoretical concepts.

Collectively these case studies contain a wealth of useful knowledge and valuable insight; knowledge and insight that are applicable in and adaptable to a wide range of other countries and contexts. Between them they cover nine different countries and 11 diverse aspects of contemporary e-government. They all reward study.

Frank Bannister
Trintiy College Dublin
Ireland

Customer Orientation in e-Government Project Management: a Case Study

Mohammed Arif
School of Built Environment, University of Salford, Manchester, UK
Originally published in EJEG (2008) Volume 6 Issue 1.

The case studies in this book all fall into both either the research or the descriptive category. Mohammed Arif describes how Dubai Municipality used an innovative approach to project management to achieve better customer orientation and understanding in the dissemination of public information (or intelligence as he calls it). This approach is based on work by Joworski and Kohli. Arif describes four major roles in this system. Of particular interest is the role of the Service Custodian (a nice concept), in effect a type of project manager whose responsibilities include post implementation follow up. The custodian is also the person that deals with client or user complaints or problems, thus adding the role of account executive to that of project manager. The system creates a powerful ownership role. The underlying structure which supports the custodian is designed, inter alia, to make the system highly responsive. The system does not wait for users to come to them with problems, but is proactive in ensuring that services and service levels are satisfied. However the same proactive approach has not been applied to intelligence dissemination, a problem currently being addressed. From this study is clear that Dubai's adoption of the Joworski and Kohli model has helped deliver considerable improvements in e-government services.

Abstract: Customer orientation is vital for success in today's competitive environment. Jaworski and Kohli (1993) proposed a model to measure customer orientation comprising three components: 1) intelligence generation; 2) intelligence dissemination; and 3) organization-wide responsiveness. This model has been applied in several sectors. This paper applies it to an e-Government organization of a municipality. To apply the model, semi-structured interviews were conducted in the organization. Some of the major findings were : 1) an absence of concurrency in the design process; 2) a lack of input in the technology selection; 3) an absence of a knowledge management system for sharing lessons learnt; 4) a reactive nature of the organization; 5) use of different personnel for design and troubleshooting; and 6) a lack of training and standardized procedures. This research accomplishes three major purposes. The first is to elucidate customer orientation, as presented in other disciplines, the second is to elucidate how elements of customer orientation relate to e-Government, and the third one is to demonstrate how customer orientation concepts can be used to suggest improvements in e-Government Project Management. All three purposes were achieved through the case study presented.

Keywords: e-government, IT project management, customer orientation

1. Introduction

e-Government initiatives worldwide have gained momentum in the past decade. Government agencies globally are trying to serve citizens through web interfaces, thus reducing or removing the need to visit brick and mortar facilities. However, this endeavour comes with challenges of its own. In an organization, prior to e-Government implementation, all the processes dealing with customers require their physical visit to the government agency (see figure 1). Different departments within the agency deal with the customers on an individual basis. Customer needs are addressed directly by the appropriate departments. However, after implementation of e-Government services, a buffer is created between the customers and the agency concerned. This buffer is the e-Government web interface (see figure 2). Although the customers and the government agency are actually farther apart, for the success of the initiative it is important that they appear to be closer to each other. In other words, customers need to feel that the web interface has added value by saving time and effort to perform a transaction, and the agency needs to realize that there is a cost saving associated with servicing the citizens online compared to a brick and mortar type of facility. In order to realize these two goals the e-Government department needs to effectively incorporate both customer and agency needs in the development of the web interface and associated process flows. Therefore, it is important that e-Government projects be customer oriented for the government agency and the end users. This customer orientation could mean an effective mechanism in order to ensure that development processes incorporate customer needs, an emphasis on usability, the incorporation of accessibility, the effective use of cultural markers. Each one of these areas is a separate research project. Therefore, for the purpose of this research efforts will be concentrated on analyzing the project management processes contributing to effectively incorporating customer needs into service design.

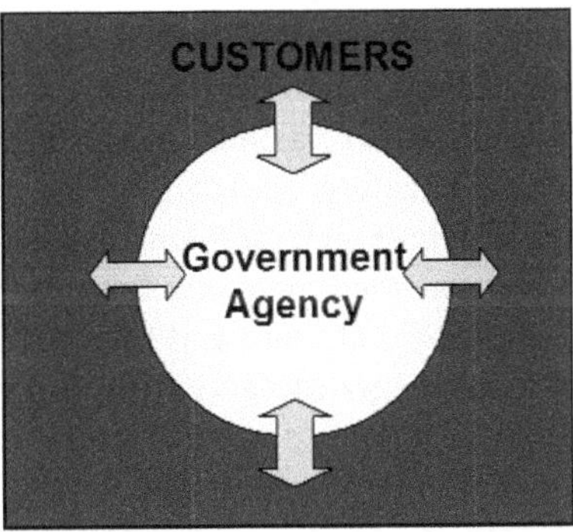

Figure 1: Agency-End User Interaction Prior to e-Government Implementation

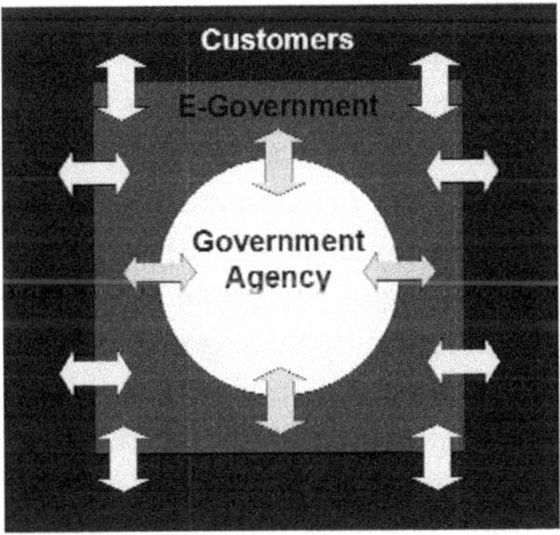

Figure 2: Agency-End User Interaction after e-Government Implementation

e-Government projects can be likened to any IT project and can draw on the lessons learnt from them. The following section presents a review of the literature in the area of risks and success factors in IT projects which can also be adopted by e-Government projects.

2. IT Project Management

IT departments in any organization occupy a significant position. However, over 60% of IT projects represent a failure in terms of exceeding the budget or deadlines, and also in terms of dissatisfied customers (Goepp et al., 2006). This underperformance represents a considerable but, to a large extent, avoidable loss of economic value (Sauer et al., 2001). e-Government projects face the same challenges as any other IT project. Literature is replete with research on the risks and challenges in IT projects of different kinds. Boehm (1991) classified software project risks into five categories: technological newness, application size, expertise, application complexity, and organizational environment. Kliem (2001) identified 38 risks in BPR projects and classified them into four categories: people, management, business, and technical. Ham and Huang (2006) as well as Wallace et al. (2004), have used a six category IT project classification that includes: user, requirement, project complexity, planning and control, team, and organizational environment. Addison (2003) highlights ten risky issues associated with e-Commerce projects: customer/user requirements issues, business and supply chain issues, methodology issues, strategic planning issues, management and user support issues, web page design issues, security issues, system integrity issues, staff issues, and technical environment issues. Mahaney and Lederer (2003), give four reasons for the failure of IT projects: the contract not being outcome based, ineffective monitoring, the failure of organizations to manage goals and conflicts, and the lack of application of regular task programmability techniques. Agarwal and Rathod (2006) point to the misalignment between the expectations of the customers and understanding of the producer (IT departments) as one of the major factors contributing to this high failure rate. King and Burgess (2006), highlight the interdepartmental and intradepartmental communication as a critical success factor in an Enterprise Resource Planning (ERP) implementation, a prevalent IT project for the past decade. Dhillon (2005) points to excessive importance on technological issues and very little to organizational issues as an important contributor towards IT failure. Procaccino et. al. (2005) rate customer satisfaction and user friendliness as key indicators of a successful IT project.

IT project management literature has also identified success factors for IT projects like: management of conflicts (Posner, 1986; Turner, 1993; Belassi and Tukel, 1996; and Wateridge, 1997); management of multifunctional teams (Kumar, 2002); good communication (Milis and Mercken, 2002); goal congruency (Clarke, 1999); teamwork (Milis and Mercken, 2002); good internal stakeholder relationship (Wilcocks, 1994); management involvement; and effective change management (Milis and Mercken, 2002).

Based on these recent findings it is important that, apart from technical competence, organizational aspects be also kept in mind while conducting IT projects. This paper presents a model that measures the organizational customer orientation of an e-Government implementation through a case study of a municipality.

3. Purpose of this paper

There are three purposes of this paper. The first purpose is to elucidate customer orientation as presented in literature from other disciplines. Second, this paper demonstrates how constructs of customer orientation relate to one another in the specific context of e-Government projects, which can also be adapted to other IT projects. Third, it demonstrates how the customer orientation concept might be used to suggest improvements to e-Government project management.

4. Customer Orientation

Customer orientation is not a new concept. Appiah-Adu and Singh (1998) have traced it as far back as 1954. In the past two decades several definitions of customer orientation have come up. Shapiro (1988) defines customer orientation as "The dissemination of information about customers throughout an organization, formulation of tactics and strategies to satisfy market needs inter-functionally and achievement of a sense of company-wide commitment to these plans". Joworski and Kohli (1990) define customer orientation as the degree to which customer information is collected and used in the business unit. Ruekert (1992) defines customer orientation as "the degree to which the organization obtains and uses information from customers, develops a strategy which will meet customer needs, and implements that strategy by being responsive to customers' needs and wants". Deshpande et al. (1993) define customer orientation as "The sets of beliefs that put the customer's interest first, while not excluding those of all other stakeholders such as owners, managers, employees, in order to develop long term profitable enterprise".

All these definitions concentrate on customer's needs and translate them into valuable outputs from producers. Jowroski and Kohli (1993) have taken the definition proposed by Jowroski and Kohli (1990) and developed a three element model of customer orientation. The proposed model measures customer orientation based on three elements: organization-wide generation, dissemination and the responsiveness of market intelligence. This model has been used by several researchers in various applications and sectors such as construction (Dulaimi, 2005), supply chain (Saiguaw et al, 1998), new product development (Kahn, 2001), hospitality and tourism (Sin et al, 2005, and Qu et al, 2005), manufacturing (Singh and Ranchodd, 2004), and non-profit service sector (Gainer, B., and Padanyi, P., 2005). Due to its simplicity, ease of application, prevalent use in past research and versatility of adoption in different sectors, this model was chosen for application in this research.

5. The Model

The case considered for this paper involves an e-Government organization which is responsible for designing, coding and maintaining the web interface as well as the back-end software functions of a municipality. It is described in more detail in the next section. The model proposed by Jaworski and Kohli (1993) has three components: 1) intelligence generation; 2) intelligence dissemination; and 3) organization-wide responsiveness. Dulaimi (2005) argues that if this model is applied to an organization, it should be able to effectively satisfy customer needs and expectations.

Intelligence generation in this model, for the case to be considered, means the generation of customer needs before the design of e-services. The effectiveness of the intelligence generation is affected by who collects the intelligence, how the intelligence is gathered, how often it is collected and the mechanism for revision as well as validation.

Intelligence dissemination in an organization can be evaluated by analyzing the process of distribution of knowledge within the organization. In the case of an e-Government organization, it is essential to collect information on customer needs and distribute it within the organization so system, webpage, and database design as well as other related technical operations can be performed.

Organization-wide responsiveness can be assessed by evaluating the product/service design process. How does the design take place, how much is the customer involved, and how often does the design need modification after the product is launched?

6. The Case

Dubai is a city kingdom located on the inlet of the Persian Gulf. It is a major port and commercial center of the Middle East, and the principal shipping, trading, and communications hub of the Persian Gulf region. Sometimes referred to as "the Venice of the Gulf," Dubai is a bustling, cosmopolitan city and a popular tourist destination. Dubai was founded as a small fishing village at the end of the 18th century. After the discovery of major oil and gas reserves in the 1960s, Dubai became a major port and a wealthy commercial town by the end of 20th century. Dubai's population is estimated to have reached 857,233. Only 19% of this population comprises the natives and the remaining 81% are expatriates who have come here seeking employment opportunities.

Dubai Municipality (DM) is regarded as one of the largest establishments in Dubai, in terms of the number of people it employs, the volume of services it provides to the public and the number of projects it executes. The municipality was established in the 1940s with three employees and housed in a one room office. However, it was not until 1965 that DM came into being officially. The municipality has continued its steady growth since its inception and now employs more than 11600 people.

In the year 2001, DM embarked on a major e-Government implementation triggered by a wider, Dubai wide government initiative to automate all government functions. The vision for the municipality e-services as defined by the ruler to use the "e-Government solution as the primary delivery channel to provide a single, easy, integrated, and reliable means of access to municipal information and services in order to continuously improve the quality of services provided for the residents, businesses, and partners, reduce internal operational overheads, enhance revenues, and promote Dubai's image as a commercial and tourism hub in the Gulf region." All government departments were given a deadline to put 90% of their services online by the year 2007.

This vision for e-Government transformed the priority of the municipality to act as a customer oriented, agile and accountable entity, rather than being a public bureaucratic organization. This was a major paradigm shift and required detailed planning by top management.

7. The Organisation

The IT department in the municipality owns the e-Government initiative. It is important that the organizational structure of this department be discussed in detail. Figure 3 represents the organizational structure of the IT department. This department performs operational tasks, provides beneficiaries support, helps in the planning and development of information systems, undertakes computer-related tasks and data processing, ensuring security. It also provides staff with equipment, programs and necessary telecommunication networks and supplies. It links all facilities and websites of the Municipality with e-Government websites and the information telecommunication network with standard specifications and protection against various risks.

Within the IT department the e-Government section has three main responsibilities: 1) To supervise, upgrade, monitor and support all computer systems of e-Government, whether externally purchased or internally developed; 2) To prepare and identify the technical criteria and standards related to the development of e-Government, databases and programming languages and implement them in the IT Department; and 3) To study and analyze e-Government systems, to determine their creation methods, to prepare the technical specifications of systems required to be developed and to prepare tenders for the system projects. These responsibilities are undertaken by three major units within e-Government. The first unit deals with the planning and design of e-Government services, the second deals with development of websites and databases and the third deals with post implementation support.

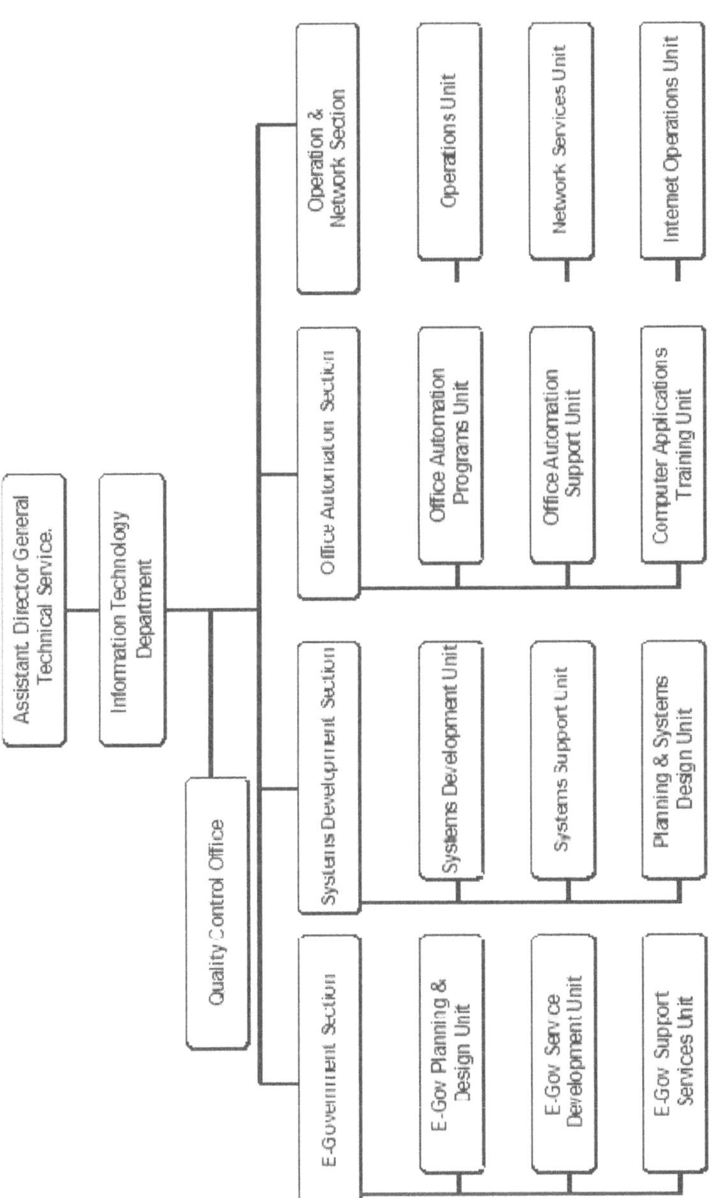

Figure 3: Organizational Structure of IT Department

The systems development section of the IT department has four major functions: 1) To propose long, medium and short term development plans for the IT systems; 2) To prepare and determine the technical criteria and standards for the development of systems, databases and programming languages, and to undertake the responsibility of implementing the same in the IT Department; 3) To perform feasibility studies of the systems which various regulatory units at the municipality are considering implementing, and to make the appropriate decision; and 4) To provide technical assistance and necessary training for the systems used or to be used at the municipality.

The office automation section of the IT department has three major functions: 1) To prepare and determine requirements of office automation programs, to perform their feasibility studies and prepare recommendations; 2) To prepare tenders and technical specifications of office programs and equipment, to communicate with companies and suppliers to evaluate submitted tenders, and to prepare the joint recommendations in coordination with the concerned regulatory units; and 3) To supervise the training of all computer users in the use of various office programs, Internet browsing, e-mail, web-mail and security aspects.

The operations and network service department within the IT department has three major functions: 1) To operate and maintain internal and external computer network and connection lines and circles; 2) To propose and execute procedures and regulations related to the security and confidentiality of information network, databases, information storage and back up; and 3) To install, transfer and maintain terminal monitor equipment, printers and connection equipment.

Each element of the IT department performs a distinct function. For the purpose of this study only the e-Government section of the IT department was considered, as that section was the only section within the IT department which produced service interfaces that were used directly by outside customers.

8. e-Government Roles

Within e-Government there are four major roles played by employees: 1) Service Custodians; 2) Business Analysts; 3) Systems Analysts and 4) Programmers.

The service custodian is in charge of a service. The municipality automates its services in phases. When a particular service is planned to be automated and is going online, a custodian is appointed for that service. The job of the service custodian is to manage the entire process of converting the service to an online service and manage any proposed changes, post-implementation.

Business analysts are responsible for documenting the process flows prior to system design and coding. Once a decision is made to automate a service and a service custodian is assigned to it, the business analyst starts the job of discussing with the relevant department within the municipality who has the ownership of the service. Based on that input the process flow is designed by the business analyst and handed over to the custodian.

Systems analysts start working after the business analyst has documented the process flow. Systems analysts are responsible for creating the data flow diagrams, entity relationship diagrams and UML diagrams. Once the system design is complete, coding of the system starts.

Programmers are involved in coding the entire service during the initial development and modifying the codes post-implementation, if required.

e-Government currently has six custodians, three business analysts, three systems analysts and two programmers on the staff.

9. e-Government Processes

e-Government has two major responsibilities: 1) Design and launch of new services online and 2) Maintaining all the e-services that have already been launched.

Figure 4 summarizes the service design process. Once the decision to go online is made, a custodian is appointed. The business analyst under the supervision of the custodian designs the process flow for the service. During this design, the business analyst works very closely with the municipal department(s) concerned. Once the process flow is designed and approved, a systems analyst is appointed to undertake the system and the database design. After the system design is complete, coding starts. Coding can be done either internally by a programmer or can be outsourced to an external vendor. Once coding is complete, the systems analyst evaluates and approves it and it then goes for the approval of the custodian. Once that approval is obtained the service goes online.

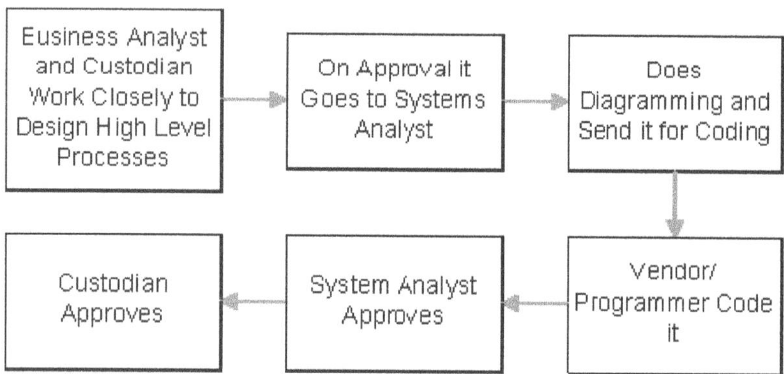

Figure 4: Service design process

Figure 5 depicts the service maintenance process. Once a service is launched both the external users and the relevant municipal department(s) can contact a help desk if they have a problem with any part of the service.

Once the problem is reported the service custodian is notified. The service custodian decides if the problem is technical or not. If the problem relates to the process then the municipal department concerned, is notified and once their change is approved by the service custodian the problem is rectified. If the problem is technical in nature then the systems analyst is notified. The systems analyst makes the decision whether there is any need for coding. If there is a need for coding then the programmer performs the coding and the changes are implemented after the approval of the service custodian. If no coding is needed, then the systems analyst makes the necessary adjustments and sends the changes for the approval of the service custodian.

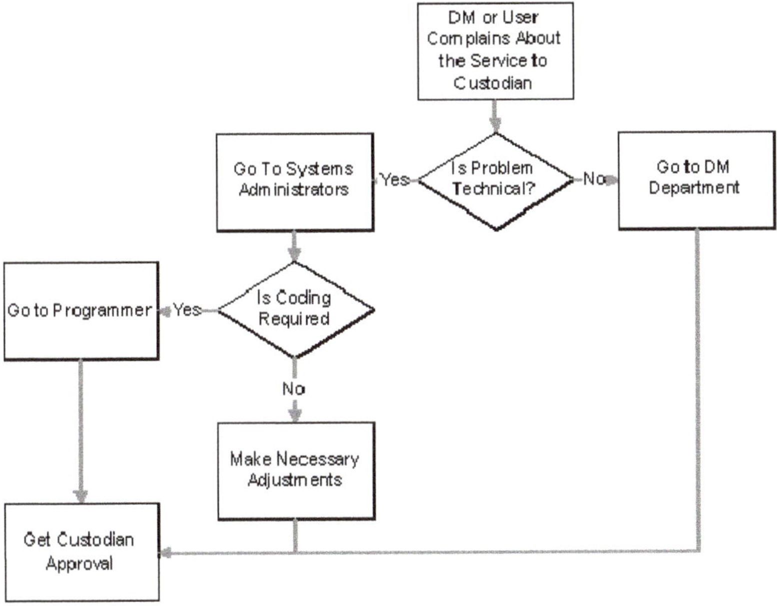

Figure 5: Service maintenance process

9.1. The Methodology

Owing to the small number of employees, it was not possible to conduct a survey and then perform quantitative analysis on the data. This led to the choice of interviews as the method for collecting data. The scope of this study covered two major customer groups, the first being DM, and the second being citizens or end-users. The interviews were conducted in a semi-structured format where participants were asked about the intelligence generation, intelligence dissemination and responsiveness, both for DM and the end-users. Two members from each type of roles were selected for interview. In addition to that, two managers were also selected. Interviews were conducted in the offices of the interviewees and lasted between 45 minutes and an hour. The purpose of this research was explained to the participants and all were promised anonymity. They were asked to support their answers in the interview with specific instances or cases, if possible.

10. Analysis

This section is divided into three parts, each part corresponding to a component of the customer orientation model.

10.1. Intelligence Generation

Intelligence generation, when it comes to DM is currently quite extensive. Service custodians and business analysts spend a considerable amount of time mapping the processes and identifying their needs. However, systems analysts and programmers do not have access to DM. They have to rely primarily on documentation provided to them by service custodians and business analysts, neither of whom have any IT background. This lack of direct contact can result in multiple iterations before a product is deemed acceptable by DM. One of the programmers interviewed described a post-implementation change project where he was at his sixth iteration and still not sure if this product would be satisfactory to the DM.

The intelligence generation for end-user needs is a relatively weaker area for a project. It is not standard practice to talk to end-users for every service being developed. On quite a few occasions this input is primarily driven by the DM department concerned which communicates to the e-Government department its perceptions of end-user needs. On some service development projects, brainstorming sessions and interviews were conducted. However, as in the case of DM intelligence generation above, all the contact currently with the end-user is done by service custodians and business analysts. The technical members of the team have no direct contact with the end-users, and have to rely primarily on the documentation of service custodians and business analysts. During the interviews the systems analysts and the programmers also pointed out that this was a frequent problem in post-implementation support as well. A lot of post-implementation changes had to go through multiple iterations, due to lack of direct contact between the complainant and the technical staff.

Currently, whatever intelligence is being generated is specific to the services being designed. No proactive intelligence about issues like perceptions and usability are being tracked. The municipality tracks two major matrices; adoption rate and the proportion of revenue generated through online versus over-the-counter transactions. Both these matrices are made available to the service custodians. However, neither of them could highlight issues like user satisfaction by changing the interface from an over-the-counter brick and mortar experience to online experience. The municipality is aware of this issue but at the moment the effort is concentrated on meeting the deadline for transferring 90% services online by 2007. The proactive intelligence generation methodology will be devised after this target has been achieved.

10.2. Intelligence Dissemination

Currently, the intelligence dissemination process is sequential. Service custodians and business analysts have the most direct contact with DM and in some cases, end-users. However, the systems analysts and programmers often feel isolated and have to rely primarily on the documentation provided to them. One more issue with this sequential nature of the process is simply the expertise. Currently, all service custodians and business analysts come from business administration backgrounds, the systems analysts come from MIS backgrounds and the programmers are computer scientists. Due to this difference in expertise it is important that the systems analysts as well as the programmers be involved in the initial process design, since that can potentially have impact on data structures, user interfaces and codes. This lack of concurrency has resulted in multiple iterations in the service design process and delays in implementation.

The second issue highlighted under the intelligence dissemination was the lack of uniformity in ways of disseminating intelligence. Even though some standard forms exist for documenting user requirements for systems analysts and programmers, they are often not used. Each business analyst and service custodian has their own format. Therefore, it is not surprising that programmers and systems analysts find it more convenient to work with some service custodians than others. As two managers pointed out, this is also due to lack of training and in some cases lack of standardized procedures. This is an area that is high on the list of to-do items on the coming year's strategic plan.

For intelligence dissemination one more issue that several interviewees pointed out was the absence of a platform or a knowledge management system where one could store lessons learnt on a project for future use. There is not even an informal mechanism for doing so. Everyone works in isolation, based on their personal knowledge and information on standard documents. This lack of knowledge sharing is counterproductive and results in the phenomenon popularly known as reinventing the wheel (Kulonda et al., 2003). The senior managers did agree that there is no such mechanism available for knowledge sharing however, one such initiative is under way that should be implemented within a year.

10.3. Responsiveness

For responsiveness, e-Government is a very reactive organization. As has been pointed out in the intelligence generation section, there is no contact between the e-Government and municipal departments or the end users unless a problem with a service is reported. In order to harness the improvement through end user feedback, a more proactive approach is needed for every service that can potentially result in incremental improvements.

The other issue is with the team structure for responding to complaints either by end users or the department in the municipality concerned. The only person who remains committed to a service is the service custodian. If some technical issue arises, then it is not necessary that the service custodian approach the same systems analyst or the programmer who has developed the service initially. This results in delay in responding to complaints. One way of addressing this issue is by keeping the entire team constant for post-implementation support. The only time this rule should be violated is when someone is on leave or has left the organization. The senior management did agree that the problem exists. Given the small size of the organization it is not an issue that can easily be resolved.

As was accepted by several participants during the interview, the responsiveness to DM complaints is considerably faster than to those of the end-users. This is primarily due to the close proximity with which e-Government works with DM compared to end-users. This proximity is due to the fact that they are physically located in the same general area and internal pressures are a lot higher from DM departments compared to end-users.

11. Summary and Discussion

Customer orientation has become a key element of organizational strategy (Dulaimi, 2005). Jaworski and Kohli (1993) proposed a model to measure customer orientation. This model has three components: 1) Intelligence generation; 2) Intelligence dissemination; and 3) Organization-wide responsiveness. The model has been used in several sectors and this paper applies the model to an IT organization dealing with the development of the e-Government interface of a municipality. Applications like e-Government or e-Commerce are important avenues for the application of this model because on implementation of the e-Government/e-Commerce initiative a buffer is created between the producer and the consumer, the buffer of the web interface. This buffer actually moves the producer and consumer farther apart, yet its function is to make them appear closer than before. Therefore it is important that any organization supporting an e-Government/e-Commerce initiative be customer oriented.

In this research the employees of the e-Government organization selected had four major roles: The service custodian who is responsible for the overall design, implementation and maintenance of any service that goes online, the business analyst who performs the business process analysis and gathers data on customer needs, the systems analyst who is responsible for system design, and the programmer who is responsible for coding.

In order to collect data, a semi-structured interview was conducted that involved two participants from each type of role and two managers. Based on the analysis of the data it was found that as far as intelligence generation is concerned, it is strong for DM but very weak for end-users. The intelligence generation is primarily a sequential process at the moment. Service custodians and business analysts are the only people dealing directly with DM or the end-users. This sequential nature of the process becomes even more of an issue because these groups of people do not have any programming or IT background. This lack of concurrency and lack of involvement of the systems analysts and programmers in intelligence generation often leads to rework. The emphasis on concurrency and having a multi-functional team at every stage is very important for IT projects like e-Government, a fact that has been identified quite extensively in IT project management literature as a success factor (Kumar, 2002; Milis and Mercken, 2002; Bai and Lee, 2003). Having concurrency in processes is a new paradigm for DM and they have not practiced it so far in any type of IT project. There is also a lack of proactive intelligence generation at the moment, due to the fact that currently the resources are concentrated primarily on meeting the 2007 deadline of putting 90% DM services online. Once most of the services are online then DM can concentrate on generating proactive intelligence on customer needs and modifying services as well as processes accordingly.

For intelligence dissemination, the sequential nature of the information transfer is an issue, the other one being the lack of standardized procedures being followed and forms being used. This points to an immediate need for the training of employees in order to ensure uniformity, a concept highlighted in IT project management literature quite often (Milis and Mercken, 2002). The emphasis on getting 90% services online has not left enough spare resources to concentrate on the development of standardized formats, forms and procedures. However, this practice needs to change and standardization should take place in all aspects of e-Government implementation. The last issue pointed out in the intelligence dissemination was the lack of knowledge management or a lessons learnt system where people can document lessons learnt that can be used for future projects. A platform like this has been identified as a key contributor to success for any IT/IS project (Pai, 2006). Discussions during the interview pointed out that most of the people interviewed were not familiar with the benefits of having a platform for sharing lessons learnt.

In the responsiveness area, it was found that the e-Government organization is a very reactive organization. The teams formed during the service design are dismantled as soon as the service is implemented and often new people have to get involved for post-implementation adjustments, thus increasing the learning curve involved with familiarization, thus the response time is delayed. This again is due to lack of resources at the moment and the emphasis on meeting the 2007 deadline. The last problem identified was the relatively faster response to DM related post-implementation issues compared to the end-user related issues. This is primarily due to physical proximity and a more diligent follow-up from the DM department that is affected by the service. There is also an increased sense of accountability towards internal departments compared to outside customers.

12. Concluding remarks

This paper had three stated objectives. The first one was to elucidate the concept of customer orientation as presented in literature from other areas. This was accomplished by choosing the Joworski and Kohli (1990) model and conducting a literature review on past work in several disciplines applying this model. The second and third purposes were to relate the constructs to an e-Government or IT project and see if application of this model can help suggest some improvements. Both these purposes were accomplished using the case of a municipal e-Government organization. The model provided an umbrella under which a wide array of issues such as communication, knowledge management, training, teamwork, and procedures could be analyzed, and areas of improvement highlighted.

References

Addison, T., (2003), "E-Commerce Project Development Risks: Evidence From A Delphi Survey", International Journal of Information Management, Vol. 23 No. 1, pp. 25-40.

Agarwal, N., and Rathod, U. 2006, "Defining 'Success' For Software Projects: An Exploratory Study", International Journal of Project Management, Vol. 24 No. 4, pp.358-370.

Appiah-Adu, K., and Singh, S., (1998), "Customer Orientation and Performance: A Study of SMEs", Management Decision, Vol. 36. No. 6, pp 385-394.

Bai, R.J., and Lee, G.G., (2003), "Organizational Factors Influencing the Quality of the IS/IT Strategic Planning Process", Industrial Management and Data Systems, Vol. 103 No. 8, pp. 622-632.

Belassi, W., and Tukel, O.I., (1996), "A Framework for Determining Critical Success/Failure Factors in Projects", International Journal of Project Management, Vol. 14 No. 2, pp. 141-151.

Boehm, B., (1991), "Software Risk Management: Principles and Practices", IEEE Software, Vol. 8 No.1, pp. 32-41.

Clarke, A., (1999), "A Practical Use of Key Success Factors to Improve the Effectiveness of Project Management", International Journal of Project Management, Vol. 17 No. 2, pp. 139-145.

Deshpande, R., Farley, J., and Webster, F., (1993), "Corporate Culture, Customer Orientation, and Innovativeness in Japanese Firms: A Quadrant Analysis", Journal of Marketing, Vol. 57, pp.23-37.

Dhillon, G., (2005), "Gaining Benefits From The IS/IT Implementation: Interpretations From Case Studies", International Journal of Information Management, Vol. 25 No. 4, pp. 502-515.

Dulaimi, M.F., (2005), "The Challenge Of Customer Orientation In The Construction Industry", Construction Innovation, Vol. 5 No. 1, pp. 3-12.

Gainer, B., and Padanyi, P., (2005), "The Relationship Between Market-Oriented Activities And Market-Oriented Culture: Implications For The Development Of Market Orientation In Non Profit Service Organization", Journal of Business Research, Vol. 58 No. 6, pp. 854-862.

Goepp, V., Kiefer, F., and Geiskopf, F., (2006), "Design Of Information System Architectures Using A Key-Problem Framework", Computers in Industry, Vol. 57 No. 2, pp. 189-200

Jaworski, B.J., and Kohli, A.K., (1993), "Market Orientation: Antecedents And Consequences", Journal of Marketing, Vol. 57 No. 1, pp. 53-70.

Kahn, K.B., (2001), "Market Orientation, Interdepartmental Integration And Product Development Performance", Journal of Product Innovation Management, Vol. 18 No. 3, pp. 314-323.

King, S.F., and Burgess, T.F., (2006), "Beyond Critical Success Factors: A Dynamic Model Of Enterprise System Innovation", International Journal of Information Management, Vol. 26 No. 1, pp. 59-69.

Kliem, R., (2001), "Risk Management for Business Process Reengineering Projects", Information Systems Management, Vol. 17 No. 4, pp. 71-73.

Kohli, A.K, and Jaworski, B.J., (1990), "Market Orientation: The Construct, Research Propositions And Managerial Implications", Journal of Marketing, Vol. 54 No. 1, pp. 1-18.

Kulonda, D.J., Arif, M., Luce, J., (2003), "Legacy Systems: Must History Repeat Itself?" Journal of Knowledge Management Practice, December, Vol. 4, Online Journal.

Kumar, R.L., (2002), "Managing Risks in IT Projects: An Options Perspective", Information and Management, Vol. 40 No. 1, pp. 63-74.

Mahaney, R.C., and Lederer, A.L., (2003), "Information Systems Project Management: An Agency Theory Interpretation", The Journal of Systems and Software, Vol. 68 No. 1, pp. 1-9.

Milis, K., and Mercken, R., (2002), "Success Factors Regarding the Implementation of ICT Investment Projects", International Journal of Production Economics, Vol. 80 No. 1, pp. 105-117.

Mullens, M. A., Arif, M., Armacost, R. L., Gawlik, T., and Hoekstra, R. L., (2005), "Axiomatic Based Decomposition for Conceptual Product Design", Production Operations Management, Vol. 14 No. 3 , pp. 286-300.

Narver, J.C., and Slater, S.F., (1990), "The Effect Of Market Orientation On Business Profitability", Journal of Marketing, Vol. 54 No. 4, pp. 20-35.

Pai, J.C., (2006), "An Empirical Study of the Relationship Between Knowledge Sharing and IS/IT Strategic Planning (ISSP)", Management Decision, Vol. 44 No.1, pp. 105-122.

Posner, B.Z., (1986), "What's All the Fighting About? Conflicts in Project Management", IEEE Transactions on Engineering Management, Vol. 33 No. 4, pp. 207-211.

Procaccino, J.D., Verner, J.M., Shelfer, K.M., and Gefen, D., (2005), "What Do Software Practitioners Really Think About Project Success: An Exploratory Study", The Journal of Systems and Software, Vol. 78 No. 3, pp. 194-203.

Qu, R., Ennew C., and Sinclair, M.Y., (2005), "The Impact Of Regulation And Ownership Structure On Market Orientation In The Tourism Industry In China", Tourism Management, Vol. 26 No. 8, pp. 939-950.

Ruekert, R., (1992), "Developing a Market Orientation: An Organizational Strategy Perspective", International Journal of Marketing, Vol. 9, pp.225-245.

Sauer, C., Liu, L., and Johnston. K., (2001), "Where Project Managers Are Kings", Project Management Journal, Vol. 32 No. 4, pp. 39-49.

Shapiro, B., (1988), "What the Hell is 'Market Oriented'?", Harvard Business Review, Vol. 66, pp. 19-25.

Siguaw, J., Simpson, P., and Baker, T., (1998), "Effects Of Supplier Market Orientation On Distributor Market Orientation And The Channel Relationship: The Distributor Perspective", Journal of Marketing, Vol. 62 No. 2, pp. 99-111.

Sin, L.Y.M., Tse, A.C.B., Heung, V.C.S., and Yim, F.H.K., (2005), "An Analysis Of The Relationship Between Market Orientation And Business Performance In The Hotel Industry", Hospitality Management, Vol. 24 No. 6, pp. 555-577.

Singh and Ranchodd, (2004), "Market Orientation And Customer Satisfaction: Evidence From British Machine Tool Industry", Industrial Marketing Management, Vol. 33 No. 2, pp. 135-144.

Slater, S.F., and Narver, J.C., (1994), "Market Orientation, Customer Value And Superior Performance", Business Horizons, Vol. 37 No. 2, pp. 22-27.

Standish Group International, Inc., (2004), 2004 Third Quarter Research Report.

Turner, J.R., (1993), The Handbook of Project-based Management, McGraw Hill, New York.

Wallace, L., Keil, M., and Rai, A., (2004), "Understanding Software Project Risk: A Cluster Analysis", Information and Management, Vol. 42 No. 2, pp. 115-125.

Wateridge, J., (1997), "Training for ICT Project Managers: A Way Forward", International Journal of Project Management, Vol. 15 No. 4, pp. 283-288.

Wilcocks, L., (1994), Information Management: the Evaluation of Information Systems Investments, Chapman and Hall, London.

The Effectiveness of E-Service in Local Government: A Case Study

Mehdi Asgarkhani
Faculty of Commerce, C.P.I.T., Christchurch, New Zealand
Originally published in EJEG (2006) Volume 3 Issue 4

In this paper Mehdi Asgarkhani describes how a local government authority in New Zealand assessed citizens' views of the effectiveness and success of its e-services. He discusses a number of conceptualizations of effectiveness and how it might be measured in online public services and democracy. After an extensive and informative discussion of a whole range of concepts and ideas surrounding e-effectiveness, Asgarkhani then examines how one local government authority in New Zealand went about measuring the effectiveness of its own services. This included looking at usage of its web services and using a survey to investigate how users judged those services. The Council also looked at the types of services that citizens would like to see, but which are not currently available. The list of concerns is illuminating with data security and confidentiality heading the list by a wide margin.

Abstract: E-technology has become a catalyst for enabling more effective government through better access to services and the democratic process. As public interest in the Internet and e-technology solutions continues to grow, there is an increasing expectation that they will be utilised in national and local governments for not only more efficient governance but also improving public access to information and services. This paper, based on a case study discusses some of the key aspects of electronic government and e-service. It examines the value and the effectiveness of e-services within the public sector with a focus on four specific facets of effectiveness: the view of management and ICT strategists; social, cultural and ethical implications; the implications of lack of access to ICT; and the customers'/citizens' view of the usefulness and success of e-service initiatives.

Keywords: E-Technologies, E-Service, E-Government, E-Readiness, Local Government

1. Introduction

The most prominent of the recent advancements in Information and Communications Technology (ICT) has been the emergence of the Internet, Web-based technologies (e-technologies) and global networked economies. Today, e-technologies play an increasingly significant role in our day-to-day lives. They have fundamentally transformed the technological, economical, political and social landscapes.

The competitive imperative of the private sector has driven businesses into the digital world. To deliver the products and/or services in a timely and cost effective manner, the private sector has had to increasingly streamline business processes. As a result, the private sector has steadily set higher standards of service (through the application of e-business and e-service solutions) both domestically and internationally. The most significant reform in the private sector has been that of revolutionizing the supply chain management and the value change management through the application of e-technologies. However, as public interest in the application of e-technology solutions grows, there is an increasing expectation that they will be adopted within both national and local government organizations alike. Public sector organizations (including local governments) deal with complex networks of suppliers (and distributors) and sophisticated value chain systems on an ongoing basis. Within the last decade, many public sector strategists have acknowledged the strategic value of e-technologies (Figure 1). They also recognize the need for improved efficiency of business processes, enhanced citizens' access to information and services, and more productive relationships with both citizens and private sector agencies alike. Consequently, many innovative public sector agencies world-wide (e.g. Canada, the UK, Australia, New Zealand, Singapore, Hong Kong SAR – to name but a few) have had to create new ways in which to use e-business and e-service solutions (known as electronic or digital government) so as to respond to the need for change (Heeks 1999). Local, regional and national governments throughout the world are attempting to broaden service delivery and citizen involvement by providing effective e-services. This reflects a growing acceptance that achieving excellence in customer service is just as critical for the public sector as it is in private companies.

The introduction of e-service solutions within the public sector has primarily been concerned with moving away from traditional information monopolies and hierarchies. What's more, e-service and e-business (through digital government) have fundamentally transformed the ways in which the logistic processes and supply chain dynamics are managed within the public sector. However, e-service remains a challenge to both citizens and public sector agencies alike. Governments must not only maximize the benefits that are offered (through the application of digital government and e-service) but must also avoid the many pitfalls (economical, social and cultural) associated with rapid technological change. That is to say, despite advancements in technology solution, the challenges to effective government within today's knowledge society are profound.

Efficiency	
Time	Accelerating business processes and activities
Distance	Reducing geographical and distance inhibitors/barriers
Creativity	Enhancing existing business processes and activities
Effectiveness	
Time	Improving the flow of information and business intelligence throughout the supply and the value chain components
Distance	Enabling integrated control of the supply and the value chain processes
Creativity	Enabling new (and/or modified) processes
Growth	
Time	Obtaining early market entry/presence
Distance	Introducing new products to new markets
Creativity	Developing new products and services

Figure 1: The Strategic Value of e-Technologies

Within the past few years, there has been much debate (e.g. Accenture 2001b, Asgarkhani 2002b, Asgarkhani 2003a, Asgarkhani 2004, Heeks 1999, Nath 2003 and Reschenthaler et al 1996) over the effectiveness of e-service in the public sector. Technology is undoubtedly the backbone of the infrastructure that is required to support electronic government initiatives. Yet there is a danger in placing too much emphasis on the technology aspect of e-services. What's more, political and financial support for e-service projects can be accompanied by political rhetoric and hype. The potential benefits of e-technologies in the public sector can only materialise when they are introduced as part of a well-planned and properly supported social, cultural and political environment. There is also a need for performance measures in order to assess progress (and effectiveness) and ensure that rhetoric of e-service is matched by reality. If citizens are to benefit from the efficacy and potential cost-effectiveness of e-service, it is essential that traditional public sector structures and conventional governance paradigms are revised.

This paper elaborates on the strategic role, the value and the effectiveness of digital government that enables e-service. Four specific facets of effectiveness have been examined:

- Effectiveness from the point of view of management and ICT strategists (concerning the implications of ICT and e-service in the public sector).
- Effectiveness as it concerns social, cultural and ethical implications of e-service and e-business.
- Effectiveness with reference to differences in access to ICTs (digital inclusion/exclusion).
- Effectiveness from the point of view of citizens - a preliminary study of the citizens' view of e-service and e-business.

The paper is presented in two parts. Part one (based on a review of previous studies and analysis of digital government and e-service cases (Accenture 2001b, Asgarkhani 2002b, Asgarkhani 2005a, Asgarkhani 2005b, Asgarkhani 2005c, Asgarkhani 2003c, Bhatangar et al 2001, COMNET-IT 2000, Heeks 1999, Lin et al 2001, Orrego et al 2000, Radics 2001 and Perri 2000) reviews the fundamental concepts of digital government and e-service followed by discussing the effectiveness as outlined in (a), (b) and (c) above. Part two is based on a case study of a digital local government and e-service project within the Canterbury region of New Zealand. The case study examines the effectiveness of e-service as outlined in (d). The methodology for gathering information included interviews with project sponsors (and a number of other stakeholders) and a combination of formal interviews and surveys of several focus groups of users.

2. E-Technologies and e-Service in the Public Sector: An Overview

Electronic government forms the foundation for digital or electronic service (e-service) and depends upon a sound technology infrastructure. However, e-service is not a technical exercise, but rather an attempt to improve the political and social environment and to drive a fundamental change in the ways in which functions are performed. The introduction of ICT in order to automate public sector functions and introduce e-service will not automatically create a better or more open government - unless it is based on policies to promote the effective utilization of technology. E-service initiatives inevitably need to take into consideration issues such as new models of policy formulation; alternative forms of citizenship; different patterns and trends of relationship and power; new solutions for economic development; and alternative approaches for connecting people to the political process.

Extensive research has been conducted by various practitioners (e.g. Asgarkhani 2004, Asgarkhani 2003c, Asgarkhani 2003a, Samaranayake 2003, Radics 2001, Tapscott 1997 and Wiener 1984) in an attempt to answer questions about the key issues concerning the adoption of ICT and e-service. What's more, certain advisory and interest groups have been formed in order to provide answers to some of the issues that were mentioned above (e.g. International Centre for e-Governance – www.icegov.org).

As the application of ICT in governments within developing nations becomes widespread, a progression through the various stages of e-government and/or e-service can be observed (Asgarkhani 2002b, Asgarkhani 2003a):

- *Basic Internal Functional Efficiency* - Improving internal functional efficiency through the application of ICT.
- *Improved Internal Communications* – Improving internal communications (through the application of electronic mail) and introducing workflow management systems for increased process efficiency.

- *Improved Access* - Providing access to information concerning services and the democratic process.
- *Electronic Interconnection of Services* - Putting in place applications that would not only enable citizen participation through feedback, but would also allow for transactions between citizens to government (C2G), businesses to government (B2G) and government-to-government (G2G).
- *Electronic Democracy* - Introducing digital democracy - technological solutions that would enable participatory action and democratic processes.
- *Total Electronic Service Integration* - Introducing integrated electronic or digital governance services through one central e-service hub.

A review of various case studies of e-government and e-service (e.g. Webster 2001, Radics 2001, NIC 2000, Asgarkhani 2003b, and Asgarkhani 2004) suggests that local government objectives in introducing e-service are likely to concentrate on:

- *Prompt, accurate service* – as local governments potentially receive millions of calls per year, setting a target to resolve a high percentage of these calls the first time they occur (through establishing a customer contact centre) can result in significant efficiency gains and cost savings.
- *Improved quality of service* (by reducing redundancy in service) - One client of a local government can potentially generate up to dozens of files in different locations. Local governments are seeking to convert these to one secure and accessible file - helping to provide continuity and coordination of local government support.
- *Removing barriers and tackling social exclusion* – Local governments are aware that many clients do not have the skills to use electronic services, yet seem keen on setting up networks of learning centres in libraries and community centres that teach people relevant Internet and Web technology skills.
- *Local access points* – It appears (Webster 2001) that up to 20% of customer queries cannot be addressed immediately. Clients often need to meet with a 'professional' Local governments can benefit from setting up community access points to let clients meet 'professionals' through online video links.

Today, e-services appear in various shapes and forms. Typical applications (within both local and national governments) can include: providing access; connecting to a service or a process; facilitating consultation; and enabling active citizen participation (Figure 2)

Type of Electronic Service	Typical Application(s)	Phase
Providing Access Making information accessible to citizens (public kiosk, Internet, CDs, and so on)	• Citizen access to general information • Directory and directions to parks and community centres • Calendar of city-sponsored events and activities • Manual of policies and procedures • Phone directories	Improved Access
Connecting to a Process or Service Provide information and/or access to government ICT-based systems, information management solutions and true web-based services	• Property information • Licence renewal and payment • Payment of parking tickets, court fines • Registration for class and sports activities • Online permits, business licences, court documents • Online auctions • Electronic posting of commodity products with purchase order and invoice transactions • Sales tax collection • Job postings; online application forms • Self-service benefits administration	Improved Access Electronic Integration of Services
Raising Awareness Provide information about the political process, services, and options that are available for the decision making process	• Government functions and services • Citizen services • Business services (information) • Employee services • Employee newsletter • Legislative agenda and pending legislation	Improved Internal Communications Improved Access

Type of Electronic Service	Typical Application(s)	Phase
Facilitating Consultation and/or Communication Initiate and develop means of capacity building, exchanging prior gained experiences, access to experts, and any other information/knowledge of mutual interest.	• Posting of RFPs (Request for Information) and Bid Documents • Distance learning resources • Web casting of City/County Council Meetings •	Improved Access Electronic Integration of Services Electronic Democracy
Active Citizen Involvement/Participation Involve citizens in government decision-making, problem solving and election processes.	• Digital democracy • Communications with Council Members	Electronic Integration of Services Electronic Democracy

Figure 2: Typical applications of digital government and e-service

3. The Value of e-Service: Management and ICT Strategists' View

A review of various viewpoints over the implications and effectiveness of e-government and e-service (e.g. Perri 2000, Asgarkhani 2002b) indicates that there are at least four schools of thought: pure optimism; optimism with some concerns; pessimism; and those who view technology as a tool only - but not a driving factor on its own.

The optimists argue that the use of ICT in governance represents a major once-and-for-all improvement in the capabilities of governance through a more effective management of all domains (Wescott, 2001). The only cost is the investment and the day-to-day operational running costs. They believe that e-government can reduce the costs of decision making, management and day-to-day operational activities (such as acquiring, ordering, coding, organising, selecting, managing and using information) steadily over time. That is to say, the initial investment costs would be compensated through the cost savings and efficiency gains that are likely to be achieved over the lifetime of the systems (Reschenthaler et al 1996). This optimistic view appears to be based on the classical cybernetic theory (Wiener 1984) that views information as control.

The second group (optimists who have some concerns) accept at least the possibility of greater control, quality and rationality in decision-making. However, they dispute that the efficiency gains achieved through e-government come at a price. That is to say, unless safeguards are put in place, e-government may result in compromising citizens' rights - such as the right to individual liberty and privacy, the right to influence governmental decision-making (Perri 2000 and Raab 1997) and the loss of control over politicians' decision-making agendas (Zuurmond 1988).

The pessimists argue that e-government actually compromises the quality of decision-making and that excessive demand for policy analysis (based on many categories of information) will cause delays in action – 'paralysis by over-analysis'. There is a fear that due to mechanical rule following (as suggested by overly simple data interpretations, overly simple modelling and overly simple expert system flows from analysis to recommendation) the cultivation and the exercise of judgement in decision-making will be downplayed.

The last group view technology as a tool only and argue that the impact of ICT solutions cannot be viewed in isolation - where it concerns technical or political rationality of decision-making. They view both continuities and changes in governance as being driven socially and politically, not by technology itself. Technology is seen as a tool for either changing or preserving the *style of governance* – e.g. *conservative* and *radical* styles of governance (Mackenzie et al 1985 and Bijker 1997).

Each theory that has been mentioned above has some empirical support - although most empirical studies have been of a rather limited scope and are not in general designed to test, let alone falsify these rival theories. It is fair to say that applying these theories in a unified manner to every case across the board would be unrealistic. These theories need to be discussed with reference to: social and cultural aspects; the technological infrastructure; experience with the application of ICT; and the level of education and interest in the political process.

4. Social, Cultural and Ethical Implications of e-Service

The perceived effectiveness of e-service can be influenced by the public's view of the social and cultural implications of e-technologies and e-service.

Impacts on Individuals' Rights and Privacy – as more and more companies and government agencies use technology to collect, store, and make accessible data on individuals, privacy concerns have grown. Some companies monitor their employees' computer usage patterns in order to assess individual or workgroup performance (Asgarkhani 2002a). Technological advancements are also making it much easier for businesses, government and other individuals to obtain a great deal of information about an individual without their knowledge. There is a growing concern (e.g. Asgarkhani 2002b) that access to a wide range of information can be dangerous within politically corrupt government agencies.

Impact on Jobs and Workplaces - in the early days of computers, management scientists anticipated that computers would replace human decision-makers. However, despite significant technological advances, this prediction is no longer a mainstream concern. At the current time, one of the concerns associated with computer usage in any organization (including governments) is the health risk – such as injuries related to working continuously on a computer keyboard. Government agencies are expected to work with regulatory groups in order to avoid these problems.

Potential Impacts on Society – despite some economic benefits of ICT to individuals, there is evidence that the computer literacy and access gap between the haves and have-nots may be increasing. Education and information access are more than ever the keys to economic prosperity, yet access by individuals in different countries is not equal - this social inequity has become known as the digital divide.

Impact on Social Interaction – advancements in ICT and e-technology solutions have enabled many government functions to become automated and information to be made available online. This is a concern to those who place a high value on social interaction.

Information Security - technological advancements allow government agencies to collect, store and make data available online to individuals and organizations. Citizens and businesses expect to be allowed to access data in a flexible manner (at any time and from any location). Meeting these expectations comes at a price to government agencies where it concerns managing information – more specifically, ease of access; data integrity and accuracy; capacity planning to ensure the timely delivery of data to remote (possibly mobile) sites; and managing the security of corporate and public information (Asgarkhani 2001).

5. The Implications of e-Readiness

Access to ICT is critical for economic and social development. There is much optimism that we are facing a myriad of digital opportunities where the means exist to broaden participation in the network-based economy and to share its benefits. At the same time, differences in diffusion and the use of ICT appear to be deepening and intensifying the socio-economic divisions amongst people, businesses and nations. Differences in access to and use of ICT and electronic networks can lead to: divides between countries; social divides within countries; divides within countries related to income, education, age, family type, and location; and business divides related to sector, region, and firm size.

Overall, developing effective e-service solutions depends on the state of the ICT industry and e-readiness within countries, organisations and societies (e.g. Information Society Index 2002 [www.idc.com], Workshop – Digital Divide – OECD 2000, META Group 2000 and Asgarkhani 2002b). That is to say, the digital divide can be considered as a barrier to the successful rollout of e-government initiatives. Some of the causes of the digital divide that can limit the successful implementation of e-service include:

- lack of telecommunications and network infrastructure and limited PC access
- lack of financial resources for developing an infrastructure
- lack of ICT literacy and cultural resistance
- limited networking and Internet access (lack of infrastructure or high cost)
- high cost of business investment
- strategic business impediments – applicability; the need to reorganise; the need for skills, security and privacy considerations

The digital divide can potentially limit the success of e-service initiatives. Even though governments in a number of developing countries receive funding and support for introducing e-government solutions and e-service, the effectiveness of these solutions is limited – unless the barriers to e-readiness within these countries are addressed.

A review of some of the studies on the digital divide and e-readiness (e.g. UN E-Government Report 2001, Accenture 2001a, COMNET-IT 2000, META Group 2000 and UNESCO/COMNET-IT 2000) indicates that there are significant differences in the level of ICT adoption and network economy worldwide. In this section we review a small sample of these studies with a focus on the Asia Pacific region.

In 2000, the META Group (META Group 2000) examined the digital commerce competitiveness of 47 countries in an attempt to establish a digital economy index. The author, Howard Robin wrote, "Traditional industrial age measures of production and performance have lost relevance in the information age. Currently, information processing capability is a better indicator of national competitive advantage." The countries were ranked in five different categories in order to establish an overall 'information age technological competitiveness' - knowledge jobs; globalisation; economic dynamism and competition; transformation to digital economy; and technological innovation capacity. The results (with regards to the overall technological competitiveness) as they concern some of the countries within the Asia Pacific region (including New Zealand and Australia) are: Japan (2nd); Australia (8th); Taiwan (10th); New Zealand (11th); Hong Kong SAR (15th); Singapore (17th); Philippines (25th); Malaysia (33rd); India (34th); China (37th); Korea (38th); Thailand (46th); and Indonesia (47th).

The 2002 Information Society Index published by the IDC (www.idc.com) considered 23 parameters to compile a ranking list of 55 countries. The countries that featured in the ISI index were classified under four categories (along with examples of Asia Pacific countries that featured in the 2002 ISI index) – Figure 3.

Skaters	Countries in a strong position to take full advantage of the information revolution, as they appear to have advanced ICT and social infrastructures. Asia Pacific countries that were classified under this category included: Australia (ranked 9th); Taiwan (ranked 10th); Hong Kong (ranked 11th); Japan (ranked 12th); and Singapore (ranked 13th).
Striders	Countries that appear to be moving purposefully into the information age with much of the necessary infrastructure in place. This category included New Zealand (ranked 17th) and Korea (ranked 18th).
Sprinters	Countries that are moving forward in spurts before needing to catch their breath and shift priorities due to economic, social and political pressures. Malaysia (ranked 30th) was the only Asian country in this group.

Strollers	Those moving ahead but inconsistently, due to limited financial resources in relation to their vast populations. Countries that were considered under this category were: the Philippines (ranked 45th); Thailand (ranked 46th); China (ranked 52nd); India (ranked 53rd); Indonesia (ranked 54th); and Pakistan (ranked 55th).

Figure 3: Categories of the ISI index

The first eight countries in the 2002 ISI index were: Sweden; Norway; Switzerland; the United States; Denmark; the Netherlands; the United Kingdom; and Finland.

This relatively small sample of previous research cannot be applied to all countries. However, it appears that many countries (including some Asia Pacific governments) are still at the early or half-way stage of adopting ICT in order to introduce e-service.

Studies (e.g. UNESCO/COMNET-IT 2000, Webster 2001, Wescott 2001, Asgarkhani 2003b and Asgarkhani 2003c, Lau 2004, Jenkins 2003, Muller 2004 and Nordby 2003) indicate that numerous other factors can hinder the successful introduction of e-government and e-service initiatives including: lack of ICT skills; inadequate resources; too many initiatives; resistance to change; low take-up; and lack of public access.

6. The Value of e-Service: A New Zealand Local Government Case Study

In December 2001, one of the local governments within New Zealand introduced an e-service initiative. This particular local government (referred to as the Council hereafter) aims to introduce e-services through the implementation of its electronic governance initiative in an attempt to facilitate improved two-way exchange of information and enhance its public image as a professional customer service oriented organisation. The Council acknowledges that successful implementation of electronic governance does not result in merely automating the collection and distribution of information, but results in the flow of useful information between the government organisation and its citizens.

The Council measures the success of its e-service project on an ongoing basis – by looking at: website hits; customer feedback; and quantifiable efficiency benefits.

Customer Feedback: The Council monitors customer feedback from facilities on the service websites. Feedback is assessed to measure customer satisfaction and service level impact. Suggestions may also result in changes to the services provided.

Website Hits: are monitored to determine the utilization of services.

Quantifiable Efficiency Benefit: Services provided by the e-service project are intended to contribute to a reduction in operating costs. Services must continue to meet the desired levels of efficiency – which includes cost savings, time saving, and service level impact.

Overall, *Web-site hits* are not an effective measure of the usefulness and usability of a web site – unless it is combined with statistics concerning the number of users who actually proceed to access services past the home page. Customer feedback through service websites can be a more effective measure of user satisfaction. However, it would be beneficial to include feedback from other sources (e.g. phone calls).

A combination of surveys and interviews (focus groups) were considered in order to assess public knowledge and opinion of this particular e-service initiative. Participants were chosen from various age groups - more specifically, 61% of the respondents were 18-34 years, 26% were aged between 35 and 49 and the rest were over 50 years. It appeared that 76% of the respondents were aware of the e-government services that are provided by the Council online whilst 87% of those who were already aware of the Council's online services viewed the electronic delivery of services as being useful. From those who were previously unaware of the Council's web site, 81% considered online local government services desirable.

Results indicated that from those who knew of the Council's online services, the majority (49%) became aware of the Council's website through word of mouth. Web surfing or search engines were second (32%) whilst 19% of them knew of electronic service delivery solutions through advertising. Those respondents, who provided additional information, seemed to have used the following services: library information/catalogue (42%); services and hours of operation (38%); events in the city (32%); maps (31%); community services and events (30%); rates information (25%); bus timetables (23%); permits (13%); art gallery (12%); job advertisements/applications (11%); water resources (10%); and population statistics (7%).

Most respondents (who had used the website services) rated the Council's online service as being effective. Those who provided additional information stated the following reasons: immediate access to information anytime/anywhere (77%); saving time – no need for time consuming phone calls and/or visiting the Council (55%); access to information with reasonable details, simple to follow (40%); high level of usability (27%); links to relevant and useful pages and sites (25%); and easy to navigate (20%).

One respondent mentioned that the website did not work correctly. Other difficulties mentioned by those who had used the Council's website included: could not find the required information (9.5%); download time slow (26.2%); access time slow (32.1%); and navigation was difficult (8.3%).

Overall, participants did not have any major problems in locating the information they needed. This can be due to participants' familiarity with the basic requirements of using a computer and launching and navigating Web-based applications as well as the local government website's ease of use.

Participants suggested that the following services should be considered for online availability: rates payments (37%); other council fee payments (27%); additional general and contact information for the Council's service departments (25%); online submission of applications - e.g. building permits (30%); interactive services: online forums and discussion groups (23%); multimedia: streaming video and audio of local events (30%); and online voting facilities (23%).

Participants were asked to state their concerns about using online services. It appeared that data security was the greatest concern (71%); followed by confidentiality of data (66%), document compatibility (6%) and the technical infrastructure and speed of access (26%). However, 19% of participants had no concerns over using the Council's online services.

On a scale of 1 to 10, (10 being the greatest), the rating for the website contents was 7.18. Overall, on the scale of 1 to 10 (10 being highly desirable), results showed the average rating of the Council's online services was 7.52. Furthermore, respondents gave the importance of access to online services (in general, not just the Council's services) a score of 7.5 (10 being highly desirable).

The results of this pilot study have not yet been finalized. However, it appears that this particular digital government and e-service initiative is rated as being reasonably effective - in enhancing public access to services and facilitating the democratic process. The results of this study to date appear to be consistent with New Zealand's state of access to ICT and its e-readiness - as outlined in Section 5. We cannot assume that the preliminary outcome of this study is applicable to every digital government solution across the board. However, there is room for optimism with caution.

7. Conclusions

Within the past few years, much has been debated over the use of e-technologies and their effectiveness in reform within the public sector. Some of the key issues concerning e-government and e-service (as discussed in this paper) can be summarised as follows:

- E-government is to encompass the reform in public management through the improvement of service delivery to the citizen, the creation of economic activity and the safeguarding of democracy.
- E-government must be oriented towards the citizen. As the citizen does not need to be aware of who exactly in the government provides the required service, inter-agency and intergovernmental e-governance dimensions are essential.
- E-government requires electronic or digital citizens (e-citizens). That is to say, before we can call an e-service initiative effective, it must be made available to all citizens - not just to a minority who can afford to have access to the required electronic infrastructure.
- E-government can provide opportunities for building viable and sustainable partnerships between the private and the public sectors whereby each party would be responsible to provide electronic infrastructure (e-capacity) so a competitive economic advantage can be achieved.
- E-government can be effective if it is adopted alongside business process re-engineering. That is to say, merely automating existing services is inadequate and does not necessarily produce results.

> The benefits of e-government and e-service can only materialise when they are introduced within an environment that supports public access to information and services.

We examined the value of e-service and e-government by considering the different aspects of effectiveness – including:

- The view of management and ICT strategists with regards to the implications of e-government – ranging from the optimists who view e-government as being an effective tool (without concerns) to those who view technology as a tool only (arguing that technology on its own cannot be a driving force for effectiveness).
- Social, cultural and ethical aspects of e-service and e-government – including the impact on information management, workplaces and individuals' right and privacy - to name a few.
- The implications of the digital divide and e-readiness – the effectiveness and success of e-service in a country rely on the country's state of e-readiness and the ways in which the barriers to the 'digital divide' can be overcome.
- A case study of citizens' views of the usefulness and success of e-government initiatives in facilitating public access to information and services – initial results of a study of focus groups indicate that citizens rate e-government solutions that were offered as being effective. However, these results are not yet final and are not applicable to all e-government initiatives across the board.

It appears that practitioners and management scientists tend to agree that the trend for government transformation and public sector reform through e-service is irreversible. However, technical innovation on its own is not enough to drive the development of effective e-service. E-government is a tool and regardless of its potential power, it has limited value and relevance on its own. In other words, access to the right technology for enabling e-service is essential but insufficient. Undoubtedly, most of the shortcomings (as they concern the effectiveness of e-service) can be resolved by improving the technology infrastructure and access to e-technologies. Nevertheless, technology by itself does not necessarily result in better, more efficient and socially inclusive government. E-technology solutions are only effective if they are considered alongside other key parameters such as: social structure; cultural values and attitudes; governance process re-engineering within governments; and ethical issues.

References

Accenture (2001a) "e-Government Leadership – Realizing the Vision", [online] http://www.digitalopportunity.org.

Accenture (2001b) "Governments Closing Gap Between Political Rhetoric and e-Government Reality", [online] http://www.accenture.com/xd/xd.asp?it=enWeb&xd=industries/government/gove_study.xml.

Asgarkhani, M. (2001) "Managing Information Security: A Holistic Business Process", *Proceedings of the 20th IT Conference*, Sri Lanka, pp93-100.

Asgarkhani, M. (2002a) "Strategic Management of Information Systems and Technology in an e-World", *Proceedings of the 21st IT Conference*, Sri Lanka, pp103-111.

Asgarkhani, M. (2002b) "e-Governance in Asia Pacific", *Proceedings of the International Conference on Governance in Asia*, Hong Kong.

Asgarkhani, M. (2003a) "A Strategic Framework for Electronic Government", *Proceedings of the 22nd National IT Conference*, Sri Lanka, pp57-65.

Asgarkhani, M. (2003b) "The Effectiveness of Digital Government as a Tool for Improved Service Delivery", *Proceedings of the International Information Technology Conference*, Sri Lanka.

Asgarkhani, M. (2003c) "Electronic Service Delivery in Local Governments – A Strategic Tool for Service Quality Improvement in the Information Age", *Proceedings of the International Symposium on Service Charters and Customer Satisfaction in Public Services*, City University of Hong Kong.

Asgarkhani, M. (2004) "Digital Government: From Vision to the Reality of Strategy Implementation", *Proceedings of the International Conference on e-Governance*, Sri Lanka, pp36-46

Asgarkhani, M. (2005a) "The Reality of e–Service in the Public Sector", *Proceedings of the 2005 IEEE International Conference of e–Business, e–Commerce and e–Service* (published on CD-ROM)

Asgarkhani, M. (2005b) "The effectiveness of e–Service in the Public Sector: A Local Government Perspective", *Proceedings of the 2005 European Conference on Electronic Government* (published on CD-ROM)

Asgarkhani, M. (2005c) "Digital Government and its Effectiveness in Public Management reform: A Local Government Perspective", *Journal of Public Management Review*, Vol. 7. No. 3, September 2005, pp 465-488.

Bhatnagar, S. and Dewan, A. (2001) "Gyandoot project: ICT Initiative in the district of Dhar Madhya Pradesh", [online] http://poverty.worldbank.org/files/14649_Gyandoot-web.pdf.

Bijker, W.E. (1997) "Of Bicycles, Bakelites and Bulbs: Toward a Theory of Sociotechnical Change", *Inside Technology, Massachusetts Institute of Technology Press*, Cambridge, Massachusetts.

COMNET-IT (2000) "Country Profiles of E-Governance", [online] http://www.digitalopportunity.org.

Heeks, R. (1999) Reinventing Government in the Information age: International Practice in IT-enabled Public Sector Reform, Routledge, London, 1999.

Jenkins, G. (2003) "Observations from the Trenches of Electronic Government", [online] http://www.acm.org/ubiquity/views/g_jenkins_1.html

Lau, E. (2004) "Strategic Implementation of e-Government in OECD Countries: Major Challenges", *12th NISPAcee Annual Conference,* [online] unpan1.un.org/intradoc/groups/ public/documents/nispacee/unpan017775.pdf

Lin, M., Zhu, R. and Hachigian, N. (2001) "Beijing's Business E-park", [online] http://www1.worldbank.org/publicsector/egov/zhongguancun_cs.htm,

Mackenzie, D. and Wajcman, J. (1985) *The Social Shaping of Technology: How the Refrigerator Got its Hum*, Open University Press, Buckingham, 1985.

META Group (2000) "The Global E-Economy Index", [online] http://www.ecommercetimes.com.

Muller, E. (2004) "From e-Government to e-Governance: The OECD Experience", [online] http://unpan1.un.org/intradoc/groups/public/documents/CAFRAD/UNPAN015841.pps.

Nath, V. (2003) "Digital Governance", [online] www.cddc.vt.edu/digitalgov/gov-cases.html.

NIC (2000) "E- Government A Strategic Planning Guide for Local Officials", [online] www.nicusa.com.

Nordby, K. (2003) "e-Accessibility – Meeting a Growing Demand", [online] http://www.e-europestandards.org/articles.htm

Orrego, C., Osorio, C. and Mardones, R. (2000) "Chile's Government Procurement E-System", [online] http://www1.worldbank.org/publicsector/egov/eprocurement_chile.htm,

Perri, 6. (2000) "E-governance: Weber's Revenge?" Proceedings of the Annual Conference of the Political Studies Association.

Raab, C. (1997) "Privacy, Information and Democracy", in Loader BD, ed, 1997, *The Governance of Cyberspace: Politics, Technology and Global Restructuring*, Routledge, London, 1997, pp155-174.

Radics, G.A. (2001) "Cristal: A Tool for Transparent Government in Argentina", [online] http://www1.worldbank.org/publicsector/egov/cristal_cs.htm,

Reschenthaler, G.B. and Thompson F. (1996) "The Information Revolution and the New Public Management", *Journal of Public Administration Research and Theory*, Vol 6, No. 1, pp125-143., 1996.

Samaranayake, V.K. (2003) "The Reality of Digital Government", *Proceedings of the 22nd National IT Conference*, Sri Lanka, pp1-9.

Tapscott, D. (1997) "The Digital Media and the Reinvention of Government", *Canadian Public Administration*- 40, pp328-345.
UN E-Government Report (2001) "Benchmarking E-Government: A Global Perspective – Assessing UN Memberstates" [online] http://www.upan1.org/e-government2.asp
UNESCO/COMNET-IT (2000), "Global Survey of Online Governance", [online] http://www.digitalopportunity.org,
Webster, A. (2001) "Message Beyond the Medium", [online] ww2.audit-commission.gov.uk/publications/ e-government2.shtml,
Wescott, C.G. (2001) "E-Government in the Asia-Pacific Region", UNPAN Asia Pacific, [online] http://www.unpan.org,
Wiener, N. (1984) Cybernetics: The Emerging Science at the Edge of Order and Chaos, Simon and Schuster, New York.
Workshop – Digital Divide – OECD (2000), "The Digital Divide: Enhancing Access to ICTs", [online] www.oecd.org/dataoecd/22/11/2428340.pdf,
Zuurmond, A. (1988) "From Bureaucracy to Infocracy: Are Democratic Institutions Lagging Behind?", *Public Administration in an Information Age: a Handbook*, IOS Press, Amsterdam, 1988, pp259-272.

Trust and the Taxman: A Study of the Irish Revenue's Website Service Quality

Regina Connolly
Dublin City University, Ireland
Originally published in EJEG (2007) Volume 5 Issue 2

Regina Connolly here provides an account of what was work in progress at the time this paper was written. It describes a project to measure the website service quality of the Irish taxation authority's award winning Revenue Online Services (ROS). While the ROS system has been a tremendous success story in terms of winning awards and take-up, the question addressed in Connolly's research is how do the customers feel about the system? To find this out, she uses a modified version of the widely used customer service quality measuring instrument SERVQUAL developed by Parasuraman and others. The adapted instrument, called E-S-QUAL, has been modified for testing website service quality. There are two interesting aspect of the article: the ROS case itself and the discussion of how to measure online service quality, the latter including a detailed review and critique of available tools for doing this.

Abstract: This paper describes an ongoing study into the quality of service provided by the Irish Revenue Commissioners' online tax filing and collection system. The Irish Revenue Online Service (ROS) site has won several awards. In this study, a version of the widely used SERVQUAL measuring instrument, adapted for use with online services, has been modified for the specific case of ROS. The theory behind this instrument is set out, the particular problems of evaluating revenue collecting online are examined and the rationale for this approach is explained.

Keywords; e-government, taxation, online, quality of service, SERVQUAL

1. Introduction

Benjamin Franklin once said that only two things in life are certain: death and taxes. It is no surprise therefore that the computerisation of taxation has been at the leading edge of e-government for many years. In surveys of e-government carried out over the past five years, (Accenture 2005, 2006; CapGemini 2001, 2005, 2006) the computerisation of taxation services is one area in which all European countries score highly. One aspect of collecting tax online is making the process attractive to citizens. While governments and tax authorities can provide various inducements (such as later payment dates) for citizens to file online, a key factor in the success of such systems is the design quality of the public interface. Perceived service quality has become a critical determinant of website success in all areas of commercial life. It is even more critical on a site that requires the citizens to declare their income and/or assets and possible pay over some of their hard earned cash to the state. Studies show that many consumers view the service quality delivered by commercial websites to be unsatisfactory (Gaudin 2003; Lennon and Harris' 2002). There is as yet no significant evidence to suggest that citizens' view of e-government service quality differs. Accenture (2005, page 4) comment that:

> *"While governments have certainly seen some value in terms of increases in citizen satisfaction and internal efficiency and some reductions in costs, none has been transformed by e-government alone. e-government simply has not led to the reinvention of service delivery."*

It is therefore essential that government bodies seeking to encourage citizens to use their online services understand the dimensions of website service excellence that their citizens value.

This paper will discuss an investigation of the Irish Revenue Commissioners' Revenue Online Services (ROS) web site. The study is expected to provide interesting insights and have implications for Revenue at a number of levels including an understanding of the dimensions of service that are valued by Irish citizens who use the online service to file their tax returns. It also expected to:

- provide evidence that Irish citizens' perception of online revenue service quality is driven by specific factors, all of which it is possible for government to manage, and
- establish the dimensions of service quality that create, or in their absence inhibit, citizen trust in Revenue Online Services.

While the online delivery of a government service may appear to be more user-friendly than that delivered by traditional means, an Information Society Commission e-government report (Information Society Commission 2003) repeatedly emphasizes that those charged with implementing e-government need to give careful consideration to the perceptions and expectations of its users.

2. The Computerisation of Taxation Services

Whatever the list of tentacles of government that have been computerised in any country, it is certain that the collection of tax revenues is one of them. As one senior tax official once put it, it is much easier to persuade governments in general and Treasuries/Ministries of Finance in particular to part with taxpayers' funds for investing in ways to collect money than it is to get them interested in putting money into ways to spend it. In Ireland, the body that collects taxes is called the Revenue Commissioners, usually referred to as Revenue. This is the equivalent of the Internal Revenue Service in the US or the Inland Revenue in the UK.

The Revenue Commissioners have a long record of leadership in the use of information and communications technology. They were first in the Irish public sector to make extensive use of computing and in 1964 purchased the public sector's first ever mainframe computer (Pye 1993, Connolly 1986). In subsequent years the Revenue have continued to be at the cutting edge of computing although, in a manner common to public sectors the world over, the systems that they developed tended to be in silos. In particular, for many years, the functions of tax collection and excise duty collection remained separate.

In 1993, the Revenue launched a ten-year project entitled CONTAX (for Consolidated Tax project). This ambitious project set out to re-engineer all of the computer systems in the Revenue, moving away from the mainframe world towards a modern distributed system. This modernisation effort was almost entirely internal. The first step by the Revenue to what is commonly (if rather unfortunately) termed e-government came with the launch of Revenue Online Services or ROS in September 2000 (Revenue Commissioner, 2001). Heretofore, it had been possible to submit tax return information to the Revenue electronically. However this had been a largely batch process and restricted to companies with the technical knowledge to manage the complicated interfaces involved. ROS was part of Revenue's drive to eliminate paper, simplify the processing of making returns and increase levels of tax compliance, particularly filing by the return deadline.

Online filing of tax returns had several important differences from most other types of online e-government transaction. Important aspects are:

- The exceptionally high level of security involved;
- The annual surge in the volume of transactions;
- The need to provide users with a variety of tools.

The first of these is self-evident. Tax returns contain a large amount of commercial and personally sensitive information. A system therefore needs to provide strong encryption (whilst also being simultaneously easy to use). Citizen trust in the system is essential if it is to succeed. While the Revenue can provide incentives for people to file online, it is not in a position to make this mandatory. It needs to lure people to the web and reliability and trustworthiness are key components of its strategy to do this.

Secondly, the system needs to be able to deal with large volumes of transactions over short periods of time. It is in the nature of companies and people to file tax returns at the last possible moment (sometimes there is no alternative but to do this). The resultant spike in transaction volumes caused ROS problems in 2003, its third year of full operations (TALC 2004). This problem was subsequently solved and has not recurred despite enormously increased volumes (see Table 1).

Thirdly, such a system needs to provide users with a number of offline tools with which to work. Many companies and individuals may wish to try out various ways of classifying financial information on their tax returns. While it would be helpful if there were only one right way to complete a return, there are often several options and more sophisticated users, particularly tax specialists like to undertake 'what if' type analysis before they submit the return. While this might be done online, a worry could be that the Revenue's computer might be keeping a record of customer's actions. To overcome this, offline tools would have to be provided.

ROS went live properly in 2001. Initially it was only for companies and for the self-employed. There were several reasons for this. One of the more important was that there was a considerable cost involved in generating digital certificates, so extension to the general run of pay-as-you-earn (PAYE) taxpayer would be expensive. Also, it was felt, at the time, that many PAYE taxpayers would not have computers with online access so there was little point in setting up a system for the small number of such taxpayers that might use it[1]. In 2006, after three years of successful operation, ROS was extended to PAYE earners. This brought a new, and much larger, group of customers into the system.

With this extended audience of private citizens, it has become even more important that the Revenue, and by extension all government bodies seeking to encourage citizens to use their online services, understand the dimensions of website service excellence that their citizens value. This has the potential both to improve the uptake of services and increase citizen satisfaction with public administration.

The scale of government investment in electronic services can be gauged from the various benchmarking reports on e-government (see, for example, Accenture 2005, 2006; CapGemini 2001, 2005, 2006). As already noted, when looking at progress to date, it is not surprising to find that the aspect of e-government which tends to be most developed and most widely used is online tax filing. According to the US Internal Revenue Service, 73 million taxpayers filed online in 2006 (Internal Revenue Service, 2007). In the UK, 2 million business and agents filed online in 2005 (HM Revenue and Customs, 2007).

The design of an online tax filing system must address a number of specific challenges that are not usually factors in the design of other types of online government services. Two have already been mentioned, namely

---

[1] In 2007, the number of Irish homes with PCs online was still only about 50% with (as of December 2006) only 23% having broadband (OECD 2006).

the need for exceptionally high security and the ability to handle large surges in the number of transactions at certain times of year. The system must also reflect the composition of its customer base. This ranges from professional tax advisor and agents to citizens who may have only a hazy notion of the tax laws. The system must be able to meet the needs of both these constituencies as well as several others. Furthermore, it needs to be able to hand a variety of different forms of taxation including income and corporation tax as well as VAT and different forms of capital taxation. The ROS website and service has been one of the notable successes of Irish e-government and has won a number of awards (Revenue Commissioners 2004). A measurement of the effectiveness of ROS can be seen in Table 1 below (reproduced from Revenue Commissioners 2005)

Table 1: Increase in use of ROS 2004-2005

Tax/Tax Form	**2005**	**2004**	**Increase**
V.A.T.	234,288	136,246	71.95%
Employers' Monthly PAYE Returns	211,924	122,099	73.56%
Employers' Annual PAYE Returns	42,201	21,421	97.00%
Cessation Certificate	187,773	135,916	38.15%
Income Tax Self Assessment Returns	248,967	194,544	27.97%
Corporation Tax Self Assessment Returns	49,992	30,151	65.81%
Vehicle Registration Tax Registrations	194,045	155,049	25.15%
Relevant Contracts Tax	67,185	29,427	128.31%
Relevant Contracts Tax –	4,603	1,693	171.88%
Customs Declarations	859,232	838,261	2.5%
Total No of all ROS Returns	2,100,210	1,664,807	26.15%

According to Accenture (2005), ROS also reported savings of €600,000 in postage alone and 30 man-years per annum in processing effort in 2005 .

This study described in this paper has three objectives:

1. It is seeking to identify the dimensions of website service quality that are valued by Irish citizens who use the Revenue Online Service to file their tax returns.

2. It is examining the degree to which website service excellence influences consumer trust in electronic government.

3. By applying the newly operationalised e-S-QUAL measurement instrument, it is exploring the relevance of this instrument in the evaluation of e-government website service quality generally.

The approach is to use a modified version of a well-established service quality tool. This is described in the following section.

3. Service Quality

Service quality is one of the most researched topics in the area of service marketing. Although research into the dimensions of website service quality that are valued by online consumers is in an embryonic stage, it is a topic of considerable importance. Research into online services quality is in a relatively early stage in comparison with the well-established tools used in service marketing. However, as online competition intensifies, the need for vendors is not only to differentiate their website, but to ensure that they do not shoot themselves in the foot as a result of poor web design. Anybody who has used a variety of web service sites will be aware of sites that are poorly laid out and frustrating to use. Good design has therefore become a differentiator. Because there are so many poor sites out there, a vendor can still gain competitive edge by having the basics right. The question is what are those basics? What is it that consumers look for, consciously or unconsciously, when they visit a web page? When competing for customer loyalty, a key indicator of success in a crowded online market, this is a critical thing to know.

Service quality can be defined as the difference between customers' expectations for service performance prior to the service encounter and their perceptions of the service received (Asubonteng et al, 1996). When performance is not up to expectations, people will consider quality to be low and when performance exceeds expectations, the perception of that quality improves. So in any evaluation of service quality, customers' expectations are fundamental to that evaluation. Moreover, Asubonteng *et al.* (1996) suggest that as service quality increases, satisfaction with the service and intentions to reuse the service increase.

Customer services requirements have two aspects: what the customers want and what standards must be met. Both need to be measurable and this is where the problem arises. For example, Swartz and Brown (1989) distinguish between the consumer's post-performance evaluation of 'what was delivered and the delivery process itself. The former evaluation is referred to by a number of different names including 'outcome quality' (Parasuraman *et al.*, 1985), 'technical quality' (Grönroos, 1983) and 'physical quality' (Lehtinen and Lehtinen, 1982). The latter evaluation, i.e. the evaluation of the services process, has been termed 'process quality' by Parasuraman *et al.,* 'functional quality' by Gronröos and 'interaction quality' by Lehtinen and Lehtinen respectively.

The most widely cited measure of service quality is SERVQUAL. This instrument was developed by Parasuraman *et al.* (1985, 1988). It has been used to measure service quality in a variety of settings such as:

- health care (Babakus and Mangold, 1992; Bebko and Garg, 1995; Bowers et al, 1994);
- large retail chains (Teas, 1993; Finn and Lamb, 1991);
- fast food restaurants (Cronin and Taylor, 1992)
- a dental clinic;
- a tyre store;
- a hospital (Carman, 1990).

SERVQUAL is designed to measure service quality from a customer perspective. It comprises five basic dimensions each representing one of the service attributes that consumers use to evaluate service quality. The five dimensions are:

- Tangibles;
- Reliability;
- Responsiveness;
- Assurance;
- Empathy.

As already noted, in their model, Parasuraman *et al.*, (1985; 1988) suggest that it is the gap between consumer expectations and actual service performance that informs service quality perceptions. Consequently, it is this performance-to-expectations gap that forms the theoretical basis of SERVQUAL. Again, as already noted, Parasuramam *et al.*, observe that the evaluation of service quality is not based solely on the service outcome, but also on the evaluation of the *process* of service delivery.

Notwithstanding its wide usage, SERVQUAL remains contentious and there have been criticisms about its validity and accessibility. One criticism is of the supposed causality of the link between service quality and satisfaction (Wolfinbarger and Gilly, 2003; Bitner, 1990), and the question as to whether one scale can be universally applicable in measuring service quality regardless of the industry or environment (Asubonteng *et al.*, (1996); Cronin and Taylor, 1992, 1994; Teas, 1993; Cox and Dale, 2001). A further question mark over SERVQUAL is the numerous small changes that are made to it, even by researchers that claim to be using this model (Paulin and Perrien, 1996). A number of other models for measuring service quality in an offline context have also been proposed. These include SERVPERF and the Normed Quality model. SERVPERF was developed by Cronin and Taylor in 1992 and determines service quality by measuring only performance (instead of performance and expectation like SERVQUAL). The authors argued that this would provide a better reflection of customers' perceptions of service quality. The Normed Quality model that was proposed by Teas (1993) measures service quality by the gap between perceived performance and the ideal amount of a feature, rather than the customers' expectations presented by SERVQUAL. While each of these models are valuable and provide a new perspective on how service quality can be measured, it is worth noting that they were developed specifically for the measurement of service quality in the offline context and therefore whether and to what degree they are applicable to an online context remains undetermined.

4. Website Service Quality

Website service quality, often termed e-service quality, has been defined as:

- "...consumers' overall evaluation and judgement of the excellence and quality of e-service offerings in the virtual marketplace" (Santos, 2003), and as:
- "the extent to which a website facilitates efficient and effective shopping, purchasing and delivery" (Zeithaml, 2002).

The quality of e-service does not stand still. Because it is so easy to copy in the online world, any feature introduced by a company can be quickly matched by its competitors. The result is an accelerated form of evolution with new ideas emerging, changing, surviving or dying at a rapid rate. Quality is honed by competition (Trabold *et al.,* 2006). Notwithstanding evidence of continuing consumer dissatisfaction with service delivered through the Internet (Gaudin 2003; Ahmad, 2002), studies of e-service quality remain limited and frequently employ instruments that were developed for use in a traditional environment (such as SERVQUAL. See, for example, Van Lwaarden *et al.,* 2004). This despite the obvious problem that SERVQUAL and similar instruments were and are not designed to examine quality factors in online environments. In such circumstances, the results must be, at the very minimum, questionable. This is not to say that 'offline' models contain nothing of value. They can provide a useful platform or starting point for an online equivalent (Van Riel *et al.*, 2001), but there is now an increasing awareness that the SERVQUAL instrument is limited in terms of its ability to measure e-service quality, particularly as there are dimensions of service quality that are unique to the electronic context (Cai and Jun, 2003; Li, *et al.,* 2003). Cox and Dale (2001) argue that dimensions of service quality specific to a traditional environment such as:

- competence,
- courtesy,
- cleanliness,
- comfort and
- friendliness

They are either not important and/or not relevant in the electronic retail environment. Other dimensions are not measured by SERVQUAL, for example:

- accessibility,
- communication,
- credibility and
- appearance

which are much more significant. Long and McMellon (2004) support this view. They argue that factors such as geographic distance and the facelessness of the experience form part of the online service experience and should therefore be part of any e-service quality measurement instrument.

Several researchers have proposed scales to evaluate websites. Unfortunately, many of these scales do not provide a comprehensive evaluation of the service quality of the website. For example:

- The objective of the WebQual scale (Loiacono *et al.*, 2000) is to provide website designers with information regarding the website (e.g. informational fit to task) rather than to provide specific service quality measures from a customer perspective;
- Barnes and Vidgen's (2002) WebQual[2] scale provides a transaction-specific assessment rather than a detailed service quality assessment of a website;
- The SITEQUAL scale (Yoo and Donthu, 2001) excludes dimensions central to the evaluation of website service quality as does Szymanski and Hise's (2000) study;
- The eTailQ scale proposed by Wolfinbarger and Gilly (2003) has been the subject of some reservations expressed by other researchers (Parasuranam *et al.*, 1995).

Recently however, many of these concerns have been addressed by the original authors of the original SERVQUAL instrument. A new instrument has been developed called E-S-QUAL (Parasuraman et al. 2005). This is a four-dimensional, 22-item scale instrument designed to capture the core dimensions of service quality as found in the current literature. The four dimensions are:

- Efficiency,
- Fulfilment,
- System availability, and
- Privacy.

There is also a special accompanying subscale, E-RecS-Qual, specifically designed for customers who have had non routine encounters with an online service provider (such as service problems or breakdowns). E-RecS-Qual consists of a three-dimensional, 11-item scale, the three dimensions being:

---

[2] Unfortunately both of these WebQual instruments have the same name but they are different.

- Responsiveness,
- Compensation, and
- Contact.

Both of these scales have been subjected to reliability and validity tests and demonstrate good psychometric properties.

As E-S-QUAL is a relatively new measure it has yet to be used extensively in online service quality research. However, Kim *et al.,* (2006) used it with online clothing retailers. With the instrument, they were able to identify successfully the exact e-service dimensions on which online apparel retailers are failing and thus identify the key factors that contribute to customer dissatisfaction. Needless to say, this type of information is highly valuable to vendors.

5. Research Methodology

Having reviewed the relevant literature, the decision was taken to employ the E-S-QUAL questionnaire for the ROS study using a web-based online survey to be sent to all ROS users. The survey was divided into two sections. In section one a varying number of questions were asked regarding specific dimensions of online service quality as identified by Parasuraman *et al.* (2005). These dimensions and the number of items used to represent them are outlined below in Table 2.

Table 2: Quality dimensions measured by the survey

Quality Dimension
Efficiency
System availability
Fulfilment
Privacy
Responsiveness
Compensation
Contact
Perceived value
Loyalty intentions

As part of the instrument design, ROS requested that a number of statements be added to the survey in order to acquire information on certain specific aspects of their service. An example of these is the statement that the ROS website:

"enables me to complete the filing of my tax returns quickly".
In addition, a number of statements on the influence of each service quality dimension on citizens' trust beliefs were included. For example, in relation to the dimension of website efficiency, citizens were asked to agree or disagree with the statement

"The ease of use of a website increases my trust in the online vendor."
The purpose of these questions was to investigate which dimension of website service quality provides the strongest influence on citizens' trust in ROS. In total, section one of the survey contained 31 statements. Section two of the survey collected relevant demographic information.

In order to run the survey, the Revenue Online Service emailed all citizens who file their tax returns online, telling them about the study and inviting them to complete the survey. The email contained a direct link that directed the citizen to the online questionnaire. When the survey was completed, approximately 7,000 responses had been received. These responses are now being analysed.

6. Conclusion

This paper has outlined an in-progress study that aims to improve the delivery of electronic government in Ireland. The findings will, it is hoped, provide the Irish Revenue Online Service with useful insights into the key dimensions of service that are valued by Irish citizens who use their online service to file their various tax returns. It is expected that the research will provide evidence that Irish citizens' perception of ROS's quality is driven or inhibited by specific factors, all of which it is possible to manage. Secondly, it is expected to show the degree to which specific dimensions of service quality create, or in their absence undermine, citizen trust in the Revenue Online Service. Finally, it will provide an indication of the usefulness of the E-S-QUAL survey instrument for improving our understanding of the e-government services environment.

References

Accenture (2005), Leadership in Customer Service: New Expectations, New Experiences, retrieved 30th April 2007 from: http://www.accenture.com/xdoc/ca/locations/canada/insights/studies/leadership_cust.pdf

Accenture (2006), e-Government Leadership: Building the Trust, Accenture, Dublin.

Ahmad, S. (2002) Service Failures and Customer Defection: A Closer Look at Online Shopping Experiences. Managing Service Quality, 2002, 12 (1) pp 19-29.

Asubonteng, P., McCleary, K.J., Swan, J. (1996) Servqual Revisited: A Critical Review of Service Quality, *Journal of Services Marketing*, 10 (6) pp 62-81.

Babakus, E., Mangold, G.W. (1992) Adapting the SERVQUAL scale to Hospital Services: An Empirical Investigation, *Hospital Services Research*, 26 (6), pp 767-86.

Barnes, S. J. and Vidgen, R.T. An Integrative Approach to the Assessment of E-Commerce Quality, Journal of Electronic Commerce Research, 2002, 3 (3), pp 114-127.

Bebko, C.P., Garg, R.K. (1995) Perceptions of Responsiveness in Service Delivery, *Journal of Hospital Marketing*, 9 (2), pp 35-45.

Bitner, M.J., (1990) Evaluating service encounters: the effects of physical surroundings and employee responses, *Journal of Marketing*, 54 (2), pp 69-82.

Bowers, M.R., Swan, J.E., Koehler, W.F. (1994) What Attributes Determine Quality and Satisfaction with Health-Care Delivery?, *Health Care Management Review*, 19 (4), pp 49-55.

Cai, S. and Jun, M. (2003) Internet Users' Perceptions of Online Service Quality: A Comparison of Online Buyers and Information Searchers. *Managing Service Quality*, 13 (6), pp 504-519.

Capgemini, Ernst & Young (2001), Summary Report: Web-based Survey on electronic Public Services. Report of the First Measurement, Directorate General for The Information Society, EU.

CapGemini (2005) Online Availability of Public Services: How is Europe Progressing? (2005), retrieved 15th June 2006 from http://europa.eu.int/information_society/eeurope/2005/doc/highlights/whats_new/capgemini4.pdf

Capgemini (2006), Online Availability of Public Services. How is Europe Progressing? Web-based Survey on electronic Public Services. Report of the Sixth Measurement, e-Europe, Available at: http://ec.europa.eu/information_society/soccul/egov/egov_benchmarking_2005.pdf

Carman, J.M., (1990), Consumer Perceptions of Service Quality: An Assessment of the SERVQUAL Dimensions, *Journal of Retailing*, 66 (1), pp 33-55.

Connolly, S. (1986) Computerisation; Some Essential Considerations – A Response, *Administration*, Institute of Public Administration, Dublin, 34, 2.

Cox, J., and Dale, B.G. (2001), Service Quality and e-Commerce: An Exploratory Analysis, *Managing Service Quality*, 1, 2, pp 121-131.

Cronin, J.J., Taylor, S.A. (1994), SERVPERF versus SERVQUAL: Reconciling Performance-based and Perception-minus-expectations Measurement of Service Quality, Journal of Marketing, 58 (1), pp 125-31.

Cronin, J., Taylor, S.A. (1992), Measuring Service Quality: A Re-examination and extension, *Journal of Marketing*, 56, pp 55-68.

Finn, D., Lamb, C. (1991) An Evaluation of the SERVQUAL Scale in a Retailing Setting, *Advances in Consumer Research*, 18, pp 483-490.

Gaudin, S. (2003), *Companies Failing at Online Customer Service*, Datamation, retrieved 30th April 2007 from http://itmanagement.earthweb.com/erp/article.php/1588171

Grönroos, C. (1983) *Strategic Management and Marketing in the Service Sector*, Marketing Science Institute, Cambridge, MA.

IRS (Internal Revenue Service) (2007), Public Information Site, retrieved 30th April 2007 from: http://www.irs.gov/efile/article/0,,id=118508,00.html

Information Society Commission (2003) *e-government Report*, retrieved 27th April 2007 from http://www.isc.ie/downloads/e-government.pdf

HM Revenue and Customs (2007) *Do It Online*, retrieved 30th April 2007 from: http://www.hmrc.gov.uk/employers/onlineguide.htm

Kim, M., Kim. J-H., and Lennon, S.J. (2006), Online Service Attributes Available On Apparel Retail Websites: An E-S-Qual approach. *Managing Service Quality*, 16 (1), pp 51-57.

Lehtinen, J.R and Lehtinen, U. (1982), Service Quality: A Study of Quality Dimensions", Unpublished working paper, *Service Management Institute*, Helsinki.

Lennon, R. and Harris, J. (2002) Customer Service on the Web: A Cross-Industry Investigation, *Journal of Targeting, Measurement and Analysis for Marketing*, 10(4), pp 325- 328.

Li, Y., Tan, K., and Xie, M. (2003), Factor Analysis of Service Quality Dimension Shifts in the Information Age. *Managerial Auditing Journal*, 18:4, pp 297-302,

Loiacono, E, Watson, R.T., Goodhue, D. (2000), WebQual: A Web Site Quality Instrument, Working paper, *Worcester Polytechnic Institute*.

Long, M., and McMellon, C. (2004) Exploring the Determinants of Retail Service Quality on the Internet, *Journal of Service Marketing*, 18:1, pp 78-90.

OECD (2006) OECD *Broadband Statistics to December 2006*, retrieved 30th April 2007 from: www.oecd.org/document/7/0,2340,en_2649_34223_38446855_1_1_1_1,00.html

Parasuraman, A., Zeithaml, V.A., and Malhotra, A. (2005) E-S-Qual: A Multiple Item Scale for Measuring Electronic Service Quality, *Journal of Service Research*, 7, (3), pp 213 – 233.

Parasuraman, A., Zeithaml, V.A., Berry, L.L. (1988) SERVQUAL: A Multiple Item Scale for Measuring Customer Perceptions of Service Quality, *Journal of Retailing*, 1988, 64 (1), pp 12-40.

Parasuraman, A., Zeithaml, V.A., Berry, L. A. (1985) Conceptual Model of Service Quality and its Implications for Future Research, Journal of Marketing, 49 (Fall), pp 41-50.

Paulin, M and Perrien, J. (1996) Measurement of Service Quality: The Effect of Contextuality, in Kunst and Lemminck (eds.) *Managing Service Quality*, London, Chapman.

Pye, R. (1992) *An Overview of Civil Service Computerisation*, 1960-1990, Economic and Social Research Institute, Dublin.

Revenue Commissioners (2005) *Annual Report 2004*, retrieved 15th April 2006 from: http://www.revenue.ie/annualreport/annualreport_2004/en/anrep_04.pdf

[33] Revenue Commissioners (2001) Annual Report 2000, retrieved 15th June 2006 from: http://www.revenue.ie/annualreport/annualreport_2000/anrep_00.pdf

Santos, J. (2003), E-Service Quality: A Model of Virtual Service Quality Dimensions. *Managing Service Quality*, 13 (3), pp 233-246.

Swartz, T.A., Brown, S.W. (1989). Consumer and Provider Expectations and Experience in Evaluating Professional Service Quality, *Journal of the Academy of Marketing Science*, 17, pp 189-95.

Szymanski, D. M and Hise, R. T. (2000), e-Satisfaction: An Initial Examination, *Journal of Retailing,* 76 (3), pp 309-322.

TALC (Taxation Administration Liaison Committee) (2004) *Minutes of meeting held on 10th February 2004*, retrieved 30th April 2007 from: www.revenue.ie/doc/minstalc100204.doc

Teas, K.R. (1993), Consumer Expectations and the Measurement of Perceived Service Quality, *Journal of Professional Services Marketing*, 8 (2), pp 33-53.

Trabold, L.M., Heim, G.R. and Field, J.M. (2006), Comparing e-Service Performance across Industry Sectors: Drivers of Overall Satisfaction in Online Retailing, *International Journal of Retail and Distribution Management*, 34 (4), pp 240-257.

Van Iwaarden, J., Van der Wiele, T., Ball, L., Millen, R. (2004), Perceptions about the Quality of Websites: A survey amongst students in Northeastern University and Erasmus University", *Information and Management*, 41 (8), pp 947 – 959.

Van Riel, A.C., Liljander, V, Jurriens P. (2001) Exploring Customer Evaluations of e-Services: A Portal Site. *International Journal of Services Marketing*, 12 (4), pp 359-377.

Wolfinbarger, M. and Gilly, M.C. (2003) eTailQ: Dimensionalizing, Measuring, and Predicting Retail Quality, *Journal of Retailing*, 79 (3), pp 183-198.

Yoo, B. and Donthu, N. (2001) Developing a Scale to Measure the Perceived Quality of an Internet Shopping Site (Sitequal), *Quarterly Journal of Electronic Commerce*, 2 (1) pp 31-46.

Zeithaml, V.A. (2002) Service Excellence in Electronic Channels, *Managing Service Quality,* 12 (3), pp 135-139.

Mypage and Borger.dk: A Case Study of Two Government Service Web Portals

Karin Furuli[1] and Sigrun Kongsrud[2]
[1] **Sogn og Fjordane University College, Norway**
[2] **Norway.no, Leikanger, Norway**
Originally published in EJEG (2007) Volume 5 Issue 2

Early on in the emergence of Web based e-government, having a national portal became *de rigueur* for governments. There has been some study of portals, but the work done by Karin Furuli and Sigrun Kongsrud in comparing the impact of two such web portals, one in Norway and one in Denmark, is one of the few deep comparisons of this sort in the literature. The authors analyse why the two portals have diverged in a number of ways ranging from their primary goals to their use of authentication technology. They derive a framework for examining portals from work by Richard Heeks and use this to compare the two sites. Some of the differences between the two portals, especially for two countries that one would expect to be similar in culture and politics, are quite striking, but much of the value of this paper lies in the analysis of the goals, and the logic and thinking behind them.

Abstract: This case study investigates the development of national portals offering online public services to citizens. Norway and Denmark are leading the way in developing online public services for citizens. In this study the development of the citizen portals Borger.dk in Denmark and Mypage in Norway will be examined. At present, documented research on national citizen portals is limited. Comparing the similarities and differences of citizen portals is an important part of e-government development. We have used a framework for comparing the portals. The research questions to be answered in this case study are: Why are citizen portals created? How does one deal with matters of security? How is portal development organized? This study is also intended to bring to light factors that have led to the differences in the development of Borger.dk and Mypage. The study is based on published and unpublished reports from the two countries in question, together with interviews with key persons.

Of additional interest, in conducting this study, is the opportunity to gain greater insight into the development of online services provided by the public sector. This case study also raises further questions relating to e-government to be used in future research.

Keywords: e-government, e-services, framework for comparing citizen portals, citizen portal, online public services, Borger.dk, Mypage.

1. Introduction

Governments are now positioning themselves to be part of the internet revolution (Butt and Persuad, 2005). As e-commerce matures and its tools and applications improve, greater attention is being given to its use to improve the business of public institutions and governments (Turban et al., 2006). Around the world, a variety of e-government initiatives are being taken to improve the efficiency and effectiveness of internal operations, communication with the public and engagement in transactional processes with individuals and organizations (Warkentin et al., 2002).

This research project has been carried out as a case study. Case study is a useful method when how, who and why questions can be asked about a contemporary set of events (Remenyi et al., 1998; Yin, 1994). Case studies can be used to explain and understand complex phenomena, and allow for meaningful exploration of real-life events (Remenyi et al., 1998). We considered case study a suitable research method because we wanted insight and in-depth understanding about the two citizen portals. The research questions defined for our study are formulated as why and how questions. We focus on simultaneous activities and have no control over behavioral events in the two projects. By using case study as a method we were able to get a deeper insight into the topic citizen portals in a controlled and limited manner, within a short period of time. A case study can also bring us to formulate new research questions.

Our research is based on interviews with key persons in the Borger.dk and Mypage projects. In addition a document and literature review has been performed. National e-government strategies and plans from Norway and Denmark have been undergoing thorough reading in the literature and document review. Evidence to answer our research questions was collected through the interviews and literature and document review. The findings are presented in section 4.

The structure of this paper is as follows: firstly, we present our understanding of the term e-government, followed by a description of the framework used to compare Borger.dk and Mypage. We then use this framework to compare the two portals and give a conclusion. Accordingly, in section 2 we provide a literature review to give an understanding of the term e-government and different maturity models of e-government. Section 3 describes our framework for comparing two citizen portals. In section 4 we present the cases and compare the portals, using the framework described in the previous section. Section 5 contains a conclusion. At the end of the paper in section 6, we address the possible limitations of our study and also propose focus for future research in this area.

2. Literature review

Before we begin to describe the framework for comparing the two portals, we will examine topical literature in order to define the term e-government, and to ascertain which agents are involved in e-government and at what stages of maturity e-government can be placed.

2.1. Definitions of e-government

E-government (electronic government) is a global phenomenon which is of interest for many operators: public administrations, politicians and citizens. There are many definitions of e-government, and these stress different aspects of governments' use of ICT.

It has been argued that e-government has many similarities with a socio-technical information system (Heeks, 2006), and that it consequently is not a new phenomenon. E-government can also be defined as the application of e-commerce technologies to government and public services for citizens and businesses (Chaffey, 2007). Heeks (2006) argues that it is not possible to transplant private sector ideas into the public sector. Governments are not businesses and are not investing in ICT to make a profit (Bannister and Walsh, 2002).

Definitions of e-government vary from having a narrow focus on use of ICT (and particularly the Internet), to delivering better governmental services, to wider definitions focusing on transforming government (Grant and Chau, 2005). From a set of identifying characteristics they define e-government as follows:

> *"A broad-based transformation initiative, enabled by leveraging the capabilities information and communication technology: (1) to develop and deliver high quality, seamless, and integrated public services; (2) to enable effective constituent relationship management; and (3) to support the economic and social development goals of citizens, businesses, and civil society at local, state, national and international levels." (Grant and Chau, 2005, p 9)*

The European Union (EU) also has a focus on e-government. In the e-government Action Plan there are five objectives for e-government (EU, 2005):

- No citizen left behind
- Making efficiency and effectiveness a reality
- Implementing high-impact key services for citizens and businesses
- Putting key enablers in place
- Strengthening participation and democratic decision-making

Grönlund and Ranerup (2001) found, in a review of definitions of e-government, that these definitions typically mention three goals: 1) better information and services to citizens, 2) improved citizen involvement in democratic processes, and 3) more efficient government.

E-government can involve relationships between government and different levels of constituents. The relations can be between:

- government and businesses (G2B)
- government and other government institutions (G2G)
- government and employees (G2E)
- government and citizens (G2C) (Long and Siau, 2006; Hiller and Bélanger, 2001).

There are many operators in e-government: from the individual citizen as a private person, to a business which has interests in the government's priorities for the private sector.

2.2. Stages of integration

Various benchmarking studies have been carried out in order to monitor the development of e-government (Accenture, 2005; CapGemini, 2004). These studies use different indicators for evaluation, and the studies are not necessarily comparable.

A number of e-government maturity models exist, focusing on how far integrated governmental services are. Various levels of e-government reflect the degree of technical sophistication and integration with users (Hiller and Bélanger, 2001). The models range from two to five maturity stages, and the names of the stages vary from model to model (Hiller and Bélanger, 2001; Reddick, 2004; Layne and Lee, 2001; Kaylor et al., 2001). The models indicate that e-government differs in complexity and levels of integration. An often referred-to maturity model is Layne and Lee's model, which operates with four stages:

- Catalogue (online presence, catalogue presentation, downloadable forms)
- Transaction (services and forms online, databases supporting online transactions)
- Vertical integration (local systems linked to higher level systems, within similar functionalities)
- Horizontal integration (systems integrated across different functions, real one stop shopping).

Hiller and Bélanger (2001) introduce political participation as a fifth stage in their model. Moon (2002) also uses a fifth stage model with political participation in his study of e-Government in municipalities. As a step in making information and services available to citizens, many nations establish a citizen portal which, among other things, will render government information and services easily accessible. Offering citizens a one-stop-shopping operation, with both horizontal and vertical integration, seems to be a suitable goal to work towards.

3. A framework for comparing citizen portals

A portal can be described as a website that offers numerous services such as e-mail, search engines, news and local information (Davis and Benamati, 2003). A portal often serves as the user's initial home page. A distinction is often made between horizontal and vertical portals. Horizontal portals define their market space to include all users of the Internet, and vertical portals are focused around a particular subject matter or market segment (Laudon and Traver, 2001). A citizen portal can be viewed as both a horizontal and vertical portal. Horizontal because it aims at reaching all citizens and vertical because the portal is restricted to the delivery of information and services from the government.

The two portals can both be described as citizen portals; it is the relationship between the government and the citizen that are in focus. The citizen can have different relations to the government (and to different parts of government). The citizen can act as a taxpayer and in other settings the citizen can act as a parent.

In our comparison, we have used a framework influenced by different sources. We have a bottom-up approach since our comparison is based on an application, a citizen portal, and subsequently this is seen in relation to specific strategy.

In a comparison of citizen portals there are many factors that can be compared. Our starting point was to see the citizen portal in relation to the authorities strategic focus on e-government. We could however have looked at the success of the citizen portals, and used the model of IS success from DeLone and McLean (1992). They created six categories of IS success (1) system quality, (2) information quality, (3) use, (4) user satisfaction, (5) individual impact and (6) organizational impact. The model has later been updated. Intention to use is included, individual impact and organizational impact are replaced by net benefits. Service quality is also included in the updated DeLone and McLean model of IS success (DeLone and McLean, 2003).

Another starting point could be to compare on the basis of the development process of the citizen portals, from not integrated e-services to integrated e-services gathered in a citizen portal.

In the following section we will give an account of the factors we have used in comparing the two portals.

3.1. Strategic level

The initiative for national plans for e-government may originate from different parts of the government, depending on the national organization. Likewise the focus on e-government will vary according to political priorities.

E-government can be thought of in terms of three distinct spheres: the administrative sphere, the civil society sphere, and the formal politics sphere (Grönlund, 2005). Since the three spheres are interrelated, a change can influence all spheres. E-government strategies have impact on the way governments interact with citizens (Chen et al., 2006). The development and implementation of e-government also causes impact and change in the structure and functioning of public administration (Snellen, 2000).

Establishing a citizen portal can be one of many ways in achieving strategic goals.

3.2. Main focus areas for a citizen portal

Larger departments and local authorities often have a portal established for citizens to access information and self-service operations. The inhabitant must have prior knowledge concerning who offers which service and then find the right portal. The establishment of portals may be cost efficient for governmental agencies, and they can introduce a higher service level for the citizens.

The focus on and establishment of portals can be part of a marketing process (Marche, 2003). The portal can play a role in making the department known to citizens. The citizen on the other hand, may first and foremost want to find information or carry out a service, without necessarily knowing who is offering the service. The administrative focus has gradually changed to become customer-focused, serving citizens and trading partners directly by providing electronic services, information and transactions online through the Internet (Devadoss et al., 2002). This has together with the desire to co-ordinate and simplify aspects of government, led to many countries establishing a national citizen portal.

The establishment of a citizen portal is a comprehensive task. A well developed infrastructure, culture and resources to undertake the task is among other things necessary to get it done. In addition, internal organizational changes in the departments may be required to gain full benefit from offering electronic services and information to the customer, i.e. the citizens. The citizens' adoption of electronic services also depends on many different factors, and extensive research exists in this area (Ajzen and Fishbein, 1972; Davis, 1989; Rogers, 1995).

Citizen portals can be pure information portals that give citizens access to public information and links to services. At the other end of the scale one finds portals requiring authentication and providing access to personalized services. It is our opinion that most citizen portals are somewhere between these extremities and offers a combination of information and services requiring authentication.

The establishment of a citizen portal may have both a democratic perspective and the perspective of the participant. The portal may create opportunities for easy contact and communication between citizen and government. A citizen portal can also be a step in improving privacy protection, because it can give citizens opportunities to access information and administrative processes concerning themselves.

3.3. Characteristics of citizen portals

A citizen portal can be viewed as an information system which is established as a step by authorities towards more focus on e-government. As with other information systems, a citizen portal cannot be seen in isolation, without connection to its surroundings. A model of an e-government system can be as follows:

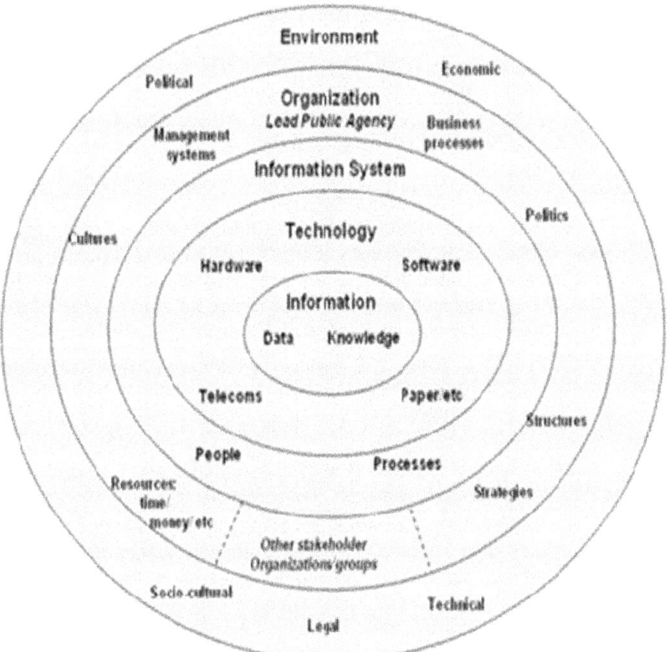

Figure 1: Full model of e-government systems (Heeks, 2006, p 5)

We choose to view a citizen portal as an information system. Heeks makes arguments for the same case in his work (Heeks, 2006). Therefore it is possible to look at specific characteristics of an information system as a basis for our comparison. Figure 1 shows the different elements of an e-government system, where elements of Heeks' checklist are included. Our checklist, or characteristics of citizen portals, is adapted from Heeks, and presented in table 1.

The list of characteristics in table 1 is influenced by what Heeks calls the ITPOSMO-checklist (Heeks, 2006). In short, these are elements used to describe and understand an e-government system and stakeholders' organizational context. The key items Heeks describes are Information, Technology, Processes, Objectives and values, Staffing and skills, Management systems and structures, and Other resources (Heeks, 2006).

Table 1: Adapted checklist for use in this case study

Keyword	Description
Goals	What are the articulated goals for a citizen portal?
Information	We are interested in the content of the citizen portal. What kind of services does a portal contain? We will also look at how the services are gathered and presented. In addition, it is of interest to examine the demands to make services available on the portal. A citizen portal can be viewed as a collection of information and services from numerous service suppliers. A lot of information has to be exchanged between these operators. The number of services on the citizen portal may be a result of this exchange of information.
Technology and security	Details of security and technology are usually not available to the general public. It is therefore not our purpose to go in-depth in relation to technical details in this research. Authentication is required to access personal information and services. How is this solved in the two citizen portals?
Processes (the organization of development)	The establishment of a citizen portal may involve changes to many of the processes which involve its various users and operators. The citizens will acquire new channels for carrying out a service or finding information. The government may have to change internal processes when its contact with the public is moved to new channels. Internal tasks will be changed as a result of offering services and information through the portal. Because of the high number of potential users and service suppliers, and because of their diversity, it will be difficult to say something with exactitude about the processes among the different users and operators. We have focused on the process of system development through which the two citizen portals have been established. It is of interest to look at the various participators and their respective roles in the projects.
Administration and operation	After the development process is completed and the citizen portal is deployed, there will be a need for an administration of the everyday management of the portal. How is the administration of the citizen portals arranged after implementation?
Implementation	We use the term implementation in connection with the introduction of the citizen portal to the public. This is of interest to us because it can tell us something about the government's active role and priorities in the launching of the citizen portal. What steps has the government taken to promote the citizen portal?

4. Cases and comparing

In our comparison we use the framework described in chapter three with subchapters. The content of table 2 is a brief account of our framework, and the table will be described in the sections following. Finally, under each point in the framework, we will say something about the differences between the two countries.

Table 2: Comparing citizen portals – a brief account

	Borger.dk (Denmark)	**Mypage (Norway)**
Strategic level (Ref. chapter 3.1)	Effective and coordinated public sector, high service quality, central focus on citizens and the private sector.	Knowledge society, exploit the potential of ICT, an easier life for individuals and businesses, value creation, best possible services for available resources.
Main focus area (Ref. chapter 3.2)	A more complete user experience, overview over the new Denmark, easier and faster for the citizen, promote use and access to digital citizen service, insight into public sector.	An easier everyday life for citizens, common entry to electronic services and dialogue with the public sector, access to own information.
Characteristics of citizen portals: (Ref. chapter 3.3, table 1)		
Goals	Making contact with the public sector on the Internet easier.	A public service office on the Internet, electronic services with secure authentication.
Information	Thematically based information plus a self-service solution. Those who deliver the service are responsible for it.	Thematically based structure with access to personalized services. Those who deliver the service are responsible for it.
Technology and security	Authentication with digital signatures. Single sign-on. A minimum of stored information.	Authentication with pin-codes. Single sign-on. A minimum of stored information.
Processes	Local authorities were an important partner in the first phase. Subsequent development as a cooperation project between Ministry of Science, Technology and Innovation (VTU) and KL (our explanation: federation of local authorities).	Developed in cooperation between many public departments, lead by Ministry of Government, Administration and Reform (FAD).
Administration and operation	A coordinating editorial office and a contact center	An administration organization established.
Implementation	Staff at libraries and municipal service as ambassadors.	Press releases and advertisements in media.

4.1. Strategic level

The strategy for digital government in Denmark is written in Strategy for Digital Government 2004-2006 (Regjeringen et al., 2004). This strategy was discontinued at the end of 2006, and Denmark is now working on a new strategy with duration to 2010. The vision for digital government is:

> *"Digitalization shall contribute to an effective and coordinated public sector with high service quality, where citizens and the private sector are in the center." (Regjeringen et al.,2004, p 4, our translation)*

The Danish strategy is regulated by five prescribed target areas with goals for each area (Regjeringen et al., 2004). Keywords for the five target areas are:

- The public sector shall deliver coordinated services with focus on citizens and the private sector
- Digital government shall lead to increased service quality and release resources
- The public sector shall cooperate and communicate digitally
- Digital governments shall have a coordinated and flexible ICT-infrastructure
- Public leaders shall lead the way in ensuring that their organization can carry out the vision

The responsibility for e-government in Denmark is exercised through a set of institutional arrangements overseen by the Joint Board of e-government. The Board is chaired by the Parliamentary Secretary to the Ministry of Finance, with membership from state, regional and municipal government. The Board leads the national e-government program, Project e-government. Delivery of the project is the joint responsibility of The Digital Taskforce (OECD, 2005).

The establishment of Borger.dk is not explicitly mentioned in the strategy for 2004-2006. The first version of Borger.dk is a result of cooperation between VTU and KL.

In Norway the strategy on e-government can be found in the document eNorway 2009 – the digital leap. There is no detailed vision proclaimed here, but the main thoughts are:

> *"The government wishes to create a knowledge society in which everyone can participate and which exploits the potential of information technology. Norway's advanced use of technology shall provide its population and businesses with an easier life and contribute to promoting value creation, thereby ensuring prosperity and welfare for future generations. Information technology shall support the advance of a public sector that provides the best possible services, based on resources it has at its disposal. The needs of its population, its businesses and industry shall be at the heart of the development of the digital Norway." (Moderniseringsdepartementet, 2005, p 2)*

The plan continues the previous eNorway plans, and it describes three target areas (Moderniseringsdepartementet, 2005):

- The individual in digital Norway
- Innovation and growth in businesses and industry
- A coordinated and user-adapted public sector.

The establishment of a citizen portal as a step in offering digital services to citizens is described in the plan. The Government has recently presented a report to Parliament concerning information society and e-government (Fornyings- og administrasjons-departementet, 2006b).

The Government's coordination of ICT policies is the responsibility of FAD. Responsibility for telecommunication politics, ICT research and the ICT industry is divided between several departments. It is up to each ministry and department to translate the common vision into concrete plans. A few coordinating forums in the ICT-sector have been established and one of these is the Coordinating body for E-government.

FAD (previously known as the Ministry of Modernization) is responsible for establishing the Norwegian citizen portal Mypage.

As we see it, Denmark emphasizes the importance of having a coherent public sector. Norway wishes to use technology to make everyday life less complex and to promote the building of value capacities, whilst digital administration in Denmark will provide increased quality of service and release resources. Both visions are oriented towards businesses and citizens.

4.2. Main focus areas for a citizen portal

In 2005 a comprehensive survey was carried out in Denmark to give an account of digital communication between the public sector and the general public (Videnskabsministeriet, 2005). The survey revealed that citizens want public information to be presented to them with their life situations as starting point, rather than the governmental organization.

As a result of this it was decided that a citizen portal should be established and replace the municipal portal Netborger.dk and the governmental portal Danmark.dk. In Denmark it is emphasized that the process of developing a citizen portal is a long-term activity constituting several phases and milestones. The current Borger.dk version is a milestone in a course planned to end in 2010 with a 100% complete Borger.dk (Den Digitale Taskforce, 2006), similar in function to Mypage.

The vision of Borger.dk is to give a more coherent user experience of public digital services and to provide a view of the new Denmark as a result of the municipal reform. The vision is also to make it faster and easier for the citizen to become self-served through the Internet, to encourage the use of and the knowledge of digital citizen services, and to give an insight into the public sector and its democratic work (IT- og Telestyrelsen, 2006). By 2008 Borger.dk will according to the plan consist of a citizen guide and a Mypage- unit with coordinated and coherent access to digital self-service solutions and the individual citizen's own data.

Mypage was launched in December 2006, after two years of intensive work. The vision of Mypage is to contribute to a simpler and more effective dialogue between citizens and the public sector. Another aim is to give an overview of what information the individual departments have concerning the individual citizen (Moderniseringsdepartementet, 2005). Mypage is part of Norway.no, which acts as a gateway to the public sector in Norway.

The vision for the Danish citizen portal may look broader than the Norwegian vision. Denmark has recently completed a municipal reform that was implemented in January 2007, and the citizen portal is to be a navigational aid after the reform. The Danish portal also emphasizes the promotion of digital self-service and insight into the public sector, while the Norwegian portal emphasizes insight into and access to the public sector's information about the individual.

4.3. Characteristics of citizen portals

This section references keywords presented in section 3.3, table 1.

4.3.1. *Goals*

Both portals have their articulated goals. The goals shall support the vision for the citizen portal and for the nation's vision for e-government in general.

The superior object with Borger.dk is to simplify citizens' contact with public government.

According to the eNorway-plan, Mypage shall be an online electronic public service, allowing the general public to access services from a personalized window with a secure logon. Mypage shall be a user-defined service in which relevant information about each individual is available in one place (Moderniseringsdepartementet 2005, p 10).

We wish to point out that the given objectives for Borger.dk are based on the present version, and that these are likely to be elaborated with the introduction of the customized Mypage- part of the portal, in the new strategy for digital government. While the Danish portal intends to simplify communication with public government through the Internet, the Norwegian portal has elaborated its objectives, in the sense that the pages are customized and the citizen can access electronic services with a secure logon. The reason why this is not mentioned in the Danish vision is probably a result of the fact that Denmark is at an earlier stage than Norway, regarding implementation of the personalized part of the portal.

4.3.2. *Information*

The Danish Borger.dk currently contains an information section about public administration. The information is structured thematically, with 18 topics, but the user can choose to view it alphabetically. In addition to this the portal contains a self-service component where the user can link up to different public authorities and agencies that offer interactive services. Self-service can vary from printing out a form, to electronically reporting relocation to a new address in the national register. The service also includes an option for selecting municipality. The personalized part of the Danish portal will be organized thematically, and will include themes like MyPension, MyHouse etc.

The menu in Mypage consists of different topics, each containing different services. Mypage offers different types of services, such as register and transaction services. Transaction services allow the user to carry out an actual service linked to an agency or local authority. The register services will display information stored about the citizen in various departmental registers. Examples of such information are MyAddress, MyProperties or MyFamilyDoctor. In Mypage you can select one or more municipalities and a link to the municipality's home site and services. Mypage does not contain public information, as its function is to give access to personalized services, while the mother portal, Norway.no, contains public information and functions as a guide to such information.

Both register and transaction services will be carried out on the agencies' own website (a municipal or governmental website). The owner of the service has full responsibility for it.

In Norway the task of getting more municipalities and agencies to take part and make their services available on Mypage is given continuous priority. The idea being that the more services that are included in Mypage, the more value Mypage will have for the citizen.

The Danish portal secretariat experiences that municipal and governmental agencies take a strong interest in having links to Borger.dk, seeing their role as partners that can help citizens in search of the right information. The integration of new services is not a particular focus, since the portal is under development.

4.3.3. *Technology and security*

According to the initial Norwegian plan, authentication and logon to Mypage should be based on a common public security portal. However, the business model was not accepted by the vendors of PKI (public key infrastructure), and the general agreement concerning security portal services was discontinued. Instead, it was replaced by a temporary solution based on PIN-codes from the Directorate of Taxes (Fornyings- og administrasjonsdepartementet, 2006a). A revised strategy on eID and e-signatures in public sector is out on hearing by February 2007.

At Borger.dk, authentication for the self-service operations requires the user's PIN-code or digital signature, and the service vendor decides which authentication is required. When the Mypage section is integrated in Borger.dk, authentication will be solely through digital signature.

Both portals are based on single sign-on, and the citizen can use all the services that reside in the portal. The amount of data stored in the portals is kept to a minimum.

Privacy protection has been given high priority during the development of Norwegian Mypage, and it has also been focused on during the development of Borger.dk. The major difference regarding authentication is that while Denmark has chosen digital signatures, Norway is still searching for a permanent solution.

4.3.4. *Processes*

The development of Mypage in Norway has been organized as a reception and a vendor project. The vendor project consists of the vendor developing the technical solution. The reception project, directed by the Ministry of Government Administration and Reform, comprised representatives from a number of public agencies. These were responsible for the specification and clarification of all circumstances tied to the project solution.

In Denmark, the further development of Borger.dk will be supervised by a broadly based project group, directed by the Ministry of Science, Technology and Innovation, and KL. The project group will be responsible for specification, deliveries and coordination (Den Digitale Taskforce, 2006).

Common to both cases is that a broad compound collaboration has been established between the authorities and the various agencies. The municipalities however do seem to have been involved to a larger extent in Denmark than in Norway.

4.3.5. *Administration and operation*

An administration has been established to manage, operate and further develop Mypage, with close links to the public service that operates Norway.no. Tasks will include adding new services to the portal, and maintaining contact with vendors and government.

In Denmark there are plans for establishing a coordinating editorial office and a contact center for user support and guidance. These two units will work with editorial guidelines for the citizen portal, cooperation with municipalities and agencies, and user support and guidance (Den Digitale Taskforce, 2006).

4.3.6. *Implementation*

The Danish Borger.dk had approximately 250 000 users two weeks after the portal had been deployed (Borger.dk, 2007), while Norway's Mypage had 100 000 users three weeks after being deployed (Fornyings- og administrasjonsdepartementet, 2007). In Denmark, users of the old portals, Netborger.dk and Danmark.dk, are redirected to Borger.dk. This may be one of the reasons for the higher numbers in Denmark. The difference may also be ascribed to the fact that Mypage does not include public information, as is the case with Borger.dk.

In Denmark there are plans for assigning staff at libraries and municipal service centers the task of being ambassadors for Borger.dk (Den Digitale Taskforce, 2006).

When Norway's Mypage was launched, an information letter and PIN-codes were distributed to 4 million citizens, and this was followed by press releases and advertisements in the media.

5. Conclusion

We have compared two citizen portals similar in the sense that they both provide services to the public. The Norwegian Mypage is a collection of personalized services, where authentication is required in order for the individual user to access his or her own services. Denmark has chosen to gather both public information and self-service operations in one portal, Borger.dk.

Why are citizen portals created? Our findings indicate that citizen portals are developed to give a more open government administration and to give citizens easy access to public information and services.

How does one deal with matters of security? Denmark wants to use digital signature for authentication, and there is a long-term strategy that supports this as one of many common components in the citizen portal. Norway is still working towards a mutual security solution for the public sector. There is a strategy on PKI in the public sector, and an ongoing strategy work on eID and e-Signatures. A temporary system for authentication is in use on Mypage at the present time.

How is portal development organized? The development of the two portals has been organized in much the same way. In both countries the projects have been broadly based, with participants from the authorities and different underlying agencies. It seems that greater attention has been paid to the municipalities in Denmark than in Norway.

6. Limitations and future research

We have compared the portals as they were at the time we undertook the comparison. In Norway, Mypage is already developed and deployed. In Denmark, the Mypage part of the portal is still being developed. It may be important for the result of our comparison that there are differences in stages of development, with regard to the personalized part of the citizen portals.

Our research has been performed as a case study. The case study evidence was used in presenting and comparing the citizen portals. Interviews and other types of documentation are inevitably colored to a certain extent by the views of the interviewee and those who have written the documentation. Our subjective interpretation of statements and literature will also characterize our presentation. We also bring with us a predisposed attitude because of our involvement in the development of the Norwegian portal. We have, however, aimed at objectivity regarding our findings and our presentation in general.

We have focused on only two citizen portals, and these two have many similarities. Our focus has been to compare only parts of the portals, excluding other aspects such as infrastructure, technical construction, and the transition from development to administration. We can in no way generalize our findings to be valid for anything other than the two specific citizen portals. With more time and resources available to compare a larger number of citizen portals we believe it is possible to create a more comprehensive and credible research result.

In future research we therefore recommend that a larger study with comparison of a larger number of portals is conducted. In doing so one might receive findings that can be generalized in a broader way. A possible future research on our own part is to continue developing the initial framework presented in this paper, and then conduct a more comprehensive study.

We believe future research should undertake a study with focus on portal users. Possible research questions might be: Are there differences in the number of users, frequency of use, the attitude of the users and/or the various services used? What might be the reasons behind differences discovered? It could also be interesting to find out if there are connections between development and initial deploying activities, and citizens' adoption of the portals.

We are under the impression that there have not been any comprehensive studies of citizen portals earlier. Future research should therefore focus on specific public services and different aspects of these services. One could also look at service providers in the portals as a starting point and look at their role in the development of electronic services. We believe a study of the different operators and stakeholders in the development of citizen portals also could make an interesting case. Another phase of interest in such a study could be the implementation phase.

References

Accenture (2005). Leadership in customer service: New expectations, New experiences, [Online]. Available: http://www.accenture.com/ [Last seen: 12. January, 2007]

Ajzen, I. and Fishbein, M. (1972). Attitudes and normative beliefs as factors influencing intentions. Journal of Personality and Social Psychology, 21, pp 1-9.

Bannister, F. and Walsh, N. (2002). The virtual public servant: Ireland's public services broker. Information Polity, 7 (2002) pp 115-127, IOS Press.

Butt, I. and Persuad, A. (2005). Towards a Citizen Centric Model of E-Government Adoption. Proceedings from 3rd International Conference on E-Governance, Lahore Pakistan.

CapGemini (2004). Online availability of public services: how is Europe progressing? [Online] Available: http://europa.eu.int/information_society/eeurope/2005/doc/all_about/online_availability_public_services_5th_measurement_fv4.PDF [Last seen: 31. January, 2007]

Borger.dk (2007). Flyvende start for Borger.dk, præssemeddelelse 18.1.2007 [Online]

Available: http://www.borger.dk/forside/aktuelt/faktaside?p_nyhedid=141 [Last seen: 20. January, 2007]

Chaffey, D. (2007). E-Business and E-Commerce Management. Third ed., Prentice Hall, Essex, England.

Chen, Y.N., Chen, H.M., Huang, W. and Ching, R.K.H. (2006). E-Government Strategies in Developed and Developing Countries: An Implementation Framework and Case Study. Journal of Global Information Management, 14(1) pp 23-46 January-March.

Davis, F. (1989). Perceived usefulness, perceived ease of use and user acceptance of information technology. MIS Quarterly, Vol 13 No 3, pp 319-340.

Davis, W. and Benamati, J. (2003). E-commerce basics Technology Foundations and E-Business Applications, Addison Wesley, USA.

DeLone, W. H. and Mc Lean, E. R. (1992). "Information systems success: the quest for the dependent variable". Information Systems Research, 3, 1 pp 60-95.

DeLone, W. H. and McLean, E. R. (2003). "The DeLone and McLean Model of Information Systems Success: A Ten-Year Update". Journal of Management Information Systems, Vol 19, 4, pp 9-30.

Den Digitale Taskforce (2006). Analyse av fællesoffentlig borgerportal [Online]. Available: http://e.gov.dk/ [Last seen: 15. January, 2007]

Devadoss, P.R., Pan, S.L. and Huang, J.R. (2002). Structional analysis of e-government initiatives: a case study og SCO. Decision Support Systems, 34, pp 253-269.

EU (2005). "i2010. "i2010 – A European Information Society for growth and employment". Commision of the european communities, Brussels [Online]. Available: http://ec.europa.eu/information_society/eeurope/i2010/index_en.htm [Last seen: 19. october 2007].

Fornyings- og administrasjonsdepartementet (2006a). Underveisrapport for eNorge 2009 –status for måloppnåelse og tiltak-oktober 2006 [Online] Available: http://www.regjeringen.no/ [Last seen: 2. February, 2007]

Fornyings- og administrasjonsdepartementet (2006b). Stortingsmelding nr 17 (2006-2007) Et informasjonssamfunn for alle. Fornyings- og administrasjonsdepartementet, Oslo, Norge.

Fornyings- og administrasjonsdepartementet (2007). Over 100 000 brukarar på Minside – pressemelding 8.01. 2007 [Online]. Available: http://www.regjeringen.no/nb/dep/fad/pressesenter/pressemeldinger/ [Last seen: 15. February, 2007]

Grant, G. and Chau, D. (2005). Developing a Generic Framework for E-Government. Journal of Global Information Management, 13(1), pp 1-30, Jan-March 2005.

Grönlund, Å. (2005). What's In a Field – Exploring the eGoverment Domain. Proceedings from the 38th Hawaii International Conference on System Sciences, Hawaii, USA.

Grönlund, Å. and Ranerup A. (eds) (2001). Elektronisk förvaltning, elektronisk demokrati Visioner, verklighet, vidareutveckling. Studentlitteratur, Lund.

Heeks, R. (2006) Implementing and Managing e-government. SAGE Publications, London.

Hiller, J. and Bélanger, F. (2001), Privacy strategies for Electronic Government. In Abrahamson, M.A. and Means, G.E. (eds), Rowman and Littlefield Publishers, Oxford.

IT- og Telestyrelsen (2006). eDanmark om kommunikation, innovation og teknik – eDanmark nr 2 2006 [Online]. Available: http://www.itst.dk/wimpdoc.asp?page=tema&objno=115891331 [Last seen: 20. February, 2007]

Laudon, K.C. and Traver,C.G. (2001). E-commerce business technology society, Addison Wesley, USA.

Layne, K. and Lee, J. (2001). Developing fully functional E-government: A four stage model. Government Information Quarterly, 18, pp 122-136.

Long, Y.A. and Siau, K. (2006). Using social development lenses to understand e-government development. Journal of global management, 14 (1), pp 47-62, Jan-March 2006.

Kaylor, R., Deshazo, R. and Van Eck, D. (2001). Gauging e-government: A report on implementing services among American cities. Government Information Quarterly, 18, pp 293-307.

Marche, S. (2003). E-government and e-governance: The future isn't what it used to be. Canadian Journal of Administrative Sciences, Vol 20, No 1, pp 74-86.

Moderniseringsdepartementet (2005). eNorge 2009 – det digitale spranget. Moderniseringsdepartementet, Oslo, Norge.

Moon, M. J. (2002) The evolution of E-Government among Municipalities: Rhetoric or Reality? Public Administration Review, Vol 62 (4), pp 424-433.

OECD (2005). OECD Peer Review of e-Government in Denmark, Pre-publication draft version 2-25. September 2005 [Online] Available: http://ec.europa.eu/idabc/servlets/Doc?id=23133 [Last seen: 14. January, 2007]

Reddick, C.G. (2004). A two stage model of e-government growth: Theories and empirical evidence for U. S. Cities. Governmental Information Quarterly, Vol 21, pp 51-64.

Regjeringen, KL, Amtsrådsforeningen, Københavns kommune and Fredriksberg kommune (2004). Den offentlige sektors strategi for digital forvaltning 2004-2006 – realisering av potentialet. Den digitale Taskforce, København, Danmark.

Remenyi, D., Williams, B., Money, A., and Swartz, E. (2003). Doing Research in Business and Management. SAGE Publications Ltd., London.

Rogers, E. (1995). Diffusion of innovations. The Free Press, New York, USA .

Snellen, I. (2000). Electronic commerce and bureaucraties. Proceedings of the 11th International Workshops on Database and Expert System Application, pp 285-288.

Turban, E., King D., Viehland, D. and Lee, J. (2006). Electronic commerce: A Managerial Perspective. Pearson Prentice Hall, New Jersey.

Videnskabsministeriet (2005). Digital kommunikation mellom det offentlige og borgerne [Online]. Available: http://videnskabsministeriet.dk/site/forside [Last seen: 19. February, 2007]

Warkentin, M., Gefen D., Pavlou, P.A. and Rose, G.M. (2002). Encouraging Citizen Adoption of e-Government by Building Trust. Electronic Markets, Vol 12, No. 3, pp 157-162.

Yin, R.K. (1994). Case study research Design and Methods. SAGE Publications, California.

Case Study: e-Youth City Council Project an Alternative e-Government for Young People

Gemma Gibert i Font
Town Hall of Sant Andreu de Llavaneres, Catalonia, Spain
Originally published in EJEG (2009) Volume 7 Issue 4.

Experiments are not the most common form of research in information systems, partially because they are hard to do properly, are time consuming and often require lots of volunteers. In this case study, Gemma Gibert i Font describes, to use her words, an explanatory analysis of an experiment in the Catalonia region of Spain into engaging young people in the processes of government. This included a mock election campaign with electronic voting and use of hard and electronic media to try to convince the voters. Those elected were empowered to run the Youth movement in the town. Gilbert i Font then examines what happened next and in particular how the voting system worked. Her conclusions include that to engage young people in politics, electronic tools are not enough, something that some of the more enthusiastic advocates of e-democracy might note. This case and the one following make a complementary pair of studies which are worth reading in tandem.

Abstract: This article presents an explanatory analysis of an e- Youth City Council project held in the town of Sant Andreu de Llavaneres, Catalonia, during the year 2008. The main objectives of this programme were to increase citizen participation, improve good governance and through it, the possibility of consolidating and strengthening democracy by ICT use. This case study was based on a survey of 628 young people aged between 14 and 18. The aim was to motivate and enable them to play an active role in politics and to take up positions of genuine authority and responsibility, within local decision making, as pre-voting citizens. In this way, the young people engaged to develop all stages of the electoral process, participated in an e-voting system and were empowered in local government for 15 days. In this case polity was translated into practice and created a successful partnership between young citizens and the local political parties. The focus of this ICT research was, basically, which tools the youngsters used and the influence they had on electorate participation. In this way, the ICT acquired a new perspective relating to this study group who are considered a generation raised in a computerised era and who are leaders in the fields of innovation and communication, used as a common tool in their social life and work. The analysis is described and evaluated by explanatory variables such as: population, age, ICT use and access, number of voters and abstentions, the ajuntamentjove.cat website, political party blogs, electoral campaign spots and meetings, the electronic voting system and finally the video "Youth Government Constitution" broadcast by internet into the school classroom. Electronic voting was incorporated as a pilot test, consisting of a voting system of closed lists with a choice of up to two preferential candidates.

Keywords: e-Government, young citizens, participation, ICT, democracy and policy, e-voting

1. Introduction

1.1. Background

Sant Andreu de Llavaneres is a small town located 40km from Barcelona, Catalonia. It has a population of about 10,120 residents. The study group was made up of teenagers ranging from 14 to 18 years, representing an electoral roll of 628 people (value of 6,28% of the population). The study group can be divided into two groups with different characteristics: 14 to 16 year olds in compulsory secondary education and the 16 to 18 year olds, sub-divided into those who continued in higher education and those who went into the working world. The school group was made up of 57% (358 pupils); personal data and information about this group was taken from the school and teachers while personal information pertaining to the working group came from the council register.

1.2. Objectives and goals

The young were given a voice to make decisions on the city council.

The main objective of the project "e-Youth City Council" was focused on developing a mechanism by which the youngsters could learn about the electoral process, public administration, local government and the responsibility of being a citizen. Through this work, the youngsters were provided with the tools and resources to design their own policies and demands and also to empower the governing body to carry them out.

1.2.1. *Creation of a Youth Commission*

To create the Council of Youth as a new body:

- To inform, consult and make proposals to design a policy on youth.
- To plan activities which encourage young people to participate in community life.
- To be the interlocutor between the young and the city councillors.
- To bond the young collective of the town.
- To carry out the negotiations and management of the Llavaneres Youth town-ship.

1.2.2. *Educational Framework.*

Educational law has currently introduced two subjects into secondary schools for the academic year 2008/9, *Citizenship* and *Philosophy and Education for personal development and citizenship.* The content of these subjects treats themes on concepts of the democratic system, cultural participation, interaction and relations between citizens and the government, its operation and governance. While studying these subjects the students are viewed as real citizens.

Our aim has been to give an opportunity to administration, pupils, teachers and schools to put what they have learnt into practice and evaluate this experience of local democracy. This programme was planned with the collaboration of the school director, pedagogic coordinator and teachers who believe that the project created activities to give young people a learning experience in democracy.

1.2.3. *Direct Political youth participation.*

> *"Our political system is based on a representative concept of democracy ... we should not forget that the representative system is also exposed to a series of dangers... excessive prominence on behalf of political representatives can easily undermine the central role that citizens should play in all good democratic systems..., it is thought more convenient to encourage mechanisms for participative democracy, that is, an instrument by which citizens can express*

their opinions and become involved in the complex world of political decisions. In effect, its objective is that citizens not only express themselves in very distant periods of time but rather that they play a leading role in the daily adoption of decisions on behalf of the corresponding administration."[1]

In the last decades, some of the main roles and institutions of representative democracy have suffered a constant loss of confidence from their citizens. It is known as disaffection and some studies say that the indicators of this situation are "loss of interest in policy, fall of electoral participation from the eighties (OECD countries) distrust towards institutions, authorities and representatives and the decrease of partisan and union affiliation". (Dalton and Walberg, 2000; Putnam 2003; Huse, 2003)[2]

Studies on disaffection propose various measures to try to change these attitudes through explicitness, transparency and support, participation, responsibility and accountability.[3]

For these reasons the project was an attempt to build up a culture of participation. This line of participation is based on direct involvement by the citizen which, from our point of view, means that they can identify with policy when taking part in decision making. However, the mechanism that enables citizens to participate politically requires a culture of political commitment that those implicated can only obtain when participation is put into practice. From our perspective, participation is best taught by active involvement and being given the channels and resources to apply it.

Finally, the small population of the town of Llavaneres permits a comfortable relationship between the governing body and its citizens and it is best

---

[1] Electronic Democracy and Citizen Participation, a sociological and legal report on Citizen Consultation, Dr. Jordi Barrat, and Reniu, Josep Mª,OVE, University of Leon,September2004. http://www.epractice.eu/files/upload/gpc/document/1612-1181135609.pdfMadrid (page 38/77)

[2]www.uoc.edu/idp/6/dt/esp/borge_colombo_welp.pdf2 Blanco Ismael i Mas Pau, La Desafecció Política a Catalunya, Fundació Jaume Bofill, novembre 2007.

[3] Blanco Ismael i Mas Pau, La Desafecció Política a Catalunya, Fundació Jaume Bofill, novembre 2007.

if we refer to the study group. It should be remembered that small towns have administrations that are close to their citizens.

1.2.4. *Promoting ICT among Llavaneres youth.*

The eruption of the use of ICT is influenced, as some studies report, by the rapport between the citizens and their representatives, promoting civil participation and making changes in public administration. It is necessary to be aware that the local area favours participation due to the proximity of the local government which promotes dialogue with those involved (Schneider*).*In this manner, the participants and the citizens are integrated into the processes of decision making and public management; a mechanism to increase efficiency and to favour the implementation of policies. (Riley, 2003; Goss, 2001; Kooiman, 2005; Brugué y Gomà 1998)4

Moreover, the youth collective is considered to be a group with more access to and awareness of these new forms of communication because they were born into the IT generation.

The project used ICT in:

- Electronic voting.
- Official Youth Website; www.ajuntamentjove.cat
- Entry to the political Blog.

We consider these tools are not purely political participation channels but also media facilitators as an alternative mechanism to participate.

2. Planning the project

This plan was divided into several parts:

---

[4] Revista d'Internet, dret I Política, Borge, Rosa, Colombo, Clelia, Welp Yanina " Explanatory analysis of electronic and presentational citizen participation in the municipal areas of Catalonia" Open University of Catalonia.. IDP Number 6 (2008) I ISSN 1699-8154: http://www.uoc.edu/idp/6/dt/esp/borge_colombo_welp.pdf

2.1. First part "Acquiring basic democratic concepts"

2.1.1. *Activities and workshops.*

The purpose of this section was to provide enough knowledge for policy and the system to be understood, thereby bringing the voice of the younger generation to the government.

These activities were:

- Video Youth Council. (www.youtube.com//watch?v=9NJjP7Uzoqc)
- The video e-youth city council was made by the group of members of the 1st edition of the project. These members explained the steps of the electoral procedure and invited young people into the experience.
- Two conferences were given by the present councillors and the youngest councillors (aged up to 30 years).
- Informative sessions. An informative session was planned with twelve classrooms where technicians from the city council (about 20 people) explained what their work consisted of and how they developed their policies. The second session was given by municipal technicians and described the function of the Youth Council, their services and the project.
- City Council workshops. The specialists prepared five workshops on culture, the environment, urbanism, psychology and education, where pupils could participate and put into practice the concepts acquired during the informative sessions. The workshops were not compulsory and the overall attendance was 60 youngsters.

2.2. Second Part "Focusing the Knowledge"

2.2.1. *Making proposals.*

Pupils from the twelve classrooms made their claims and demands to improve activities and issues in the municipal government. They made 97 proposals of which 21 were approved by the municipal plenary and were included in the current budget. Most of these proposals were listed on the electoral program. The Youth department would work, together with members from the list of candidates, in a committee to develop these policies.

2.3. Third Part. "Electoral Process"

2.3.1. *Electoral Campaign*

The period of the electoral campaign was seven days from the 3rd to the 10th November 2008.There were five lists of candidates: one list composed of people of 14 years old, another mixed list of young people between 14 and 15 years old, a list of 16 year olds and two others of 17 to 18 year olds. Each list was composed of a minimum of seven members and the rest were substitutes. The political parties held meetings during school breaks, in the town, in the town hall and through the media of local and county digital television. They also published leaflets and programs to try to convince voters. They created specific blogs with

- Statements and achievements.
- Electoral programme
- Publicity spots (www.youtube.com/watch?v=3FX3i5EZPu8)
- Surveys of their electoral programme proposals.

There were 5 lists of candidates and the blog site was housed on the official website linked by frame: http://ajuntamentjove2008e.blogspot.com/

The addresses of the parties' blog sites are:

- http://jovesambidees.blogspot.com/ (Youth with Ideas)
- http://futures-promises.blogspot.com/ (Futures promises)
- http://3viles.blogspot.com/ (3 Viles Group)
- http://alternativaperllavaneres.blogspot.com/ (Llavaneres Group)
- http://podemmillorarllavaneres.blogspot.com/ (We can Improve Llavaneres)
- The Content of the Youth website (www.ajuntamentjove.cat) consists of:
- e-youth City Council News: Containing news, event calendar, activities they can do and summaries of their achievements with photos.
- e-youth City Council blog site with the candidates' blogs.
- e-youth City Council elections. This site contains a guide to the e-voting process pilot test with demonstrations, the results and news of the electoral process.

The official website has had 7,225 visitors.

3. Electronic voting

3.1. Why electronic voting?

During the last elections held by the Youth City Council, the number of voters was about 62%; we showed that this percentage of voters was similar to that of the local municipal elections.

This new addition put to the test whether technology provided a useful mechanism to engage young people democratically and increase the electorate and therefore the number of voters.

The e-youth City Council is the first pioneering project in electronic voting in the whole of Catalonia and includes a pilot test designed by the political commission of the Public Administration Department of Catalonia. The project was financed by the Catalan government, *La Generalitat de Catalunya.*

Therefore, the overall objectives of electronic voting are:

- To increase the number of voters in the Youth City Council elections.
- To evaluate the impact of the ICT on this group.
- To evaluate the disaffection of the pre-voters.
- To guarantee the rights of voters; secrecy and a transparent process of voting.

3.2. Requirements and features to make use of electronic voting

- The Youth electoral role was about 628.
- Election of a list of candidates among several. Closed lists.
- The election supports both types of election (ballot and remote)
- Pilot test: closed lists with preferential voting system with a choice of 2 candidates. If there were 5% of voters who voted for the same preference of candidate, that candidate took up the first position on the list.
- The requirements for voter identification were an authorization and a National Identification Card . The authorization was a code of 16 alpha-numeric characters which the voters received by post or from school.

- The voting application was housed on the youth official website.
- Remote voting allowed numerous votes, the final vote being valid.
- The ballot was allowed once and automatically invalidated the electronic vote.
- The voting application introduced the concept of the invalid vote. It was designed on small windows on the screen above the candidates' names. When the voters wrote something in the space, it invalidated the previous vote.
- The electronic voting election period ran from 5.00pm on Wednesday 12th November to 1.00pm on Saturday 15th November 2008 and the traditional voting from the 14th to the 15th November until 1.00 pm.
- There were two electoral stations, one in the school and the other in the Town Hall which remained open from 9.00pm on Friday the 14th to the 15th November 2008.
- The results of the online vote and paper ballots were posted, the day after voting ended, on the website.
- After using the e-vote, the voters were asked to fill in a questionnaire on their preferences pertaining to the type and security of the voting system.
- After making an e-vote, the application allowed a print out of a coded voting receipt as confirmation of the vote. The code did not include any personal data about the voters nor their electoral option but was a key that enabled the voters to verify the list of voters published by the website.
- Three bodies were created by the elections: The administrative electoral body who controlled the electoral process, the electoral ballot board and the electoral electronic board which were composed of well-known people such as politicians and artists.

The software applications were developed by Scytl which is a company that specialises in the development of secure electronic voting solutions. The internet voting platform provided for this election is known as *Pnyx government.*

3.3. Electoral outcome

As the results show, the level of participation in this election declined if compared with the 58% of the first edition project held in 2002. There were 112 valid votes, 36 of which were on line, the remaining 76 votes were by ballot which means that 67.8% preferred this option.

The successful candidates were "Youth with Ideas" which had 51.78% followed by "3 Viles Group", Future Promises, We can Improve and lastly "Llavaneres Group". The Hond't Law was applied to calculate the score. As a result 5 points went to "Youth Ideas" 1 point to "3 Viles Group" and 1 point to Future Promises. This political system gives advantages to the majority parties above the minority ones.

The changes to the candidate order produced by the preferential system indicates that all of the candidates, with a number of votes up to 5% of the total, will move up the list.

Table 1: Votes and the pilot test: preferential e-vote system. source: Gibert Gemma

CANDIDATURE	VOTES	REMOTE	BALLOT	5%
YOUTH WITH IDEAS	58	17	41	2,9
FUTURE PROMISES	14	6	8	0,7
3 VILES GROUP	20	9	11	1
LLAVANERES GROUP	6	1	5	0,3
WE CAN IMPROVE	11	3	8	0,55

The three most voted lists and those that had been assigned scores, were modified by the preferential voting system. It ensured that the candidates situated in the first position changed. The second and third list saw a change in candidate. While the first list maintained its candidate, the second chair sought a new candidate.

Table 2: The impact of the preferential voting system

YOUTH WITH IDEAS	Pref. Votes	YOUTH WITH IDEAS	Pref. Votes.
LEANDRO DIAZ	27	LEANDRO DÍAZ	27
ADRIÀ RINCÓN	10	MARIA RUBAL	14
MARIA RUBAL	14	ADRIÀ RINCÓN	10
DÍDAC CABELLO	2	POL RIVERA	6
POL RIVERA	6	GORKA ARANGUREN	3

YOUTH WITH IDEAS	Pref. Votes	YOUTH WITH IDEAS	Pref. Votes.
GORKA ARANGUREN	3	JOAN MARC BARULLS	3
JOAN MARC BARULLS	3	DÍDAC CABELLO	2
RAQUEL RODRIGUEZ (SUPLENT)	1	RAQUEL RODRÍGUEZ (SUPLENT)	1
XAVI LEONARD (SUPLENT)	0	XAVI LEONARD (SUPLENT)	0
JOAN MORA (SUPLENT)	0	JOAN MORA (SUPLENT)	0
REAL VOTES	58	5% OF VOTeS	2,9
FUTURE PROMISES	Pref. Votes	FUTUReS PROMISES	Pref. Votes
ANDREA CASTILLA	0	MIQUEL BERROCAL	3
CLARA SÃNCHEZ	1	ELOI CASAS	2
CLAUDIA BARREIRO	0	CLARA SÁNCHEZ	1
BEATRIZ DOBON	0	ANDREA CASTILLA	0
ARIADNA SUBIRATS	0	CLAUDIA BARREIRO	0
MIQUEL BERROCAL	3	BEATRIZ DOBÓN	0
ELOI CASAS	2	ARIADNA SUBIRATS	0
REAL VOTES	14	5% OF VOTS	0,7
3 VILES GROUP	Pref. Votes	AGRUPATION 3 VILES	Pref. Votes
ALEXANDER CLASEN	3	SERGI ARANYÓ	10
SERGI ARANYO	10	CARLES CARMONA	7
ANDREA NOGUÉS	1	MARIONA BERROCAL	4
ALBA SOLER	0	ALEXANDER CLASEN	3
ANNA RODRIGUEZ	0	ANDREA NOGUÉS	1
MARIONA BERROCAL	4	ALBA SOLER	0
CARLES CARMONA	7	ANNA RODRÍGUEZ	0
REAL VOTES	20	5% OF VOTeS	1

3.3.1. *Youth with Ideas*

The candidates on this list continued to be in the lead, nevertheless the candidates in the 3rd place through to 5th moved up in position to become councillors on the young government. This group received 5 seats.

With reference to the candidate, Maria Rubal, who arrived at 3rd place and with preferential votes, went up to 2nd position, we found that the majority of her supporters (80%,) only marked this preference, therefore the preference for this candidate was very apparent.

3.3.2. *Future promises and 3 Viles group*

These two nominations saw a variation in the order of the lists. The preferential vote moved candidates in the sixth and seventh position to the top places. We consider that having a very low number of votes gives the preferential vote a very strong influence.

4. Empower the government

Those elected were given power within the Youth government from the 21st November to the 19th December. In the beginning they had to establish the government following the articles of electoral law, they had to vote to elect the Mayor and the councillors. There were seven councillors on the government and one of them had to be elected Mayor. By consensus the Mayor was the first candidate on the list "Youth and Ideas". They assigned the departments and they started to work together with the real politicians on a daily basis. Firstly they had to get to know the specialists working in each department and the issues they were working on. One of the most important things to understand was the structure of the public budget in order to include Youth issues. Of the 91 proposals 21 were submitted, prioritised by economy and necessity. As a result these proposals were approved at a plenary meeting and the young politicians were invited to the Catalan Parliament.

5. Results and conclusion

5.1. Methodology

The methodology used to elaborate this report on electronic voting was based on a two channelled survey. On one hand, the citizens who participated in voting through the internet could choose the option to answer a questionnaire that automatically appeared on the computer once they had voted. The questions they were asked to answer were based on the type of voting they had chosen and the electronic voting system. On the other hand another questionnaire was formulated on the development of the project, the reasons to decide to vote or not, the ICT and electronic voting. This questionnaire was completed by 199 school pupils that made up 31.2% of the participants in the electoral census, an important number, when considering the tendencies reflected were representative of the collective of young people.

What happened in the first part "The acquisition of basic democratic concepts" and in the second part "Focusing the Knowledge: making proposals".

In this first part the participants in the learning process were teachers, civil servants and the students. They all evaluated the perceptions and the benefits that they believed the project had contributed. In conclusion the teachers rated the experience as positive, in as much as the students had become involved in the project and had taken responsibility for decisions taken on behalf of the young collective that they represented. The aim of this first part was to ensure that the youngsters established which civic problems were particular to the young and tried to solve them through the use of the legal democratic mechanisms that they had learnt.

From the results taken from the student's evaluation it stands out that their initial knowledge of government, municipal politics, and the structure and workings of the administration was flimsy. However contact with the civil servants changed their vision of politics. They had previously seen politics only as a way of making money with a certain level of corruption. This attitude could be influenced by the widespread idea that politics has become discredited. Nevertheless the second evaluation marked a new tendency as the youngsters were surprised at their lack of knowledge of the services provided for the citizens by the local government and the little perception thy had of the difficulties the civil servants had in implementing municipal politics.

In designing this learning programme the same standard was used for all the groups and whether, it would be better to revise and adapt it, according to school year and age.

In the second part the pupils learnt to make municipal proposals. A total of 91 proposals were made and those that stood out were those relating to sport, mobilization, city planning and culture. Once again it is proved that these demands have age related motives that form a part of their own reality, such as a Youth centre, more transport, different types of sport.

They made no reference to the housing situation or to employment as they considered these questions to be far from their present reality.

Finally the civil servants emphasised that their impression of the students was that there existed a general lack of knowledge of the municipal reality and that it was necessary to inform citizens of the functions of administration and to establish ways to communicate with them, so as to give a better understanding of how politicians make choices and what it means to develop those choices.

5.2. ICTs and the Internet

As was indicated by the data that was taken from the study group, 94.74% of this cross section had access to a computer; ownership by 1/3 of this sample with the rest sharing one with other members of their household. Internet connection was good and fast and they had ADSL (71.60%) with access available at any time of the day (78.40%). It could be considered that this study group indicated that ICT access and availability was excellent.

5.3. Blogs

The blogs were designed by the applicants and the candidates. They included information on the electoral programme, different election events and the candidates; they also inserted publicity spots for the young voters. The object was to establish a link between the young citizens and the young, future politicians. Even though the intention was to create this interaction, the length of the electoral campaign was quite short, only 7 days. They used all the traditional ways such as school meetings where they interacted directly with the students from the whole secondary school, explaining their proposals and debating them, they also used television and through the town hall, the candidates tried to activate all the possible means of communication to convince the voting citizens.

5.4. Electronic vote

According to data, motivation to vote a concrete listing is based, mainly, on the proposals made manifest in the electoral programme and the possibility that their chosen candidates would be able to carry out the said proposals during their mandate (27.79%). This election was also influenced by the appeal of the main candidates (13.20%). These criteria of selection, apparent in the young voters, are also prevalent in the municipal election voters.

5.5. Identification needed in order to apply as an elector

The elector was identified by a National Identity Card or NIE (if a foreigner) and with a password (PIN) that in this case was a code of 16 characters. Thus the elector had to introduce these two forms of identification into the programme and once authorised, the programme allowed them access into the voting system. This was the solution the company gave to ensure secure voting.

With reference to these two forms of identification we should point out different aspects that should be taken into account.

- The municipal registers where the voters DNI or NIE were obtained, should have been checked more frequently and the way the personal data was introduced into the programme should be standardized. Some of the youngsters' DNI and NIE were taken from both the electoral roll and the school. These details were coded in different ways when entered and this caused the NIE(Foreign identity number) to be missing zeros or the letter. Human error was also found in the details entered.
- According to municipal law a resident is one that has registered in the community where they have spent the majority of time over the span of a year. The electoral rolls have not been revised since 1996 and when a citizen moves it only comes to light when a notification is received from the new community, if the citizen has registered in the new area. This makes it difficult to comprehend the exact population movement. Because of this more than 80 authorizations were returned with a notification that the citizen no longer lived at the shown address (12.78% of the population did not receive their authorization). However authorizations could be obtained from the city council.
- Continuing with these classifications it is important to establish the format of entering the electorate identification into the programme (e.g. Capital or small letters, the whole number with or without spaces, etc.) and indicate the aforementioned format on the programme window or in the instructions. In these instances

the system indicated 13 errors and did not permit the elector to enter into the programme.

- This pilot test incorporated the null and void vote. Its introduction opened a new window on the computer screen under that of the electoral roll. A vote became null and void if the voter introduced a note or an express comment. The real concept of the null and void vote in normal elections comes about when various ballot papers are introduced in the same envelope, the ballot paper is marked or crossed out or when it is torn. In an attempt to introduce this new form of voting it was deemed appropriate to introduce the check box in the same window as each candidate, as it could become null and void if introduced on the candidate ballot paper.

5.6. What happened to the system established by the pilot test: closed lists and the preferential voting system

In our opinion this combination of a closed list and the preferential vote has raised some confusion. The pilot test established two voting options: voting for a list without making any preference, which meant that there was agreement with the order of the candidates, or to mark a preference. In this case it was possible to vary the order of the list by a maximum of two candidates. The modification of the candidate order became effective when 5% of the electorate manifested the same preference.

It was made obvious by the results, that the electorate who decided to mark a preference, established the 5% necessary to create the minimum parameter to vary the order of the candidates and to determine the number of seats necessary to govern. The non-preferential votes had no effect on the first two candidates on the list but they were indirectly weakened because the votes were added to the general list.

The preferential voting system did not include the order of preference of the chosen candidates (option, 1st candidate or 2nd candidate). However this order was established following the true order of the candidates on the list. This did not allow all the candidates to have the same opportunity to be favoured.

5.7. What was the participation?

As was mentioned before, participation was very low and as the survey showed, the pupils commented that it was difficult to enter into the programme and that it was very slow (about 32% out of 197 students questioned). This information was compared with the company responsible for the electronic vote who, finding no technical error, argued that during voting, internet connection collapsed on various occasions.

The main reasons that the young people did not take part in the electronic vote were the following:

- Decided not to vote (33.70%)
- Lost their authorization (13.04%)
- System did not work (14.13%)
- Form of identification not accepted. (2.17%)
- Not having Java programme.(4.35%)
- The system was very slow. (1.09%)
- Considered the request exploitation. (3.26%)
- Were unable to pass from the first page of the system (6.52%)
- Lack of time (21.74%)

5.8. According to the youngsters, what advantages did the electronic vote have?

The advantages, according to the study, of the e-vote are that the system is fast and easy (44.58%), it can be accessed from anywhere (16.27%) and it is possible to increase participation. The young people assert that, why improve e-voting when there is already a good e-voting programme (38.42%), that there should be more public computers available (31.64%) and that access to the internet should be more efficient.

5.9. Mandate

The mandate started on the 21st November with the Youth government constitution, that by consensus, voted that the head of the most voted list "Youngsters with Ideas" would be the mayor. The remaining six members became youth councillors and the municipal council briefs were handed out. Each of the young members elected, worked together with the town councillors and they saw exactly how municipal decisions were made and how different projects, underway at that moment, were developed.

The youth proposals were treated taking into account:

- The viability and technical possibilities of each proposal.
- The economic cost of every proposal
- The immediate, real necessity of the proposals
- The departments that would have to participate to develop the proposal.
- Criteria for priority relating to the cost and the need.

Of the 91 proposals collected from the young population 21 were approved in the Youth plenary session where the town councillors agreed to follow the proposals through and gave them an estimated budget. These 21 proposals were selected by the Youth government as the most important and necessary for the young population.

Another task that the young councillors worked on was a general town budget, which, at the time they entered into the government, had been finalised. The young members of the council were also present and involved, together with the town council, in the Sant Andreu de Llavaneres "Major" festival activities.

This co-operative governing has created a new link between the youth of Llavaneres and local government; in fact, the youngsters have taken the initiative to create a youth council with the aim to follow through the rest of the municipal proposals during the year 2009. Furthermore, the presence of the youngsters in the town council has modified the local politicians' view in that the young people have made real and valid proposals and that now they have a more concise idea of their demands. As was commented, being young politicians has enabled them to comprehend that politics is a difficult job and to decide what is best for the town and its population is, at times, very complex, as there are many factors to take into account.

6. Final considerations

Although the present government is making a great effort to adapt to an innovative and technological society there is still a long way to go to arrive at an era of technological communications. For that reason it should be noted that the electronic vote, according to results, ought to be accompanied by the traditional voting system. The majority of the candidates on the lists manifested that they would have liked to be physically present to vote, as they believe that the electorate have a right to see the evidence of their candidates' vote.

Nevertheless, this pilot test might be more suitable for primary elections where the candidate to head the party is chosen. The test has shown that the preferential system had a strong influence and that the two primary candidates were easily toppled. On the other hand, not giving priority to the candidates did not determine the real preference of the electorate.

With reference to electorate identification we consider that it is necessary to establish more valid methods of authenticity to avoid human error and maybe, in the long term the electronic identification document could correct this. It should also be noted that to implement a good technological system, such as e-voting, it is necessary for the programme to adapt to the technological resources available and also that it is simple to use.

At the same time, we should take into account that the youngsters should previously be involved in an indispensable process of participation and education so that the groups of youngsters can learn how democracy works and become involved in municipal responsibilities and arrangements. The participation process has helped the young people to decide for themselves if they wanted to be a part of this project and has, therefore, been fundamental in the creation of the five candidates, in their electoral programmes and in the belief that they can improve their town.

Finally, in conclusion, to involve and awaken youngsters' interest in politics, electronic tools are not enough. However channels of communication need to be established or a new figure which we have called "Participation and Mediation Agent", to ensure that coming generations approach public institutions.

Acknowledgements

The author would like to express her gratitude for the support provided by Joan Mora i Buch, Citizen Participation Councilor, the technicians and the Town Hall of Sant Andreu de Llavaneres.

References

Barrat, Jordi and Josep Mª Reniu (2004) "Electronic Democracy and Citizen Participation, a sociological and legal report about the Citizen Consultation" OVE, University of Leon. Madrid, 38-77. http://www.epractice.eu/files/upload/gpc/document/1612-1181135609.pdf [Accessed 7.12.2002]

Batısta, Carlos (2003). "ICTs and Good Governance: The Contribution of Information and Communication Technologies to Local Governance in Latin America" NP³ - Núcleo de Pesquisa e Políticas Públicas. Brasilia University, Brazil . [Accessed: 08.11.2008]

Blanco, Ismael and Pau Mas (2008)" The political Disafecction of Catalonia". Fundació Jaume Bofill. *Informes Breus.*Núm. 11.Barcelona.

Borge, Rosa, Clelia Colombo and Yanina Welp (2008), " Explanatory analysis of electronic and presential citizen participation in municipal areas in Catalonia" Open University of Catalonia ", *IDP.Revista d'Internet, Law and Policy* [article online].Num. 6. Open University of Catalonia UOC. Accessed: 08.11.2008]. http://www.uoc.edu/idp/6/dt/esp/borge_colombo_welp.pdf

Borge, Rosa (2005). «La participació electrònica: estat de la qüestió i aproximació a la seva classificació». *IDP.Revista d'Internet, Law and Policy* [article online]. Num. 1. UOC. [Accessed: 08.11.2008]. http://www.uoc.edu/idp/1/dt/cat/borge.pdf ISSN 1699-8154

Castells, M. (1998). La era de la información. Vol II: El poder de la identidad. Madrid: Alianza.

Fundació Jaume Bofill (2000). Debate about E-voting with Jordi Capo and Andreu Riera. Debate Collection review.Núm.33.

Fundació Jaume Bofill (2004). «La participació ciudadana a través de les noves tecnologies. Estratègies per a la utilització de Consensus». *Finestra Oberta*. Núm. 42.Barcelona.

Oostveen, A., & Van den Besselaar, P. (2004). Internet voting technologies and civic participation, the users perspective. *Javnost/The Public*, *XI*(1), 61-78.

Oostveen, A., & Van den Besselaar, P (2007). Security as belief User's perceptions on the security of electronic voting systems In: Electronic Voting in Europe: Technology, Law, Politics and Society. Edited by A. Prosser and R. Krimmer. Lecture Notes in Informatics. Volume P-47, p73-82. Bonn: Gesellschaft für Informatik. ISBN 3-88579-376-

Valls, Núria and Andrea Borison (2007). "Youth and politcy" . Fundació Jaume Bofill.*Informes Breus.* Núm. 7.Barcelona.

The Highland Youth Voice[Accessed 5.12.2008]

http://www.wellington.vic.gov.au/e-governance[Accessed 5.12.2008]

Using SMS Texting to Encourage Democratic Participation by Youth Citizens: A Case Study of a Project in an English Local Authority

David Griffin, Philippa Trevorrow and Edward Halpin
Leeds Metropolitan University, UK.
Originally published in EJEG (2006) Volume 4 Issue 2.

Like the preceding study, the case described by David Griffin, Philippa Trevorrow and Edward Halpin is also about engagement of young people in local democracy, in this instance in a local authority in the north of England. Griffin et al's work focuses on the impact of a single technology, SMS text messaging. As with the Catalonian experiment, the authors find that, despite the almost universal access to this technology, there are many non technical barriers that get in the way of effective engagement. In their own words, they take a 'cyber-sceptic' stance. Amongst the problems that emerged during this experiment were a lack of real commitment by Council staff and a failure by the Council to provide feedback. The lack of interest in the views of young people is not just a UK phenomenon. The study raises several important issues and provides a number of valuable insights for those who wish to engage young people more in the public sphere.

Abstract: Public administrations across Europe take the view that using digital media for consultation with citizens will help to increase their democratic participation. In the UK, the Government has encouraged local authorities to experiment with new electronic communication channels for this purpose. This paper presents a case study in which one such medium, the mobile phone, is being used in an attempt to raise participation amongst young people. It evaluates a project set up to use SMS text messaging as a means of electronic consultation with young people by a council in the North of England. Specifically, it examines the effect of text messaging on democratic participation by the young and the effect of this type of consultation on the processes of the political administration. This case study identifies a number of organizational, social and cultural issues that may limit the scope for using this technology to increase youth participation and change the relationship between young people and their local elected representatives. Based on the initial evidence from this case study, we take the cyber-sceptic stance. We suggest that the mobile phone is not the 'silver bullet' for invigorating consultation with young people by the local public administration. We identify a series of potential barriers to increasing participation by youth and changing the relationship between the elected politicians and their constituents.

Keywords e-Democracy, e-Consultation, local government, young people, mobile telephony, case study

1. Introduction

The 2001 General Election in the UK highlighted the stark decline in democratic engagement over a fifty year period. Voter turnout at the election was 65% compared with 78% in 1950. Young people, in particular, appeared to be disengaging from civic involvement. MORI (2005) reports that only 37% of the 18-24 age group voted in 2001, down from 68% in the previous general election in 1997 (Couglin 2003). It has been suggested that less than a quarter of those eligible to vote for the first time actually did so (Russell 2005).

Following the 2001 election, some parliamentarians felt that new digital media should be employed to halt this decline in democratic participation by young people, as illustrated by this exchange in the House of Commons in 2002 (House of Commons Debate 12 February 2002 quoted in Parry 2004):

> *"David Taylor MP: Does the Minister agree that the wholesale abstention by younger voters in June 2001 was at least partly rooted in their sense of detachment from an institution widely seen as mired in an era of quill pens and hansom cabs? Does he believe that there is potential for e-democracy to reconnect this place with the elec-*

torate, by promoting and improving the consultation with them on matters that we debate?

Minister Twigg: I very much agree with my Hon. Friend.... Clearly, we face a serious challenge in reconnecting young people with politics. As my Hon. Friend may be aware, there is now a Cabinet committee on e-democracy. It will address many of the issues that have been raised."

The UK government has encouraged local authorities to experiment with new channels of democratic engagement in order to address the fall in participation (Cliff 2004). Electronic voting was trialled in the 2003 local elections; it was not immediately successful (Mathieson 2005). The turnout did not significantly increase and issues about security and privacy were evident. Council websites are beginning to offer facilities for electronic feedback of residents' views on service delivery and policy formulation. However, access to such facilities is not universal. 35% of UK households do not currently have Internet connectivity in their home and only 10.5% of UK Internet users have broadband access (OECD Statistics 2004). Furthermore, having access to a computer at home does not imply that all, or any, members of the family know how to use it to participate in the information society.

The mobile phone has a wider coverage than the Internet. 76% of adults (over the age of 15) in the UK own a mobile phone (Vodafone MORI 2003) and this rises to 97% of females and 92% of males in the 11-21 age group (Haste 2005a). The average age at which a UK child receives their first mobile phone is currently eight (Dhaliwal 2005). It is a tool that is extensively used by young people, especially for exchanging text messages. The mobile phone has become a *"prosthesis of the body, an extension of one-self"* (Haste 2005b p.56). It is wherever its owner is and is thus an almost immediate means of communication.

Can the mobile phone be used as a communication channel to increase the democratic engagement by young people? In this paper, we evaluate a project set up to use SMS text messaging as a means of electronic consultation with young people by a council in the north of England. We specifically examine whether it has increased the scope of participation by young people and whether it has changed the democratic process. Based on the initial evidence from this case study, we take the cyber-sceptic stance. We suggest that the mobile phone is not the 'silver bullet' for consultation with young people by the local public administration. This case study identifies a number of organizational, social and cultural issues that may limit the scope for using this technology to increase youth participation and change the relationship between young people and their local elected representatives.

The paper is organised as follows. First we define the key terms used in the paper before reviewing the literature about e-consultation, concentrating on the scope of participation and the impact on the democratic process. We then outline the research methods used to gather the empirical evidence for this research. Finally, we analyse our findings to identify the issues involved with using this medium of consultation with young people and conclude that there are several factors to be addressed to ensure its successful employment as a means of raising democratic participation.

2. Key terms

The following three terms are important in what follows:

The period of *youth* is characterised by its semi-independent state. The person is independent in that they can make their own decisions to a certain extent, but they are also dependent on other people for guidance, care and support (Coles 1995). The precise chronological age at which youth begins and ends varies considerably, for the purpose of this paper we will refer to the range 11-24 when discussing youth.

Secondly we define *electronic consultation* (sometimes referred to as electronic participation) as the use of digital technology, such as the Internet and the mobile phone, to facilitate the engagement of citizens in community policy making and service delivery monitoring (Danodaran 2005).

Thirdly, the concept of the *digital divide* is concerned with an existing, and possibly widening, gap between "*information haves and have-nots, knowers and know-nots, doers and do-nots*" (Tapscott 1998 p.11; Bucy 2000 p.50; Cullen 2001). It is the rift between those who have access, knowledge and skills to use information and communication technologies (ICTs) and those who lack access, skills and so on. Instead of closing any disparities in knowledge, or access to information, it is believed that the Internet will actually add to the exclusion of disadvantaged groups.

3. Electronic consultation

Many local administrations across Europe take the view that e-consultation should form part of the democratic process (Coleman 2004). A recent survey for the European Union (Deloitte 2004), covering 101 cities which the authors claim to be 'representative of the whole [EU] population', found that over 90% of the authorities felt that e-consultation with citizens was a good idea and believed that the use of digital technology in this way would encourage and increase participation in democracy.

There are several different viewpoints regarding the contribution of digital technology to democracy (Norris 2005). *Cyber-optimists* suggest that technology will widen the scope of participation and improve the quality of the democratic process. Examples of this viewpoint can be found on some UK government websites (e.g. www.e-democracy.gov.uk.). In addition, e-consultation provides a channel that might particularly attract young people to engage in democracy more fully (Ward et al 2005). *Cyber-pessimists* argue that digital technology will have a detrimental effect on the democratic process. It will increase the divide between the information rich and poor. The technology itself might make the discourse shallower. It might also raise expectations among those citizens who make use of the technology. They might perceive that they are communicating directly with elected representatives and expect action to be taken more quickly than currently happens (Ward et al 2003). *Cyber-sceptics* argue that there will be little change in participation, with the social divide being mirrored by the digital divide. Providing new channels of engagement will have little effect on democratic renewal. Cyberspace will become *normalise*d to be the place where normal political activity is undertaken (Margolis and Resnick 2000).

If digital technology is to have an impact on the democratic process, citizens and politicians will need to change their behaviours (Coleman 2004). Citizens must perceive that online consultation is a worthwhile means of connecting with public administration. Politicians must not just see e-consultation as a way of appearing to be part of the techno-modernity, but integrate this into their democratic processes. Some studies have suggested that *"parties have been relatively slow to develop the use of technologies for participatory purposes"* (Lusoli and Ward 2004 p.456). Coleman (2004) suggests that the ultimate measure of the success of e-consultation will be the degree to which it leads to better policy and practice. However, in the 'top-down' model of politics, this communication between the elector and the elected is controlled by those in power. Dahlberg (2001) argues that these information flows need to take place in an environment which is autonomous of the public administration. Blimer and Gurevitch (2001) echo this concern as they warn about the powerful commercial interests trying to bend the Internet to their own end. Similar concerns could be raised about the mobile telephony channel of communication.

4. Research methodology

In this study, we examine two aspects of e-consultation, the scope of participation and the impact on the democratic process. Accordingly, the two objectives of the study are:

Objective 1: To examine the scope of participation in the SMS text messaging project by participants;

Objective 2: To examine the project's impact on the democratic processes of the council.

The research method was to undertake a case study in an English metropolitan borough council. The Youth Services Department in this council had initiated a 'Youth Participation Project', and installed a SMS text messaging system, to be used in a one-year trial. This investigation started eight months into the project and was concluded at the end of the one-year period.

The case study method is appropriate for dealing with contemporary situations, such as tackling youth participation, in which the intervention being applied is difficult to distinguish from the context (Yin, 2003). In this study, we take the stance that technology is socially situated, is bounded not just by the artefact itself, but by many contextual elements including the culture of the organization, the skills of the staff and so on. There is not a simple causal relationship between the technology being employed and the organization applying it. Organizational characteristics have to help shape the technology (Fleck and Howells, 2001).

The case study method uses a variety of sources of data to investigate a situation (Keddie, 2006). These sources may include: documentation, interviews, physical artefacts, archive material and observation (Yin, 2003). While this study of the Youth Participation Project uses all five of these data sources, interviews provided the main data source.

Semi-structured interviews were held with staff in the council responsible for the service being investigated. The interviews lasted between 45 and 90 minutes and were recorded for subsequent transcription. The interview topics are listed in Appendix A. The interviewees comprised of the project leader, the Head of Youth Services for Students and Communities, the Youth Service Manager and the Deputy Chief Executive. In addition, an interview was held with the Member of the Youth Parliament (MYP) representing the young people in this local education area. Hand-written notes were produced from this interview, rather than recording the discussion, in order to put the young person at ease.

At the time of our investigation 100 young people were registered as participants in the Youth Participation Project. This total population was surveyed via text messages, using the council's SMS texting system, to elicit their views about the project. The survey questions are listed in Appendix B. The research instrument presented some challenges to the researchers. Firstly, the system will only allow a message of 160 characters. Consequently it was decided to send one question at a time and to restrict the survey to 4 questions. Secondly, the conventions and practices of young people using text messaging require a less formal language set. Every effort was made to convert the questions to reasonable 'text-speak'.

In addition, the following source material was also utilised:

- The results of a survey conducted by the MYP of 100 young people shopping in the town centre;
- The electronic consultation processes documented on the council's website;
- The SMS text messaging system supplier's website;

- A demonstration of the computer system by the supplier

The case study method is sometimes criticized for providing subjective results (Yin, 2003). In this study, we have followed Yin's suggestions for assuring the validity and reliability of the study and have used the tactics described in Table 1 below.

Table 1: Issues of validity and reliability of the study (adapted from Yin, 2003)

Test	Definition	Tactics employed
Construct validity	Establishing appropriate measures for issues being studied	Several sources of data were used to provide data triangulation at appropriate points; attention has been given in this article to making the steps in the development of our argument as transparent as possible; the draft article was submitted to the Head of Youth Services for approval. At the conclusion of the one-year trial, the findings of this study were presented to the chief executive of the council.
External validity	Establishing how to generalize from the case study findings	We studied a single local authority. No attempt was made to suggest that these findings were representative of authorities elsewhere. Serendipity played a part in the choice of the case study. We became aware of this experiment and took the opportunity to study the workings of the Youth Participation Project. External validity may be achieved through four types of generalization: theory, implications, concepts and rich insight (Walsham, 1995). Here the external validity was achieved through the first two of these types of generalization. This case study identifies implications that might be relevant for practitioners elsewhere who are considering taking similar action to that of the case study authority. To a lesser extent, it also explores theories relating to the application of technological innovation for the purposes of youth participation.

5. The Case Study - the Youth Participation Project

5.1. Background information

The case study borough in the north of England had 193,200 residents in mid-2003 (National Statistics 2003). It is a multi-cultural area with 5.7% of the residents being of Asian descent. It has problems of social deprivation;

the area was ranked 86 out of 354 in the 2004 Indices of Deprivation (1 being the most deprived area).

5.2. Project success factors

The Youth Participation Project was established in October 2004 to help deliver a public service agreement (PSA) target for the local authority which was concerned with improving community cohesion. One strand of this was to improve youth participation in the democratic process by using SMS text messaging, the channel of communication that young people were employing themselves. A project leader was appointed for one year and a computer system was purchased for sending text messages to, and receiving responses from, young people registered with the project. To encourage participation, a financial incentive was offered; registered participants would receive a £10 voucher for every 50 consultation queries to which they personally replied.

According to the Deputy Chief Executive, this project was primarily about improving engagement, particularly by those young people who would not engage in other ways. She suggested that, in the first instance, consultation would mainly relate to new developments and services for children and young people.

The interviewees identified the following indications of success for the project:

- Consistently high response rate to questions from participants in the project;
- Raising issues with the participants that are meaningful to the current local authority agenda and having an impact on the local youth parliament;
- Evidence that the consultation life cycle has been completed. In particular, that the consultation has contributed to the action taken by the council and its partners in a timely manner;
- Young people in the borough report that they have confidence in the service provided locally and feel that they have an influence on decision making;
- A considerable growth in the number of participants being consulted by SMS text messaging.

5.3. Analysis of participants' survey results

The four SMS text messages were sent to the 100 young people registered with the project. The response rates were 9% for question 1, 8% for question 2, 7% for question 3 and 12% for question 4.

This low response is not specific to our survey alone as similar response rates were obtained for questions asked by the Youth Services Team. Although the sample does not provide enough data to be able to derive significant information to the questions posed, it does raise questions in itself. The fact that 100 young people have willingly signed up to the service, with the ability to withdraw their phone number at any point, and yet the highest return was 12% to an individual question, shows that the tool is not yet being used as envisaged when the project was established. The registered participants are not engaging even though it is the means of communication that they prefer and have signed up to use. Interestingly, the question which achieved the best response rate was the one that asked how the e-consultation service might be improved. The responding participants felt that two measures were equally important: consulting over issues that matter and receiving the £10 voucher more quickly.

6. Discussion

6.1. Using SMS text messaging to strengthen democratic participation by the young)

This can be considered at two levels. At the micro level, once the participant is registered, is action being taken to encourage future commitment and involvement? At the macro level, what action is being taken to encourage young people who are not already active citizens to join the participation project?

At the micro level, the council has taken steps to ensure the quality of issues raised and to reduce the possibility of consultation fatigue among participants in paper- and Internet-based surveys. All requests for consultation with young people must be submitted to a steering group. This group ensures that different departments are not repeating the same questions and it acts as a quality control gateway. However, this procedure is not being adhered to for SMS texting consultation.

The council does not feed back to participants or other residents, a summary of the action taken as a result of a specific consultation. The Deputy Chief Executive recognized that improved feedback to participants was needed, as this would encourage future participation. The council is considering the best ways of providing feedback on the action arising from consultation campaigns. As there will often be a proportion of consulted people who will not be pleased with the decisions taken, this feedback needs careful management. It is likely that it will sometimes be communicated using a different medium to that used during the consultation. For example, the decisions arising from a texting consultation might be released on the council's website.

The Head of Youth Services and the Member of the Youth Parliament warned against 'tokenism'. They felt that young people should not be consulted because it might look good to external partners, but should inform the action taken as a result of airing their views. A recent study of environmental education projects in Finland, Switzerland and France, showed that the decision makers showed no lasting commitment to young people's ideas or views. Authorities were more likely to pay lip service to youth participation than to treat it seriously (Horelli, 2001).

Finally, the discussions with council staff make it clear that there was a lack of commitment to the project by politicians and officers of the council. It had mainly been left to the project manager to develop consultation material. It could be argued that this system is an example of a technology possessing political qualities (Winner, 1999). This project has been situated in a location remote from the main council offices. The way that power and control have been exercised has directly affected the behaviour of the system and its potential to reach and engage young people in meaningful dialogue. It is inaccessible via the main telephone switchboard. It is staffed by a project manager on a temporary contract.

At the macro level, there is a lack of awareness of the Participation Project by the borough's young people. In a survey of 100 young people in the town centre carried out on Wednesday 10 August 2005 by the MYP, only 7% had heard of the SMS text messaging project. If the project is to affect an increase in participation, it needs wider publicity among the target group. It is not simply a lack of finance that has caused this. One definition of technology, which emphasizes the human and organizational characteristics of a successful operational system, is the technology complex (Fleck and Howells, 2001). According to this model, the culture of the department and the skills of the project staff are significant elements of the technology that rank alongside the software and hardware components. This system is operated by the Youth Services Department. The culture is one of promoting learning and development of young people. Had the system been placed in a department with a more commercial culture, external funding might have been sought to pay for publicity. The project manager had been involved in youth work, in various capacities, for a number of years, and admitted having difficulties with the artefact component of the system.

In summary, viewing the technology as more than just the hardware and software has given insight into the political and organizational dimensions of the system. The decisions taken about its placement and operation have limited its ability to strengthen participation amongst those who have registered. The specific resources applied (coupled with disinterest on behalf of young people in the town?) have affected the uptake by the town's youth.

6.2. The effect of SMS text messaging consultation on the processes of political administration

The interviewees in this study identified a number of consultation process improvements arising from conducting them electronically. Firstly, using digital technology made the process quicker. Previous paper-based consultations with young people in the borough had taken 3 to 6 months to complete. Electronic consultation via SMS text messaging, whilst not instantaneous, was far quicker. Secondly, there was a perception that e-consultation provided a more objective process. Traditional focus group responses could be affected by the group dynamic or by the sample invited to participate.

However, had the SMS text messaging consultation affected the back-end democratic processes? The interviewees identified several barriers impeding the project's success in this respect.

7. Resources

The resources available to the youth services-based project, funded initially for one year, have been described earlier. Our contention, applying the technology complex, is that the staff skills and organizational characteristics such as culture are all part of the technology being applied in the council. The issues identified in 6.3.3 and 6.3.4 below are, to some extent, outcomes from the particular technology complex implemented in this specific council. The MYP's survey, whilst methodologically limited, does suggest that further publicity is required to raise awareness of the participation project among young people. As the MYP noted, the larger the sample of participants, the more likely it is that their views will be taken into account.

7.1. The widening agenda

The recent introduction of the Children's and Young People's Agenda by the government had caused a restructure within the Council. This started to take effect in the early stages of the project. The Deputy Chief Executive had been appointed as the Director designate of the new service. Within the functional departments, such as Education and Social Services, change management processes were underway. As a result, this participation project was now just a small, single strand within a much wider strategy.

7.2. Political inertia

According to the Head of Youth Services, there was agreement within the council that young people's views are important. The process for development of consultation exercises has been established for paper-based surveys, if not for electronic consultation. However, having been consulted, it is possible that young people's opinions might challenge the views of the council executive team (Wallace, 2001). The interviewees felt that some elected members still considered that 'children should be seen and not heard'. The MYP had been made a member of a scrutiny and overview committee, but he felt on occasions that his inclusion was more a token gesture rather than a genuine attempt to gain input from young people in democratic decision-making.

7.3. Lack of consultation topics

A major limitation of this project to date has been the lack of actual consultation with the participants. The project manager has attempted to raise participants' interest by using the system to disseminate information about youth club activities and so on. There have been few issues consulted on and the majority of these have originated from the project manager. It was reported that participants welcomed the financial incentive, but felt that at the slow rate that texts were being sent out, they would have cancelled their membership before having received a voucher.

8. Concluding remarks

To date it would appear that the case study council has had limited success in either raising participation by the borough's young people or changing the democratic process. However, this study raises several important issues regarding electronic consultation:

The mobile phone as a technology is ubiquitous amongst young citizens (Haste, 2005a). Furthermore, it has become the normal means of communication in many situations. It tends to accompany the owners wherever they go and fits in with the *"mobility and flexibility of young people's lives"* (Haste 2005b p.63). It therefore has great potential for immediate feedback and empowerment for young people who have control of the communication.

Choice of appropriate topics is vital for the success of the consultation. Raising issues that do not matter, or seem irrelevant to the target population will reduce the likelihood of their engagement with the subject. Furthermore, with a constant population of registered participants, frequent consultation over irrelevant material may lead to consultation fatigue and adversely affect the response to future communications.

Public administrations should consider how electronic consultation impacts upon the consultation life cycle. Receiving responses more quickly may lead to an expectation that results will be available in a shorter time frame and, significantly, that action will be taken quickly. In the case study council there was no evidence of any changes to the back-end processes as a result of introducing this new approach.

This study has demonstrated the merit of considering the relationship between technology systems and the organizations in which they are applied. In this study, following Fleck and Howells (2001), our definition of technology is not limited to the artefact itself, but also includes the staff skills and organizational characteristics as well. The placement of the SMS texting system in an off-shoot office, staffed by a temporary employee, has shaped the technology itself.

There are some limitations of this study. Firstly, the timing of the study has had an effect on its outcome. Consultants have been engaged for year two of the project. This new skill set, and the learning from the experience of the first year of operation, will alter the performance of the project. Secondly, while we have endeavoured to explore as much of the case environment as was open to us, the only access to the participants that we were able to negotiate was the texting survey. A much richer understanding of participants' views would have been obtained by employing different research methods.

Following on from this study, it is intended to carry out a similar investigation in other councils using technology for consultation with the young to compare with the findings of this case study. It is also intended to undertake a survey of young people's attitudes to being consulted using the mobile phone.

References

Blimer, J. and Gurevitch, M. (2001) "The new media and our political communication discontents: democratizing cyberspace", Information, Communication and Society, Vol 4, No. 1, pp1-13.

Bucy, E.P. (2000) "Social Access to the Internet", The Harvard International Journal of Press/Politics, Vol 5, No. 1, pp50-61.

Cliff, S. (2004) "Whitehall softens 2005 e-gov targets", Computer Weekly, 8 April 2004, p9.

Coleman, S. (2004) "Connecting Parliament to the Public via the Internet: two case studies of online consultations", Information, Communication and Society, Vol 7, No. 1, pp1-22.

Coles, B. (1995) Youth and Social Policy. Youth citizenship and young careers, UCL Press Limited, London.

Couglin, S. (2003) "First time voters ignored election", BBC News Online, Tuesday 22 April 2003.

Cullen, R. (2001) "Addressing the digital divide", Online Information Review, Vol 25, No. 5, pp311-320.

Dahlberg, L. (2001) "The Internet and democratic discourse: exploring the prospects of online deliberative forums extending the public sphere", Information, Communication and Society, Vol 4, No. 4, pp615-633.
Danodaran, L. (2005) "Edemocracy: challenges for social inclusion", ITNow, July 2005.
Deloitte (2004) E-Citizenship for all: European benchmark report, [online], http://www.deloitte.com/dtt/cda/doc/content/dtt_ps_eCitizenshipforAllEuropeanbenchmark2004_lowrez_042105.pdf [accessed January 2006]
Dhaliwal, J. (2005) "Youth market is central to developing mobile", New Media Age, 21 April 2005, p9.
Fleck, J. and Howells, J. (2001) "Technology, the Technology Complex and the Paradox of Technological Determinism", Technology Analysis & Strategic Management, Vol 13, No. 4, pp523-531
Haste, H. (2005a) "Joined-up texting", Nestlé Social Research Programme, February 2005.
Haste, H. (2005b) "Joined-up texting: mobile phones and young people", Young Consumers, Quarter 2, Vol 6, No. 3, pp56-67.
Horelli, L. (2001), "Young People's Participation in Local Development: Lip Service or Serious Business?" In H Helve and C Wallace, Eds, Youth, Citizenship and Empowerment, Ashgate. Aldershot.
Keddie, V. (2006) "Case Study Research" in V Jupp Ed, The Sage Dictionary of Social Research Methods, Sage, London.
Lusoli, W. and Ward, S. (2004) "Digital Rank-and-file: Party Activists Perceptions and Use of the Internet", BJPIR, Vol 6, pp453-470.
Margolis, M. and Resnick, D. (2000) Politics as usual, Sage, London.
Mathieson, S.A. (2005) "Voting searches for the x-factor", [online], The Guardian, Wednesday 23 November 2005, http://society.guardian.co.uk/e-public/story/0,13927,1648136,00.html [accessed 01 December 2005]
MORI (2005) MORI Final Aggregate Analysis, [online], http://www.mori.com/polls/2005/election-aggregate.shtml [accessed November 2005]
National Statistics (2003) Neighbourhood Statistics, [online], http:www.neighbourhood.statistics.gov.uk [accessed December 2005]
Norris, P. (2005) "The impact of the Internet on political activism: evidence from Europe", International Journal of Electric Government Research, Vol 1, No. 1, pp20-39.
OECD Statistics (2004) OECD Broadband Statistics, [online], http://www.oecd.org/document/60/0,2340,en_2825_495656_2496764_1_1_1_1,00.html [accessed November 2005]
Parry, K. (2004) e-Democracy Standard Note, House of Commons Library, London.
Russell, A. (2005) "Political Parties as Vehicles of Political Engagement", Parliamentary Affairs, Vol 58, No. 3, pp555-569.

Tapscott, D. (1998) Growing Up Digital. The Rise of the Net Generation, McGraw-Hill, New York.

Vodafone MORI (2003 The British mobile communications survey, January 2003.

Wallace, C. (2001) "Youth, Citizenship and Empowerment" in H Helve and C Wallace, (Eds), Youth, Citizenship and Empowerment, Ashgate, Aldershot.

Walsham, G. (1995) "Interpretive case studies in IS research: Nature and method", European Journal of Information Systems, Vol 4, pp74-78.

Ward, S., Gibson, R. and Lusoli, W. (2003) "Online participation and mobilization in Britain: hype, hope and reality", Parliamentary Affairs, Vol 56, pp652-668.

Ward, S., Gibson, R. and Lusoli, W. (2005) "The promise of 'virtual representation': the public view", ESRC e-Society Programme report, NOP opinion survey of online political transactions in the UK, February 2005, Salford: ESRI and ESRC eSociety Programme.

Wilhelm, A.G. (2000) Democracy in the Digital Age, Routledge, New York.

Winner, L. (1999) "Do Artifacts have Politics?" In D MacKenzie and J Wajcman (Eds) The Social Shaping of Technology, 2nd Edn., Open University Press, Buckingham.

Yin, R.K. (2003) Case Study Design: Research and Methods, 3rd Ed, Sage, Beverley Hills.

Appendix A - Interview topics

- What do you feel are the benefits of e-consultation?
- How successful have your web-based consultations been?
- What stages of policy determination are usually consulted over?
- Is the consultation always led by the council?
- How did the SMS texting project come about?
- What types of issue do you perceive should involve consultation with young people?
- What benefits do you foresee in consulting the young?
- What barriers do you perceive will restrict the use of this channel for consultation?
- Do you feel that SMS texting has the potential to strengthen participation by young people?

Appendix B – Text message survey questions

- Q 1: Do you have a PC at home?
- Q 2: Do you have internet at home?
- Q 3: Do you think Youth Participation Project is good or bad?

- Q 4: How could the service be improved, A = ask about issues that matter, B = get £10 voucher quicker, C = let you know it's had an impact, D = more texts, E = fewer texts.
-

A Social Perspective on the Implementation of e-Government: A Longitudinal Study at the County Administration of Sweden

Kerstin Grundén
University West, Trollhättan, Sweden
Originally published in EJEG (2009) Volume 7 Issue 1

An area that had been largely neglected in the e-government literature is the impact of e-government on public officials. Kerstin Grundén addresses this gap using a longitudinal study to draw lessons about the implementation of e-government in a local authority, West Gotaland, in Sweden. She studies the reactions of staff at three levels within the authority: administrative assistants, handling officers and managers in two departments: the traffic department and the legal department. Amongst the many interesting findings are that most respondents considered the implementation of e-government as being more about changing employee attitudes than about technical solutions. Unsurprisingly, older employees found it harder to adjust. As this study took place over a prolonged period, Grundén is able to track the changes in attitude as the project progresses. The insights from this, including how employees coped and made sense of changes are fascinating.

Abstract: A longitudinal study of implementation of e-Government at the County Administration of Sweden was analysed and discussed from a social perspective. Two interview studies at the legal and traffic departments were compared. Interviews were made with decision makers, handling officers and administrative assistants focussing on social consequences of work situations, work processes and quality of e-services to the clients. The MOA-model was used as a frame of reference for the study. According to the analysis, coping and sense making strategies by the respondents increased. e-Government made demands for new competencies for employees and clients. Internal and external digital divides are social consequences of the implementation of e-services. Management increased their focus on efficiency aspects related to e-Government. There is a need to integrate competence of social aspects into the development process of e-Government. The users were aware of the importance of social aspects of IT implementation. There is a need for competence development of social consequences related to IT implementation also for development personnel and different interest groups.

Keywords: Implementation, e-Government, digital divide, social consequences, coping and sense making strategies.

1. Introduction

Many countries have put a great deal of effort into developing and implementing e-Government during the last decade, even Sweden. In fact, Sweden shared the third position with US and Denmark in a recent bench marking study by Accenture (Accenture, 2007). According to a government vision formulated in a bill in 1999 (Näringsdepartementet) the country should become an information society "for everyone". The use of IT should contribute to growth, employment, a sustainable society and equality. The public organisations should be precursors in this development and contribute to increased availability of public information and services to Swedish citizens. Public authorities should be stimulated to develop "the 24h authority" (Statskontoret 2000), where public service and information should be available to the citizens at any time by using electronic self-services. The development of eGovernent also means increased electronic co-operation within and among public organisations which even puts demands on development that is not technology-oriented. The development towards e-Government involves social changes of work roles, attitudes and new competence needs.

For nearly a decade Accenture has tracked the progress of more than twenty governments in different countries that have moved towards high performance through leadership in customer service. In their eighth report (Accenture, 2007) they found governments at important crossroads. The main focus for public service organisations has been on improvements of front end services to the citizens, neglecting the importance of also aligning back end aspects, such as value, infrastructure, work force competence and cultural change. Many governments continue to underestimate the impact of their workforce and what restructuring must take place to acclimate people to new ways of working.

In this article I will present and discuss a longitudinal evaluation study of e-Government in the County Administration of Sweden, focussing especially on social aspects of e-Government. The County Administration is one of the biggest public organisations in Sweden, divided into twenty-one separate County Administrations situated in different regions. The regional administrations are responsible for different specialised areas such as environmental issues, social issues, veterinarian issues, etc. The employees dealing with matters in these areas mainly have academic backgrounds and work as handling officers in different areas of expertise.

The aim of the study was to especially focus on social aspects in order to contribute with increased understanding of the importance of these aspects for the implementation process. Implementation of e-Government has earlier been criticised for focussing too much on technical aspects (Grönlund 2001, Schedler & Summermatter 2003), thereby ignoring the importance of social aspects. The evaluation model MOA-E was used as a frame of reference for the study and will be presented in the next section. Social aspects could change during the implementation process, and therefore a longitudinal study seemed relevant.

2. The MOA-E model

The MOA-E model was developed by the author and has been used in several evaluation studies (e.g. Grundén 2001, 2004). Ideas about coordination and control influence the choice and design of technology and organisation and imply many important decisions. Important aspects that could be affected due to different designs of technology and organisation are work situations of the staff, work processes, and services provided to the clients. Interrelated relationships between design of technology and organisation are stressed in this model. Different consequences for work processes, work situations, and quality of the services provided to the client, could arise depending on different designs of organisation and technology.

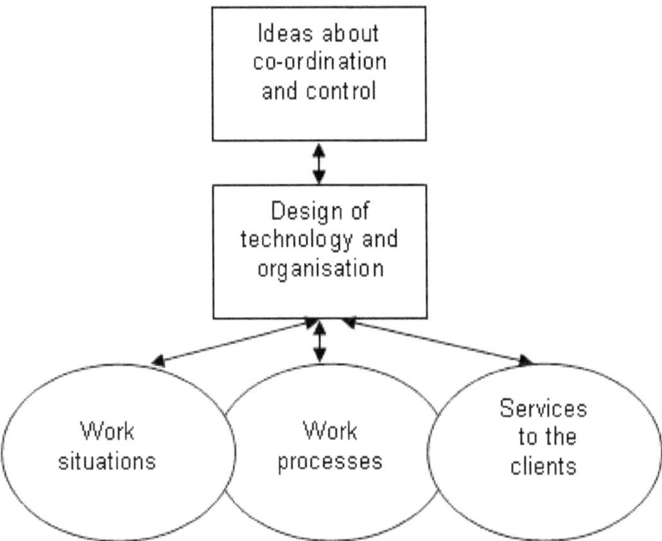

Figure 1: The MOA-E model

An evaluation study can focus on different parts of the model. In the study presented in this article, special focus is given to the social aspects of work processes, work situations and client relationships. There are complex interdependencies between work processes from a managerial perspective, work situations for the staff and the services provided to a client. An unsatisfying work situation for the personnel could negatively affect quality and efficiency aspects of the provided service. A satisfying work situation could have the opposite effect. The development of e-services and e-Government puts demands on changes or work process and work routines which in turn affect the work situation and the client relationships. New competences are needed for the personnel. Different types of consequences could be examined depending on the point of time for the evaluation (Göranzon, 1984).

The model could be used for process-oriented longitudinal evaluation studies. The organisation can be studied before, during and after implementation and use of a new system in order to examine changes in quality and efficiency aspects of the changed work process and the work situation for example. but instead of using discrete starting and ending points ("from-to"), I prefer the concepts "from-through", in order to stress the process-orientation of the study (Saldana, 2003).

3. The longitudinal study of implementation of e-Government at the County Administration

A vision and a strategy for the implementation of "e-Government 2007" were formulated early in 2005 by the County Administration of West Gotaland. National government policies for e-Government were taken as a starting point for the internal development work. A project group was appointed for the development work. According to the vision the County Administration of West Gotaland should become an e-Government authority at the end of 2007. Then work activities should be dealt with mainly by using electronic documents, electronic communication and electronic information retrieval. Electronic services to the citizens should be produced and delivered irrespective of time and geographical location. The development presupposes increased electronic co-operation with other authorities. The development process should lead to increased internal efficiency, quality and insight into work activities. The vision will influence the development of IT support, changes of the organisation as well as the work situation of the co-workers.

As a starting point of the implementation of the "Vision of e-Government 2007" there was an interest the project group to investigate aspects such as attitudes and knowledge about e-Government of the personnel and competence needs. The first interview study was made during spring 2005 (Grundén 2007), before the implementation process had taken off. The first interview study before implementation was made in the social building authority, the legal authority and the traffic authority. Each authority was located in different geographical locations in West Gotaland. The social building authority mainly dealt with municipality detail plans, survey plans and infrastructure issues. The matters were often prolonged, and involved a lot of contacts with municipality employees and local politicians. According to the terminology of Bonham et al. (2003) the main work activities in this authority could be classified as Government-to-Government (G2G) activities. This department was not affected by implementation in the same way as the traffic and legal departments, when the second study was made, and was therefore not included.

The traffic authority mainly dealt with applications for driving licences from citizens and occupational traffic matters. About 50 to 60,000 such matters are dealt with each year in the West Gotaland region. These work activities are mainly Government-to-Citizens (G2C) activities (ibid.). The legal authority dealt with miscellaneous matters such as appeals from citizens and organisations regarding municipality decisions, environmental matters such as sewage, authorization of surveillance enterprises, funeral matters, general elections, supervision of foundations.

The three different personnel categories, administrative assistants, handling officers and managers from different authorities were studied in both interview studies. In the first study five persons from the three different departments were interviewed (fifteen interviews in total). In the second study thirteen respondents from the traffic authority and five respondents from the legal department (a total of eighteen interviews) were studied. All interviews were semi-structured and took about forty-five minutes each. The interviews were tape-recorded and written down word by word. The evaluation model MOA (Grundén 2003) was used as a reference frame for the interview questions and the analysis. The model focuses especially on the different perspectives of the user's work situation, the work process, and the quality of the produced service from the client's perspective.

The results of the first interview study were presented for the project group of implementation of e-Government 2007 in West Gotaland. They then decided to initiate the development of a web-based study circle for issues related to e-Government as a way of competence development for the personnel. All personnel of the national County Administration were supposed to participate in this education. The main goal of the study circle was to give basic introduction to e-Government. The study circle was also aimed to stimulate work place discussions about e-Government related issues. The author participated in the working group developing the course. The second interview study was made during spring 2007. Most of the respondents had also participated in the course. During the second interview study, the author also evaluated the course (Grundén, 2008).

A second interview study was made during spring 2007, in the legal and traffic departments, during early implementation stages; a few e-services had already been implemented and some were ready for implementation.

A new electronic software system for dealing with official matters, Platina, was implemented in the legal authority, and the implementation of new e-services for granting driving licences was in progress at the traffic authority. The implementation started with simple matters (so-called "green matters") and will be followed by implementation of more complicated matters (so-called "red matters"). In the legal authority they had also implemented e-services for security guards and foundations. A third interview study is planned to be carried out in 2009, when more of the e-services are implemented and used in the organisation in order to examine further social changes related to the implementation of e-Government.

4. The results

In this section a summary of the results from both studies are presented. I have also included some quotations in the summary, in order to present a richer picture of some important aspects of the study. The studies are reported more in detail in Grundén (2007, 2008).

4.1. Results from interviews before the implementation – the first study

The respondents in general had not yet heard much about the Vision of e-Government 2007. The issue had been discussed at some personnel meetings, but not very much. They seem to have discussed e-Government primarily at the traffic department. Most of the respondents associated the concept of e-Government with availability of the electronic services from government to citizens 24 hours each day. Some also mentioned a need for internal reorganisation of administrative routines. The respondents seemed to have a mainly positive attitude towards e-Government, but they were also aware of some presumed negative consequences.

4.1.1. *Work situation*

Most respondents mainly thought that the implementation of e-Government had more to do with change of the employees' attitudes, work roles and culture of the work place, compared with technical solutions. One of the handling officers compares the e-Government with the internal computerisation in the eighties. He meant that at that time change of attitudes and culture seemed to be almost 100% of the development work. A handling officer mentioned that they had discussed the archive rules for about fifteen years, without making necessary completions. Some of the respondents were confused about the long time elapsed in order to make those documents more available. They did not think this is mainly a technical issue; instead personal attitudes and work culture seem to matter highly. Attitudes towards the use of paper documents instead of computer documents could also be a culture issue. People seem to like to read and keep paper documents, at least big documents and survey maps.

Some respondents feared risks for an increased work load and demands on more rapid dealing with matters, due to e-Government. The work could also be more impersonal, as a consequence of increased electronic communication.

Several respondents mentioned that the majority of employees were over 50 years old and computer knowledge was also unevenly distributed in the organisation. There seemed to be a risk that many employees were not motivated enough to change, and could resist change instead.

> *"I think it will be extremely difficult for the older employees to accept e-Government. They also show such attitudes towards smaller changes, and this is a very big change, it will be difficult to engage people. The new generation is more conscious and used to this and has no problems." (Handling officer, juridical department).*

All respondents felt that information and education about the vision of e-Government 2007 should be well rooted at the local level in different departments. They preferred a bottom-up strategy. Information adjusted to local situations was requested. The vision could be discussed at local level in group discussions and work place meetings. Some of the respondents seemed to have a negative attitude towards complete education courses mainly defined by the top level of the organisation. Instead a bottom-up strategy was requested.

4.1.2. *Work process*

Many respondents expected the implementation process of e-Government to be going on for a very long time, probably five to ten years. The respondents in the legal authority felt that electronic dealing with matters will affect existing working roles to a great extent. The time needed for dealing with each matter was expected to be reduced. When a new diary system is implemented (Platina), handling officers need to register all information regarding a matter in the system. Platina will replace the older software system (Diabas).Today many handling officers leave these work tasks to a registrar. This work division between registrars and handling officers had a long tradition in the organisation. Most of the handling officers had an academic background, and preferred to work within their fields of expertise. They did not want to put too much time into administrative work tasks. However, management wanted to change this work division, and a web-based course for dealing with Diabas was developed and offered to the handling officers. (Grundén made evaluation studies of this course, 2004.) When such work tasks are reduced fewer registrars would be needed. But some registrars could receive other work tasks such as instructors and quality work. Some of the interviewed handling officers had already started to register their own measures, and they showed a positive attitude. However, they also mentioned that other groups resisted changing these work tasks.

Implementation of electronic dealing with driving licences was expected to lead to a reduction of the work load and fewer personnel will be needed at the traffic authority. Several monotonous work tasks will be transformed to web based inquires and controls:

> *"Many work tasks should be done by the customer instead of us, similar to electronic bank services, but in return the customers will get faster handling of their matters." (Handling officer, traffic department).*

> *"We will get rid of many monotonous work tasks, thus the work will be easier. Today there are very much duplication of the applications." (Decision maker, traffic department)*

The respondents seemed to have a positive attitude towards this change and reduction of monotonous work tasks. There seemed to be a shortage of personnel in this authority, so the respondents were not afraid of losing their jobs:

> *"We have already had some discussions about the possible reduction of work tasks related to the new e-services. But you almost*

hope this will be a reality as we are so few employees in this department". (Handling officer, traffic department).

4.1.3. *Services to clients*

Most of the respondents mentioned the advantage of increased availability to e-services for the clients. Implementation of e-Government was expected to lead to increased transparency of the handling processes that could increase trust towards the authority by the citizens. Digital documentation seemed to be more secure compared with paper documentation. Some expected disadvantages with e-Government included increased vulnerability due to security problems that could occur. There also seemed to be a risk of more impersonal contacts with the clients.

External implementation and use of web-based services could be affected by computer habits and possibilities of different user groups. Younger people tend to use the internet more than older people.

4.2. Results from interviews during early implementation stages – the second study

Some of the respondents were already affected by the use of a new system for the handling process of e-services. However, most of the respondents had not started to work with e-services yet, but were affected by the overall change of the culture. They saw change of their work hitherto mainly as mental change. e-Government had been discussed at the ordinary work place meetings. Most of the personnel expected the implementation of e-Government to take a long time, probably five to ten years.

4.2.1. *The work situation:*

Most respondents showed a positive attitude towards the implementation of e-Government, and stressed that it did not work to be reluctant towards development in the organisation. A common understanding was also that *"you cannot stop the development, you have to keep up"*. There could, however, be problems for those employees who deal with manual, routine work tasks, if they did not have the capabilities to renew their competencies when their work tasks are computerized.

The users of the new e-services will probably put more demands for efficient and rapid handling of all matters, which could affect the internal prioritization of matters. Increased external demands could also lead to a more stressful work situation.

Many respondents mentioned risks for resistance towards the change by many older employees who are not motivated enough as they soon will retire:

> *"Many employees will soon retire. They doubt they are able to engage in this change work. They will still not remain in the organisation when e-Government will be implemented. Therefore they are not enough motivated to put required strain on the change work". (Decision maker, traffic department).*

Computer literacy was also unevenly distributed in the organisation. Younger people tend to use the Internet more than older people. It could be more difficult for the older generation to learn, some respondents felt. Many respondents felt that this was an important field for competence development. There also seems to be a need for both basic computer program knowledge, such as the use of Microsoft Word, as well as more complicated software and file management.

Most respondents were satisfied with the competence development possibilities at the County Administration. The personnel were used to being well informed and having access to good internal education possibilities. The County Academy for internal web-based education had offered such courses since 2002, but there were also traditional education activities taking place in the organisation. It was seen as very important to receive relevant information about the implementation for all of the staff, so they could understand the meaning of the changes, and give relevant information to the citizens about the new e-services. It was also very important to receive relevant information "just in time", when it was needed. Some of the respondents preferred individual studies, with access to an instructor when they had questions to ask. Many respondents preferred a combination of individual and group studies. An advantage with group studies could be that other participants could pose questions you had not even thought about yourself. Different educational forms could be appropriate due to different work situations. Many of the respondents preferred practical exercises instead of too much theory.

4.2.2. *The work process*

In the legal authority they had already implemented e-services for security guards and foundations. They were also implementing a new electronic system for dealing with official matters, Platina. During a test period they worked with two systems at the same time, Platina and the older system for dealing with the diary, Diabas. They had started to use Platina for dealing with foundation matters. The work with the new system Platina for electronic administration of the diary meant a lot of changes for the work, compared with the work with the older Diabas system. The registrations in the older Diabas system were mainly made by the registrars, based on information from the handling officers. In the new Platina system, the handling officers were responsible for using the system during the entire process of dealing with a matter; from initiation to termination. This meant big changes of work routines and work roles for the handling officers, compared with the earlier division of work.

The respondents stressed both advantages and disadvantages with Platina. The use of Platina gave the handling officers a better general view and control of matters. But when more handling officers use the system, there could be more errors due to different individual ways of formulations. Still many handling officers were sceptical towards the coming change of the work division between the registrars and the handling officers. Many of those who had not yet started to use Platina, seemed to fear the coming use:

> *"Many fear Platina as 'the new black cloud'...we are more or less forced to use it...I don't have the energy to learn a new computer system, I hardly master the old system." (*Handling officer, legal department).

> *"I think Platina could be difficult to handle...A work mate who uses the system, told me that the system sometimes is very tough to use... There are always growing pains with new systems." (*Handling officer, traffic department*).*

In the traffic department e-services for drivers' licence applications were developed. Such matters would be dealt with electronically that were simple with no need for supplementary information (so-called "green matters"). The implementation of these e-services had been planned to start with driving schools at the beginning of 2007, but the time schedule was revised and the implementation was instead planned to take off by the end of that year. When the "green matters" were implemented as e-services, manual judgements of the applications were no longer needed. The manual handling of these matters meant a lot of monotonous and stressful tasks. When the "green matters" were implemented time could be released for other work tasks, such as more complicated matters e.g. This would probably lead to a reduction of time needed for the total dealing with drivers' licences when the e-services were implemented, but this could be compensated by the fact that many older people soon will retire.

> *"If there were not so many employees who will soon retire, I would have probably reacted more strongly, because of the reduction of jobs." (Administrative assistant, traffic department).*

Many handling officers did not think implementation of e-Government would affect their jobs, as their work was seen as too complex and not possible to computerize:

> *"It will not be possible with automatic dealing of matters other than for very simple cases....It must be human beings who deal with more complex matters". (Decision maker, traffic department).*

But process mapping of work contents has been initiated in many units, even for more complex work, in order to analyse computerization opportunities. Most respondents expect implementation of e-Government to take a long time, probably five to ten years.

Some of the respondents who have been employed for a very long time in the organisation refer to the situation in the organisation in the eighties, when manual routines had to be computerized. They feel that if the personnel managed the hard work at that time, they will also manage the implementation of e-Government: "it cannot be worse..."

Management seemed to have great expectations on the outcomes from e-Government. They expected increased efficiency and saving of resources. Employees who are retired were not replaced e.g.:

"Top management seems to expect to save a great deal of resources due to implementation of e-Government; vacant positions are not filled; management is waiting, then the co-workers have to take over work tasks from other employees who retire...During the last year there has been more focus on efficiency aspects from management." (Handling officer, traffic department).

4.2.3. *Service to the client*

The personal services to the clients tend to be more impersonal and formal:

*"We are very service-minded today (at the local level). When you receive a phone call with a question from the customer, often you don't limit your answers to the concrete question, but also inform the customer about other related aspects that could be useful for the customer to know. But the development of customer services is moving towards a more impersonal direction; you only answer exactly about what the customer requests. Then it is up to the customer to seek for more information if needed. We have been taking good care of the client, but we will not continue with this in the future." (*Handling officer, traffic department).

Different customer groups seemed to have very different computer habits and different needs for personal service, according to the interviews. For example, there seemed to be a digital divide between younger and older clients as well as for immigrants and disabled. Younger clients demand e-services, but the elderly, immigrants and disabled need more personal support.

"The new, young people use much more e-services, they are born with a computer in their hands. The older people are not...then we have to work in two different ways, with traditional paper routines and the digital system." (Handling officer, traffic department).

The external digital divide could contribute to increased differences between different societal groups (A and B groups) as consequences from the increased dependency on computers and the development of public e-services. The dealing with a matter using e-service will probably be faster compared with traditional manual routines:

> *"I think many old people like to talk to a handling officer and bring their documents with them. But then we maybe give them the answer that we could not give them via personal assistance, because we have the electronic systems, and then I think very many people in our society such as older people, immigrants or disabled, in a way are being neglected;. Instead elite groups will win, those who manage the digital technology. It is the new generation."* (Handling officer, traffic department).

There could also be a tendency to give certain important customers ("VIP-customers", e.g. bigger companies) a faster handling process compared with other groups, which also could increase differences between different user groups.

There seemed however, to be an ambition from the authority to keep the traditional paper routines along with the new e-services, in order to satisfy all users, but probably the handling process will be slower for paper related matters. It is a challenge for the organisation to combine personal service with electronic routines. The trust for the authority from the citizens could increase if the authority succeeds in combining personal treatment with the increased use of e-services, according to a respondent.

A need for increased customer support was expected when new e-services were offered. Centralised customer support was planned. Centralised front desk support could relieve pressure from back-office work, but co-ordination between front desk and back-office customer support routines could be difficult to handle. Some respondents mentioned that customer support at the local level takes good care of the client. With the more centralised, computerized customer support, the customers were expected to take care of themselves.

Less personal contact with customers seemed to be a consequence of the new e-services. Personal contact with customers could be a motivating aspect of the job today for some handling officers. A respondent implies that for some e-services (such as simple driver's license applications), no personal contact at all is needed with the customer.

5. Analysis and discussion

In this section the two studies are compared and analysed. The focus of the analysis and comparison are changes of social aspects. The analysis is structured according to the different aspects of the MOA- model.

6. Work situations

6.1. Increased coping and sense-making strategies by the personnel

Most respondents from both studies showed a positive attitude towards implementation of e-Government, but the respondents from the second study showed more of coping and sense making strategies related to the implementation which probably are consequences of being closer to actual changes of their work situation compared with the respondents from the first study. Implementation of e-Government means a lot of work processes changes, and new competence demands, which could contribute to more stressful work situations for the employees, compared to the work before implementation. Often there are growing pains with new systems and often there is a need to work with two systems during implementation, the old and the new system, which increases the work load and stress of the work situation. People do not always articulate their feelings of stress. Instead you could identify different coping and sense making strategies in order to handle a stressful work situation, from their stories told during the interviews.

The concepts "coping" and "sense making" are interrelated, but have evolved from different traditions. "Sense making" resides in the tradition of organisational thinking (e.g. Weick 1995) and IT adaption (e.g. Henfridson, 1999) while "coping" has evolved from behavioural research focussing on stress (Josefsson, 2007). The sociologists Lazarus and Folkman (1984) evolved a process-oriented and context dependent transactional model of coping, focussing on the interaction between the individual's cognitive appraisals and the environment. Coping could also be seen as defence mechanisms towards stressful changes in organizations (Angelöw, 1991).

Henfridson (1999) argues that sense making processes affect IT-adaption. The source of sense-making could be the ambiguity people feel when they try to understand an IT artefact that is new to their work practice. The introduction of IT artefacts in organisations is an ambiguous enterprise in general, and especially for e-Government, which affects organisation, work situation, work processes and the service produced for the clients in fundamental ways. Ambiguous situations are unclear and need to be interpreted in a sense making way according to Checkland and Scholes (1990). Ambiguous situations could be very stressful for the involved employees. Sense making could reduce this feeling of stress. Thus, both "sense making" and "coping" are related to stress reduction for the individual, but from different research angles.

Some of the older respondents of the second study compared implementation of e-Government with the computerization of the early 80s, when manual routines were computerized. If they managed to deal with that change, they would probably also manage to deal with implementation of e-Government, they reasoned. This is an example of sense making; the comparison with the early computerization contributed to a meaningful understanding of the implementation of e-Government, and could thus reduce their stress with regard to coming implementation work.

Many respondents from the second study did not think their work would be affected, as they saw their job as too complicated to computerize, although process studies of even more complicated work had started in the organisation. This could be an example of "denial" as a coping strategy in order to avoid stress (Angelöw, 1991). Many older employees who would soon retire were uninterested in taking an active part in the coming implementation. This is also an example of "uninterested" as a coping strategy (ibid.). "Denial" and "uninterested" are interrelated, but the difference is that if you are "uninterested" you are aware of the needed changes, but hope that you will not be affected if you stay "uninterested" and passive.

However none of the respondents showed purely explicit negative attitudes towards implementation of e-Government. They stressed instead that it does not work to be reluctant towards development in the organisation; "you cannot stop the development, you have to keep up". The example indicates that they have accepted the overall situation, and acted in accordance with the main cultural norms of the organisation: not to be actively reluctant towards changes.

6.1.1. *Competence and participation*

Respondents from both studies stressed reduced needs for personal contact needed with the clients, and this seemed due to the use of the new e-services. Personal contact with clients is motivating and meaningful aspects of the job today for many handling officers. A respondent mentioned the fact that for some e-services (easy matters to handle such as driving licences' permissions), no personal contact with those clients was needed at all. Efficient communication with clients usually requires long term experience by the handling officers, competencies that are not needed to the same extent when e-services are used. Instead, implementation of e-Government seems to put demands on increased computer oriented competencies of the employees. There could thus be a risk of a reduction of competencies related to the personal communication with clients and increased demands of computer related competencies.

The respondents requested a "bottom-up" approach for education and information. Some respondents showed scepticism towards educational courses mainly defined by top management. A few months before the second study, the respondents had participated in a course with basic information of e-Government implementation, with group discussions, which they appreciated. The pedagogy was inspired by a study circle approach; a kind of "bottom-up" pedagogy which stimulates the participants to discuss their local experiences.

Motivation to change is a central driving force for the employees in implementation work (Angelöw, 1991). Participation could stimulate motivation, a central aspect of the so called Scandinavian tradition of systems development (Scandinavian Journal of Information Systems, 1994). The respondents requested information and education related to their local work situation. It seems to be an important challenge to integrate all employees in competence development activities stimulating their motivation and participation in the implementation work of e-Government. Participation in project groups could be a way of stimulating learning (Grundén, 2004). But in a very big organisation, like the County Administration, project development work is usually organized with representative participants as members of the project groups. Not all employees are able to participate in such groups, thus it is a challenge to find motivating educational forms stimulating participating and competence development.

The difficulties with competence development for some older employees, and other employees with problems to adapt to new demands, could be described as the *internal digital divide*. The respondents from both studies mentioned that a majority of the employees were over 50 years old, and there was a risk that they were not motivated enough to change their competences and work routines, and therefore could resist implementation of e-Government. The same aspects are stressed in the second study, but more examples of the phenomena were mentioned. Some respondents also felt that older persons could be more worried about the changes, than the younger. They could also have more problems in learning new work routines. There could thus be a need for differentiated work routines and less demands on competence development for some of the older employees, during a period of transition to e-Government.

It could also be difficult to find proper work tasks even for younger people who today deal with simple, monotonous work tasks, if they do not have the capability to renew their competences.

6.2. Work process aspects

6.2.1. *Increased focus by management on efficiency aspects related to e-Government*

According to the interviews from the second study the management expects increased efficiency gains from the implementation of e-Government. Electronic dealing with matters was supposed to reduce the time needed to handle a matter. Some electronic matters such as dealing with simple applications of drivers' licences needed hardly any human handling at all. There were a lot of older employees in the organisation that would retire, and many of them would not be replaced, due to expected efficiency gains. But in the short term, remaining employees would receive increased work load instead, until all e-services were implemented. Efficiency aspects seemed to be more and more important from a management perspective, according to some respondents.

Increased focus on the efficiency aspect of implementation of e-Government could be analysed according to Ciborra's (2002) metaphor of "hospitality". This metaphor is an alternative metaphor for thinking critically about relationships between organisation, people and technology. Many public administrations involved in implementation of e-Government have adopted structured techniques which emphasize planning and control by the host organisation, based on the more common "organic" metaphor, where power aspects are more invisible, and explained by striving for balanced homeostasis of the system (Griffin, Trevorrow & Halpin, 2007). If management and developers instead are seen as hosts, and other employees and clients are guests, striving for increased internal efficiency could be seen as reasonable, according to the hospitality metaphor, but not if we use the organic metaphor. As management and development staff have the most control of the design and implementation, their internal goals could be given much attention, such as internal efficiency according to traditional management philosophy. Then there could be a risk that other goals could become secondary goals, such as the quality of the service to the client, and a good work situation for the staff.

6.3. Services to the client

6.3.1. *Increased stress of the external digital divide*

The respondents from the second study gave more detailed examples of expected external digital divide consequences due to implementation of e-Government. There seemed to be a digital divide between younger and older clients as well as for immigrants and disabled. Younger clients demand e-services, but the elderly, immigrants and disabled need more personal support. The personal service will be more impersonal and formal. The external digital divide could contribute to increased differences between different societal groups as consequences from the increased dependency on computers and the development of public e-services. Dealing with a matter using e-service will probably be faster compared with traditional manual routines. There seemed however, to be an ambition from the authority to keep the traditional paper routines along with the new e-services, in order to satisfy all users, but the handling process will probably be slower for paper related matters.

There could also be a tendency to give certain important customers a faster handling process compared with other groups, which could also increase differences between different user groups.

A need for increased customer support was expected when new e-services were offered. Centralised customer support was planned. Centralised front desk support could relieve pressure from back-office work, but coordination between front desk and back-office customer support routines could be difficult to handle. Some respondents mentioned that customer support at the local level usually took good care of the client. With the more centralised, computerized customer support, the customers were expected to take care of themselves, which could be a further disadvantage especially for the clients who need a lot of personal support.

The results from the studies thus support the thesis that development of e-Government could reinforce a development towards an increased digital divide among different groups. There could be a risk that we are moving towards a dichotomized society, where already marginalized groups (older, immigrants, disabled) will be even more marginalized due to less availability and competence to use the new e-services compared with the "new young generation", who put demands on an even faster development of e-Government.

e-Government is not just about value-neutral technological advances in service delivery and communication, it also affects societal groups in different ways. The EC funded project eGovRTD2020 has identified some possible future scenarios using trend techniques (year 2020) of e-Government. The possible outcomes are judged on a scale of low and high impact on society and low and high uncertainty. Divisions in high and low skilled and rich and poor, as well as social exclusion of skilled, non-skilled, rich and poor and disabled people were depicted as high uncertainty and high impact (Bicking et al 2006).

In order to have more of a win-win scenario for the different interest groups of e-Government, there is a need to adjust the implementation of e-Government to be relevant for those who cannot or do not want to use e-services, by also offering manual routines and more personal contact from the authorities and to offer relevant competence development for vulnerable groups of the society. The implementation of e-Government is closely related to democratic ideals of our society and how these are realised.

7. Does knowledge about social aspects matter?

The respondents of especially the first study stressed the importance of social aspects related to e-Government implementation. They mainly had a user perspective, and no providers were interviewed. Usually they had a more technical oriented background as system developers and programmers that could affect their perspective of the implementation work. Senyucel (2005) found different views between providers and users. The providers had a more technical perspective, and the users stressed social and organisational aspects as important. The respondents of this study stressed social and organisational aspects as important for the implementation of e-Government. Most research hitherto reflects the notion of e-Government as much to be gained and little to be feared (Heinze & Hu, 2005). Articles addressing the dangers and threats are relatively sparse (e.g. Shelley et al., 2004).

The analytical split between providers users enables the notion of e-Government to be viewed from two perspectives. Congruence between providers and users is critical to the evolution and adaption of e-Government. The theories of Giddens (1998) could be taken as a relevant starting-point for such an analysis as they focus on the dialectic relationship between technology, people and organisational context. According to his theory different actors exercise power and legitimate their own behaviour in the use of their own knowledge and experiences, recourses and norms. In such a dialectic context different human activities could be both reinforced and inhibited.

There seems to be a need for providers to make solid problem analysis of the work process, organisation and work culture before implementation work. It is important to have not only a "hard systems view" on the implementation process, according to the terminology of Checkland (1991). He differentiates between hard systems thinking and soft systems thinking. According to Checkland it is important to identify "the root problem" of a problem situation and to determine whether a problem is mainly of technical or social character, in order to find proper solutions. It is not unusual to propose a mainly technical solution for a problem that mainly has a social character.

e-Government is often associated with increased transparency of work processes and information about matters from a citizen's perspective (Bonham et. al. 2003). However, transparency could also be relevant for the problem analysis process in order to find the root problem. If "the right" problem is defined as the root problem, then the problem analysis is transparent. If "the wrong" problem is defined, then the problem analysis is more obscure.

The results from my studies indicate that important implementation aspects of e-Government are closely interrelated with different social consequences. Thus it is important that relevant competence development within this field, contributes to relevant knowledge of the development personnel in order to avoid social problems during implementation and use of e-Government. But relevant knowledge and relevant competence of the developers will not be enough for a development of e-Government supporting democratic ideals of our society. We also need to use the competence in discussions and development works involving different interest groups of e-Government, in order to contribute to more well-informed clients, decision-makers, politicians and employee groups.

8. Conclusions

In the study the following social problems related to the implementation of e-Government are identified:

- Increased coping and sense-making strategies by the personnel related to increased stress during the implementation process.
- A tendency of increased internal and external digital divide among different groups.
- Increased focus by management on efficiency aspects making other goals secondary (such as the quality of the service to the client and the quality of the work situation for the staff).

Increased knowledge about social aspects and consequences could be integrated in the development and implementation process by providers (as well as other interest groups), in order to avoid social problems related to the implementation of e-Government. There is a need for empirical based research studies in order to further explore the field of a social perspective on the implementation of e-Government.

References

Accenture (2007) Leadership in Customer Service: Delivering the Promise. Electronic source: www.accenture.com

Angelöw, B. (1991) Det goda förändringsarbetet. Lund: Studentlitteratur.

Bicking, M., Janssen, M. and Wimmer, M.A.(2006) "Looking into the future – scenarios for e-Government in 2020" In Project e-society: Building Bricks. Soumi, R., Cabral, R., Hampe, J.F., Heikkilä, A., Järveläinen J. and Koskivaara, E. NY: Springer Science & Business Media.

Bonham, M.G., Seifert, J.W. & Thorson, S.J. (2003) "The Transformational Potential of e-Government: The Role of Political Leadership", In 4th Pan European International Relations Conference, UK.

Checkland, P. 1991 Systems thinking, systems practice. Chichester: John Wiley & Sons.

Checkland, P. & Scholes, J. (1990) Soft Systems Methodology in Action. Chichester: John Wiley & Sons.

Ciborra, C. (2002) The Labyrinths of Information: Challenging the wisdom of Systems, Oxford: Oxford University Press.

Giddens, A. (1998) The Constitution of Society: Outline of Theory of Structuration. Polity Press, Cambridge.

Griffin, D., Trevorrow, P. & Halpin, E. (2007) Introduction e-Government: A welcome Guest or Uninvited Stranger? In Developments in e-Government. A critical Analysis, Griffin, D., Trevorrow, P., & Halpin, E. Amsterdam: IOS Press.

Grundén, K. (2001) "Evaluation of the use of video conferences for health care planning". Health Informatics 7 (2), 71-80.

Grundén, K. (2003) "An Evaluation Model for Work-integrated E-learning", I Rossett, A. (ed.) Proceedings of E-Learn 2003, World Conference on E-Learning in Corporate, Government, Healthcare, and Higher Education. Nov. 7-11, Phoenix, Arizona.

Grundén, K. (2004) "A case study of work-integrated learning", Journal on Systemics, Cybernetics and Informatics, vol 2.

Grundén, K. (2007) "Back-office implementation of e-Government – a learning process". Proceedings of the 7th European Conference on e-Government (ECEG), Dan Remenyi (ed.) Haagse Hogeschool, den Haag, Netherlands, (21-22 June).

Grundén, K. (2008) "Evaluation of e-Government implementation from a social perspective". Accepted to ECIME2008 11-13 Sept., Proceedings of the European Conference on Information Management and Evaluation (ECIME), Royal Holloway, University of London, UK.

Grönlund, Å. (2001) "The long and winding road". In Grönlund, Å., & Ranerup, A. Elektronisk förvaltning, elektronisk demokrati. Visioner, verklighet, vidareutveckling. Lund: Stud.litt., 713-729.

Göranzon (1984) Datautvecklingens filosofi. Stockholm: Carlsson & Jönssons Bokförlag.

Heinze, N., & Hu, Q. (2005) "e-Government Research: A Review via the Lens of Structuration Theory". Proceedings of the Ninth Pacific Asia Conference on Information Systems (PACS2005), Bankok, july 7-10, 891-904.

Henfridson, O. (1999) IT-adaption as sense making. Doctoral dissertation. Research reports in informatics RR-99.01, Umeå: Umeå University, Department of Informatics.

Josefsson, U. (2007) Coping online. Patients' use of the Internet. IT. Doctoral dissertation. Gothenburg: University of Gothenburg. Department of Applied Information Technology.

Lazarus, R.S., & Folkman, S. (1984). Stress, appraisal and coping. New York, Springer. Näringsdepartementet (1999) Ett informationssamhälle för alla. Poposition 1999/2000:86

Saldana, J. (2003) Longitudinal Qualitative Research. Analyzing Change Through Time. Walnut Creek, California: AltaMira Press.

Scandinavian Journal of Information Systems (1994), Vol 6, No. 1.

Schedler, K. and Summermatter, L. (2003) "e-Government: What Countries Do and Why: A European Perspective". In The World of e-Government Curtin, G.C., Sommer, M.H. & Vis.-Sommer, V. The Haworth Political Press.

Schelley, M. Thrane, L., Shulman, S., Lang, E., Beisser, S., Larsson, T. and Mutti, J. (2004) „Digital Citizenship: Parameters of the Digital Divide", Social Science Computer Review (22:2), 75-88.

Senyucel, Z. (2005) "Towards Successful e-Government Facilitation in UK Local Authorities". Irani, Z., Elliman, T. & Sarikas, O.D. (eds.) Proceedings of the e-Government Workshop '05 (eGOV05) Brunel University, Sept. 13.

Statskontoret (2000) 24-timmarsmyndighet.. Förslag till kriterier för statlig elektronisk förvaltning i medborgarnas tjänst. Stockholm.

Weick, K., E. (1995) Sensemaking in organizations. Thousand Oaks: Sage.

e-Government and Technology Acceptance: The Case of the Implementation of Section 508 Guidelines for Websites

Paul Jaeger and Miriam Matteson
University of Maryland, USA
Originally published in EJEG (2009) Volume 7 Issue 1.

The acceptance of technology has been a favourite theme in IS research since Fred Davis first published his now famous model back in the 1980s. Paul Jaeger and Miriam Matteson, in a US based study, use a number of cases to study the acceptance of technology and the so-called Section 508 guidelines which specify disability accessibility standards. Accessibility is an important issue and the US government has been proactive in creating laws mandating that services and facilities must be usable by the disabled. Jaeger and Matteson use a five layer modified version of the technology acccp tance model (TAM) to examine adoption of the section 508 guidelines. This case identifies several possibilities for further research in the field of access for the disabled.

Abstract: This paper examines the relevance of the Technology Acceptance Model for e-Government websites at federal government level in the United States through an exploratory research study. Various unfunded government mandates over the past several years have required agencies to create websites, put services on the sites, and make them accessible to citizens, and the federal e-Government now includes tens of thousands of sites. Section 508 of the Rehabilitation Act, for example, was passed to ensure e-Government sites would be accessible to persons with disabilities. By studying the implementation of the requirements of Section 508 through a number of data collection techniques and in terms of the Technology Acceptance Model, this paper seeks to use this particular law as an example through which to better understand the processes by which government agencies adopt e-Government requirements and the actions that government managers can take to improve the implementation of such adoption.

Keywords: e-Government, technology acceptance model, accessibility, Section 508, disability, public servants, websites

1. Introduction: e-Government technologies and guidelines

Governments internationally are showing a strong preference for delivering services via the Internet, particularly as a means of boosting cost-efficiency and reducing time spent on direct interactions with citizens (Ebbers, Pieterson, & Noordman 2008). The United States has created a larger e-Government network than any other nation. While e-Government includes a wide-range of functions such as e-voting, e-procurement, data collection, management and analysis, inter-agency collaboration, intra- and inter-agency communication, e-learning, for agency staff, human resource management, a key focus of the President's e-Government Management Agenda (http://www.whitehouse.gov/omb/egov/) is on interactions between the government and citizens and many government agencies are viewing e-Government as their primary method for interacting with citizens. As such, it is extremely important for e-Government research to focus on issues of how e-Government is meeting the needs of citizens.

Citizens still show a strong preference for phone-based or in person interactions with government representatives when they have questions or are seeking services, though individuals with higher levels of education are typically more open to using online interactions with government (Ebbers, Pieterson, & Noordman 2008; Steib & Navarro 2006). e-Government services generally are limited by difficulties in searching for and locating the desired information, as well as lack of availability of computers and Internet access for many segments of the general population (Singh, & Sahu 2008). Such problems are exacerbated by a general lack of familiarity with the structure of government and attitudes toward technology and government among many citizens (Jaeger & Thompson 2003, 2004). While the e-Government Act of 2002 and President's e-Government Management Agenda have emphasized the transformative effect of e-Government, thus far it has primarily been used as a way to make information available, provide forms and electronic filing, and distribute the viewpoints of government agencies (Jaeger 2005). As commercial sites are developing faster and provide more innovative services than e-Government sites, public satisfaction with government websites is declining (Barr 2007).

For these and other reasons, the majority of citizens, even those with a high speed Internet connection at home, when seeking government information and services, prefer to speak to a person directly in their contacts with the government (Horrigan 2004). As a result of these tensions between policy, implementation, and public perception, e-Government exists as an option, but not the preferred option, of most citizens. There is a range of reasons that may deter some users—infrequent need for them, lack of interactivity, lack of availability of services or information that people really want. However, a key part of the problem is that e-Government websites are not being designed to fully implement user-oriented standards.

This paper examines this problem as a matter of technology acceptance, specifically the process by which and the extent to which agencies accept and implement standards for e-Government websites. This problem will be examined through the lens of Section 508 of the Rehabilitation Act (29 U.S.C. § 794d), which provides a set of standards to ensure e-Government websites are accessible to persons with disabilities. As e-Government websites are intended to serve as the electronic face of government and provide the majority of government services, determining how to better increase the adoption of standards for e-Government sites by government agencies is essential for improving the usage of and user experiences with e-Government websites.

2. Accessibility and e-Government

Accessibility is equal access to information and communication technologies (ICTs) for persons with disabilities. "Accessibility allows individuals with disabilities—regardless of the type of disability they have—to use ICTs, such as websites, in a manner that is equal to the use enjoyed by others" (Jaeger 2008: 24). This equal access is of utmost importance to persons with disabilities in a society where functions of government, business, and personal life are increasingly online. In the United States, 54 million people have a disability, while the number of persons with disabilities worldwide is more than 550 million, and that number will continue to grow as the baby boom generation ages (Jaeger & Bowman 2005). For ICTs to be accessible, they should: 1) provide equal or equivalent access to all users, and 2) work compatibly with assistive technologies, such as narrators, scanners, enlargement, voice-activated technologies, and many other devices that persons with disabilities may employ.

The United States federal government has created numerous laws related to accessibility of ICTs (Jaeger 2004a, 2004b). For websites, the most prominent law is Section 508 of the Rehabilitation Act, which mandates specific design requirements that reduce barriers to access for different types of disabilities and promote compatibility with assistive technologies that users may be employing. Section 508 has a detailed set of technological and accessibility requirements as well as guidance for implementation (www.section508.gov). Federal e-Government websites, in spite of the requirements of Section 508, are still often inaccessible to persons with disabilities long after the Section 508 requirements were supposed to have been implemented in 2001 (Jaeger 2004b, 2006). Some persons with disabilities have come to distrust e-Government as a result of these accessibility issues (Cullen & Hernon 2006).

Accessibility in the online environment is a relatively new development as a focus of research and is also a highly complex topic that involves policy, technical, and user issues (Jacko & Hanson 2002; Stephanidis & Savidis 2001). This combination of newness and complexity has thus kept most investigations of online accessibility at a very practical level, including most studies of the accessibility of e-Government websites. As a result, no conceptual frameworks have been established for the standards for evaluation of the accessibility of e-Government websites. Having a conceptual framework through which to evaluate the implementation of Section 508 standards on e-Government websites would be beneficial to government employees, researchers, and citizens with disabilities. This exploratory paper proposes that an extant conceptual framework is potentially useful to the study of the accessibility of e-Government websites in terms of the implementation of Section 508 requirements.

3. The Technology Acceptance Model

The Technology Acceptance Model (TAM) was originally introduced and studied as a means of understanding how users adopt and use new technology by evaluating the factors that influenced the decision to accept a new technology (Davis 1989). TAM is based on the belief "that perceived ease of use and usefulness can predict attitudes toward technology" (Lederer et al. 2000: 269). Perceived usefulness of a technology and perceived ease of use of a technology combine to create an attitude about the technology, influencing decisions on whether to adopt the technology. Figure 1 shows the most basic form of TAM. Perceived ease of use and perceived usefulness are shaped by external factors unique to the situation, while the behavioral decisions ultimately dictate whether and how a technology is used (Davis, Bagozzi, & Warshaw 1989).

Since its introduction, TAM has been tested in many studies and has been used to evaluate numerous different technologies, including email, voice mail, and many others (i.e., Dasgupta, Granger, & McGarry 2002; Gefen & Straub 1997; Straub, Keil, & Brenner 1997). Some recent studies of TAM have extended the application of the model to areas beyond a single technology, such as the study of online educational settings or the World Wide Web (i.e., Dishaw & Strong 1999; Saade & Bahli 2005; Venkatesh & Davis 2000).

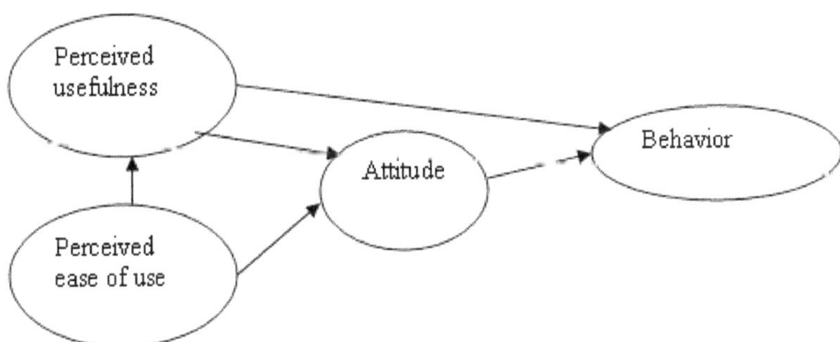

Figure 1: Basic Technology Acceptance Model

One of the extensions of TAM has been to explore decisions by organizations comprised of groups of users, instead of individual users, to adopt new technologies. These studies have examined TAM in relation to organizational adoptions of new technologies in contexts such as e-commerce, police investigations, sales force coordination, and telemedicine (Chau & Hu 2002; Colvin & Goh 205; Grandon & Pearson 2004; Olson & Boyer 2003;

Robinson, Marshall, & Stamps 2005; Yu et al. 2005). Such studies have focused on technology in numerous different forms, including software, hardware, websites, technology standards, and Internet-based activities. These types of studies of TAM within the context of organizations demonstrate the potential applicability of TAM to the acceptance of new technologies by government agencies.

Grandon and Pearson (2004), for example, explore how small and medium sized businesses accept the use of e-commerce as a part of their business activities. That study found the acceptance of e-commerce by the organizations was based on perception of the value of e-commerce in an organization, in light of certain external and internal factors, and the level of success of the adoption was influenced by a number of internal factors. The acceptance of the new technology was influenced by agency mission, actual cost, perceived cost, agency priorities, and staff interest, among others. This approach appears to have utility when applied to the process through which government agencies adopt new technologies and apply them.

4. TAM and e-Government websites

The conceptual framework tested in this study was based on the idea of a modified TAM for organizational acceptance of new technology, similar to those like the Grandon and Pearson (2004) study detailed above. The organizations studied were United States federal government agencies and the new technology at issue was accessible websites that comply with the standards of Section 508. The TAM (and its related variants) were originally developed and intended to be applied to assess the reaction and behavior of individual users of a technology. This study conceived of the federal agencies as users of the standards of Section 508 and the accessibility standards as a new technology that they were supposed to adopt. Federal agencies with e-Government websites are providers of technologies to citizens, such as websites, but they are also users of technologies, such as the elements they must use to create and provide websites. It is in this latter sense that this study approached the federal agencies, with the essential problem in this research being how agencies choose to adopt or not adopt the Section 508 accessibility standards for their websites. As such, the TAM provides a unique conceptual approach to the study of the organizational acceptance of the accessibility standards by federal agencies.

Figure 2 illustrates the preliminary conceptual framework for this study.

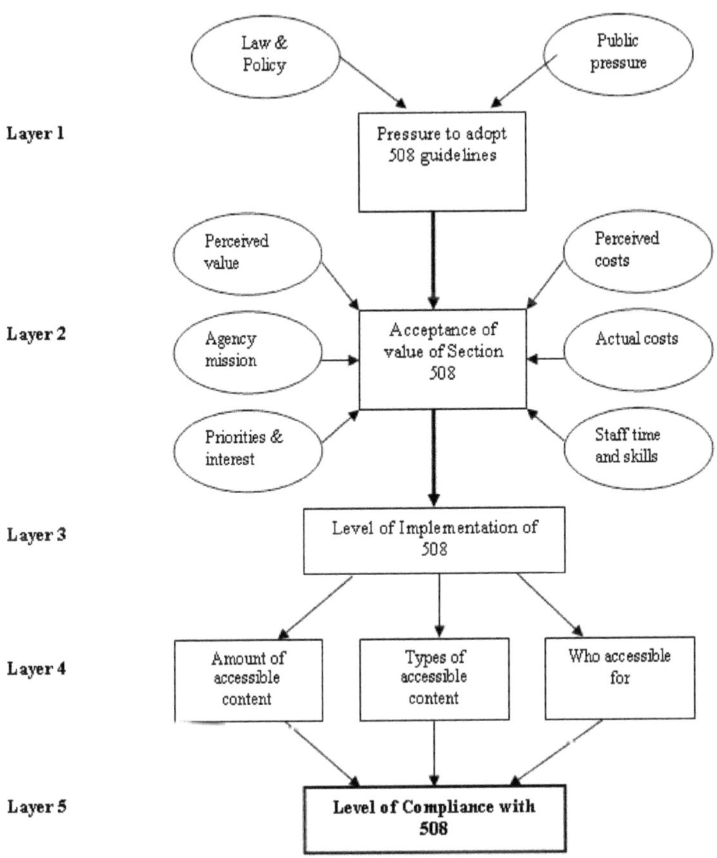

Figure 2: Conceptual framework for the study, based on modified TAM for organizations

The two upper layers of the model are contextual, while the three lower layers represent the accessibility research conducted in this study. The contextual layers are derived from extant research and professional literature about the policy environment for e-Government and issues of accessibility. The three lower layers of the framework display the research focus of this study—the mandate to implement the standards of Section 508, the ways the standards could be implemented, and the actual level of compliance that is achieved.

The top layer of Figure 2 shows the external pressures to adopt Section 508 standards for federal e-Government websites. Various law and policy instruments, including Section 508, create legal standards for accessible websites, while various types of public pressures, such as complaints, news reports, lawsuits, and research studies may create further pressure by bringing attention to the issue (Jaeger 2004a). These pressures drive the acceptance of Section 508 standards for websites as a value to which agencies adhere.

As the second layer of the figure shows, there are many internal issues related to perceived usefulness and perceived ease of adoption of Section 508 standards for websites. Issues related to culture can have a significant impact on decisions to accept and implement a technology (Straub, Keil, & Brenner 1997). Feedback within an agency has been shown to play an important role in the development of online government services (Mahler & Regan 2002). These specific internal issues are drawn from the review of relevant research literature as key factors that can influence agency decisions regarding how to adopt Section 508 standards (see Jaeger 2004a, 2004b, 2006, 2008). On the left side of the figure are the internal factors related to perceived usefulness of adoption of Section 508 standards to websites—perceived value, agency mission, and priorities and interests of the agency. On the right hand side of the middle level of the figure are the internal factors related to perceived ease of adoption of Section 508 standards for websites—perceived costs, actual costs, and staff time and awareness.

The third layer of Figure 2 examines the influences of the varying contextual factors that will shape the ultimate level of compliance with Section 508 on an agency website. The fourth layer of Figure 2 represents the extent to which the standards of Section 508 are implemented on an agency website. The amount of accessible content, the types of content that are accessible, and the types of disabilities that content is accessible for will all be influenced by decisions made regarding implementation of Section 508 standards on e-Government websites.

The fifth layer of Figure 2 focuses on compliance with the Section 508 standards for federal e-Government websites. Ultimately, the amount of accessible content, the types of accessible content, and the types of disabilities for which content is accessible demonstrate the extent to which an agency website complies with the standards of Section 508. If an agency considers adoption to be difficult or of limited value, the levels of compliance with Section 508 standards will likely be low. In contrast, if an agency considers adoption a high priority or of significant value, then the levels of compliance with Section 508 standards will be high.

5. The study of TAM and 508 standards

This framework was examined in a multi-method, user-centered study of e-Government websites for compliance with the Section 508 of the Rehabilitation Act standards for accessibility (Jaeger 2006, 2008). This study employed five data collection methods in the assessment of e-Government websites in terms of the implementation of Section 508 of the Rehabilitation Act. Selected federal e-Government websites were evaluated using policy analysis, expert testing, user testing, and automated testing, along with a survey administered to federal webmasters that assessed their views on accessibility. In the evaluation of e-Government sites, the use of a multi-method approach is optimal (Thompson, McClure, & Jaeger 2003).

The policy analysis was conducted through extensive review of legal and policy documents. The expert testing involved the evaluation by persons knowledgeable about the design of accessible websites to provide a technical evaluation of the accessibility. The user testing under the guidance of a researcher was used to provide detailed information from the perspective of users. Table 1 lists sample questions used in expert and user testing. Automated testing—the use of software designed to test accessibility of websites—was used, but proved to provide no additional information to the expert and user testing. Appendix A provides a detailed description of the data collection methods.

Table 1: Sample questions from expert testing and user testing

Sample Expert Testing Questions:

- Provides an audio/video/textual equivalent for every element related to content and services?
- Alternative formats of elements of multimedia presentations synchronized to the appropriate parts of the presentation?
- All information conveyed through color also conveyed without color?
- Provides clear navigation mechanisms?
- Does not rely on moving pictures or flash to convey content?
- Ensures user control of time-sensitive content changes?

Sample User Testing Questions:

- Are you able to navigate the site without difficulty? If not, what accessibility problems did you face in navigating?
- Are you able to use particular applications (i.e., download forms, view audio or video, fill out forms) on the site without difficulty? If not, what accessibility problems did you face in using these applications?
- Do you feel that the site as a whole is working well with the assistive technology you are using? Please specify.
- Do you notice problems that might affect people with other types of disabilities? Please specify.

The study also employed questionnaires to government webmasters about agency perceptions of accessibility. The questionnaires were sent to a diverse set of prominent government agencies that work directly with citizens. This survey received a response rate of 60%. Table 2 lists sample questions from the survey of government webmasters.

Table 2: Sample questions for government webmasters.

- Do you feel that the accessibility of your website for persons with disabilities is a priority within your agency?
- When working to make your website accessible for persons with disabilities, where do you turn for resources and guidelines?
- Do you perform accessibility testing on your website to test how well it can be used by persons with disabilities? If so, at what point in the website development process is this testing done?
- What factors (i.e., staff time, staff skills, funding, agency mission, etc.) influence the priority accorded to the accessibility of your website for persons with disabilities?
- Have you received any feedback from users of your site regarding its accessibility? If so, were the comments generally positive or negative?
- If you feel that the accessibility of your website could be improved, what resources would you find beneficial in working to improve it?

The primary finding from the study was that most e-Government websites do not comply with all of the requirements of Section 508 of the Rehabilitation Act, rendering most e-Government websites inaccessible to some or all persons with disabilities (Jaeger, 2006, 2008). Key accessibility barriers that were recurring problems across all of the sites tested included:

- Compatibility problems with screen enlargement;
- Compatibility problems with screen readers;
- Compatibility problems with alternate color schemes;
- Use of flash and moving images to convey content;
- Cluttered layout and organization;
- Audio content does not have a text equivalent;
- Graphics lack Alt tags;
- Difficult drop-down, mouse-over menus; and
- Problems with consistency and clarity of context, orientation, and navigation.

Further, the webmaster survey revealed that agency perceptions of the accessibility of these websites often did not match the actual levels of accessibility on the sites (Jaeger 2006, 2008).

The three lower levels of the proposed framework were studied through several methods of accessibility testing. Accessibility testing by users with a range of different disabilities, experts in accessibility testing, and automated tools evaluated the ways in which and the extent to which Section 508 standards have been implemented on the sites.

In addition to the testing, the questionnaires to government webmasters examined the context in which agencies are implementing accessibility on their websites. The law and policy analysis was used to examine the initial pressures to implement Section 508 standards, while the webmaster questionnaires explored the factors that influence agency perspectives and decision-making processes related to Section 508. As such, the webmaster questionnaires served to directly connect the findings of the accessibility testing to information about the agency perspectives and decision-making processes related to implementing accessible websites, explicitly linking the accessibility methods to the larger contextual issues.

The tentative conceptual framework presented in Figure 2 served as an initial guide for this study. Given the newness of accessibility research and the lack of established conceptual frameworks for studies of e-Government accessibility, this proposed framework of a TAM at least provided an exploratory conceptual basis from which to begin research.

6. Findings and modification of the TAM

The top layer, which posits that law and policy combine with public pressure to create the impetus for an agency to adopt the Section 508 standards on its website, seems sound in light of the findings of the study. The literature review and the policy analysis revealed an intertwined relationship between the development of the laws and policies and the support by the public and by particular stakeholder groups for such laws and policies. The passage and implementation of the primary disability rights laws were inextricably linked to public support and political protests by interested groups (Jaeger 2004a; Jaeger & Bowman 2005). Without sufficient public support and stakeholder intervention, the passage of the Rehabilitation Act, Individuals with Disabilities Education Act, or the Americans with Disabilities Act would not have been assured. As the policy analysis demonstrated, the passage of Section 508 of the Rehabilitation Act and the promulgation of standards were greeted with significant support from an array of stakeholder groups. Further, disability rights groups and government organizations like the Access Board and the National Council on Disability have continued to lobby for better implementation of Section 508. The data from the user testing and expert testing affirm the accuracy of the top layer of the framework, as the websites that fared the best in all of the testing were primarily agencies that focus on issues related to disability. These agencies would be most likely to be interested in and affected by public pressure from stakeholder groups on issues of disability.

The bottom three layers of the conceptual framework can also be assessed in light of the data from the study. The user testing and the expert testing methods were both focused on gathering data about the level of implementation of the standards of Section 508, the success of that implementation, and the ultimate level of compliance with the Section 508 standards on a site. From the data collected, it seems that the lower three levels of the framework represent what appears to be happening on the websites. On sites where the methods of accessibility testing found poor design in terms of persons with disabilities, the problems clearly were not the result of failed efforts to provide accessibility, but were instead the result of limited attempts to provide accessibility. These sites lacked significant evidence of attempts to meet many of the Section 508 standards, demonstrating a decision to make a minimal effort to implement the standards. In these cases, the resulting sites had limited levels of accessible content, with many different types of content being inaccessible for persons with a range of different disabilities. This finding was independently reached through the user and expert methods of accessibility testing.

The opposite situations—where the design of the website evidenced meaningful attempts to provide accessibility and, thus, the intent to implement the standards of Section 508—the sites were well designed for accessibility and fared much better in the accessibility testing. In the sites that were generally better designed for accessibility, the flaws were often implementations of the standards that were not completely correct. The sites designed with a noticeable intent to comply with the standards received much better results in the expert testing and the user testing. The primary reason for these better results was that the sites provided much higher levels of accessible content, access to most or all types of content, and accessibility for users with most or all disabilities.

For both of the sites that were poorly designed for accessibility and the sites that were well designed for accessibility, the lower three layers of the conceptual framework seemed to accurately represent the situation. However, the second layer of the conceptual framework proved more difficult to assess, due to the complexity of this level of the framework and to the limitations of the responses to the webmaster questionnaire. It is also the layer that is most tied to the TAM, as it reveals the decision making process in the agency related to acceptance.

Based on the findings of the policy analysis, the second layer seems reasonable, and the findings from the user and expert accessibility testing do not call any elements of the second layer into question. However, results of the webmaster questionnaire, the data collection method most relevant to assessing this layer of the framework, are less helpful than hoped in relation to the framework. When asked about the factors that influenced decisions related to the implementation of the Section 508 standards and when asked about the prioritization of accessibility within the agency, many responses focused on the importance of providing accessibility without giving many details related to agency process or decision-making.

Even though the top layer and the lowest three layers of the framework seem accurate based on the data gathered in the study, the questions about the second layer also raise questions about the interactions of the other layers and their relationships to one another that will need to be answered in further studies. Nevertheless, the data from this study have identified four important elements not included in the initial conceptual framework:

- User feedback – Comments from users with disabilities would influence compliance with Section 508 standards at many agencies.
- Education and training – Many federal web developers are receiving insufficient training about designing, testing, and monitoring for accessibility.
- Monitoring and enforcement – The current citizen-based monitoring and enforcement structure needs to be accounted for in the conceptual framework.
- Political climate – Accessibility is not a political priority to many agencies.

Figure 3 is a revised version of the conceptual framework that incorporates these factors.

One way to address the need for information about the second layer would be a study targeted directly at web developers at government agencies. Such a study, however, would need to have a much larger sample than the one in this study. Further research will also need to account for and evaluate the suggested additions to the revised conceptual framework. One clear finding, however, is that agency management plays an enormously important role in the adoption of Section 508 requirements.

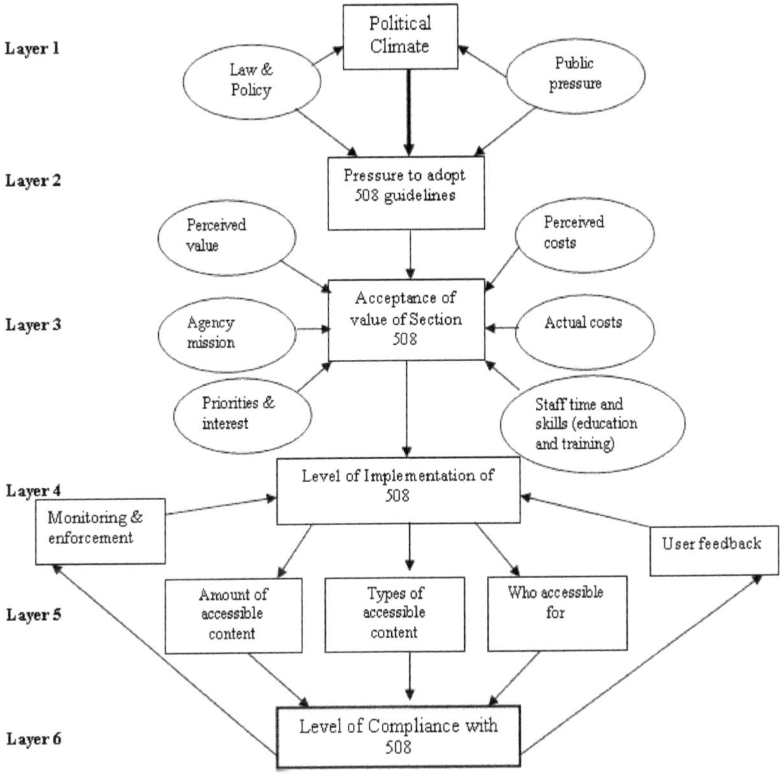

Figure 3: Revised conceptual framework of TAM for Section 508 standards on government websites

To further test the fitness of TAM as a conceptual framework for the implementation of Section 508 and other e-Government standards, future work in this area should consider the role that management plays in implementing requirements for e-Government websites. Managerial leadership and political support can be central to e-Government development (Chou, Chen & Pu 2008; Ho & Ni 2004). In specific terms of the adoption of Section 508 standards, managerial leadership and political support may offer the best means of increasing adoption of Section 508 standards among federal agencies.

Managerial influence can be explored as an external variable in the TAM, which influences the perceived usefulness and the perceived ease of use of the technology (Bhattacherjee & Sanford 2006). Alternatively, managerial influence might appear as a direct effect on a user's behavioral intention to accept the new technology. Although this relationship is not captured in the TAM, support for it can be found in other technology acceptance theories, such as the Theory of Reasoned Action (TRA) (Fishbein & Ajzen 1975); Theory of Planned Behavior (TPB) (Ajzen 1991); and the Unified Theory of Acceptance and Use of Technology (UTAUT) (Venkatesh et al. 2003). In the case of government agencies implementing Section 508 provisions for websites, agency managers may be perceived as "important others" by employees responsible for implementing the changes, and thus managerial influence might affect an employee's behavioral intent to implement the provisions.

7. Conclusion: The implications of TAM and Section 508

While this paper has focused on adoption of the Section 508 standards on e-Government websites, the general ideas and approaches explored in this paper may have relevance to the adoption of e-Government standards more widely. Given the importance placed on e-Government as a means of communicating with and providing services to citizens, improving the adoption and implementation of standards is essential for e-Government to meet the stated administrative goals. This paper has identified potential areas for further research, and further research is definitely needed to ascertain the relevance of the TAM to e-Government and the process of adoption of e-Government standards to websites. The proposed model needs to be tested with other e-Government standards, and individual factors suggested in this study will need to be tested to understand the role they play in the process. These ideas need to be researched in the context of other e-Governments—international, state, and local. The particular roles of management in the adoption of e-Government standards seem to merit specific attention. Ultimately, such research could improve understanding of the ways residents and public servants use e-Government technologies (Chang et al. 2005).

Results from TAM studies might also be useful in helping to determine the best methods for addressing the issues at hand. In terms of compliance with Section 508, TAM studies might help determine the best means for raising compliance with Section 508 requirements, such as the creation of an independent division monitoring conformance of e-services to Section 508 regulations; making conformance report an essential part of e-Government project deliverables; or the adoption of technological products and frameworks known to assist accessible content and service development. However, TAM alone will not be able to explain issues of technology adoption related to e-Government. Additional factors, such as costs and technology maturity, should be considered as well.

The United States and many other local, state, federal, and supra-national governments rely on their online presence for activities ranging from information provision to complex service delivery. Given the growing importance of e-Government and the continually increasing amounts of government information and services available primarily or exclusively on the web, the process of adoption by government agencies of e-Government standards is a significant issue that merits considerable further study. Hopefully, the ideas, approaches, and models suggested in this paper will serve to foster more research in this area.

References

Ajzen, I. (1991) "The theory of planned behavior", *Organizational Behavior and Human Decision Processes*, vol. 50, pp. 179-211.

Barr, S. (2007). "Public less satisfied with government websites", [online], *Washington Post*, http://www.washingtonpost.com/wp-dyn/content/article/2007/03/20/AR2007032001338.html.

Chang, I. C., Li, Y.-C., Hung, W.-F. & Hwang, H.-G. (2005) "An empirical study on the impact of quality antecedents on tax payers' acceptance of Internet tax-filing systems", *Government Information Quarterly*, vol. 22, pp. 389-410.

Chau, P. Y. K. & Hu, P. J-H. (2002) "Investigating healthcare professionals' decisions to accept telemedicine: An empirical test of competing theories", *Information & Management*, vol. 39, pp. 297-311.

Chou, T.-C., Chen, J.-R., & Pu, C.-K. (2008) "Exploring the collective actions of public servants in e-Government development", *Decision Support Systems*, vol. 45, pp. 251-265.

Colvin, C. A. & Goh, A. (2005) "Validation of the technology acceptance model for police", *Journal of Criminal Justice*, vol. 33, pp. 89-95.

Cullen, R. & Hernon, P. (2006) "More citizen perspectives on e-Government", in Hernon, P., Cullen, R. & Relyea, H. C., (eds.), *Comparative Perspectives on e-*

Government: Serving today and building for tomorrow*, Lanham, MD: Scarecrow Press.

Dasgupta, S., Granger, M. & McGarry, N. (2002) "User acceptance of e-collaboration technology: An extension of the technology acceptance model", *Group Decision and Negotiation*, vol. 11, pp. 87-100.

Davis, F. D. (1989) "Perceived usefulness, perceived ease of use, and user acceptance of information technology", *MIS Quarterly*, vol. 13, pp. 319-339.

Davis, F. D., Bagozzi, R. P. & Warshaw, P. R. (1989) "User acceptance of computer technology: A comparison of two theoretical models", *Management Science*, vol. 35, pp. 983-1003.

Dishaw, M. T. & Strong, D. M. (1999) "Extending the technology acceptance model with task-technology fit constructs", *Information & Management*, vol. 36, pp. 9-21.

Ebbers, W. E., Pieterson, W. J. & Noordman, H. N. (2008) "Electronic government: Rethinking channel management strategies", *Government Information Quarterly*, vol. 25, pp. 181-201.

e-Government Act of 2002, P.L. 107-347.

Fishbein, M. & Ajzen, I. (1975) Belief, attitude, intention and behavior: An introduction to theory and research, Reading, MA: Addison-Wesley.

Gefen, D. & Straub, D. W. (1997) "Gender differences in the perception and use of e-mail: An extension of the technology acceptance model", *MIS Quarterly*, vol. 21, pp. 389-400.

Grandon, E. E. & Pearson, J. M. (2004) "Electronic commerce adoption: An empirical study of small and medium U.S. businesses", *Information & Management*, vol. 42, pp. 197-216.

Ho, A. T-K. & Ni, A. Y. (2004) "Explaining the adoption of e-Government features: A case study of Iowa County Treasurers' offices", *American Review of Public Administration*, vol. 34, pp. 164-180.

Horrigan, J. B. (2004) *How Americans get in touch with government*, Washington DC: Pew Internet & American Life Project.

Jacko, J. A. & Hanson, V. L. (2002) "Universal access and inclusion in design", *Universal Access in the Information Society*, vol. 2, pp. 1-2.

Jaeger, P. T. (2004a) "Beyond Section 508: The spectrum of legal requirements for accessible e-Government websites in the United States", *Journal of Government Information*, vol. 30, pp. 518-533.

Jaeger, P. T. (2004b) "The social impact of an accessible E-democracy: The importance of disability rights laws in the development of the federal e-Government", *Journal of Disability Policy Studies*, vol. 15, pp. 19-26.

Jaeger, P. T. (2005) "Deliberative democracy and the conceptual foundations of electronic government", *Government Information Quarterly*, vol. 22, pp. 702-719.

Jaeger, P. T. (2006) "Assessing Section 508 compliance on federal e-Government websites: A multi-method, user-centered evaluation of accessibility for persons with disabilities", *Government Information Quarterly*, vol. 23, pp. 169-190.

Jaeger, P. T. (2008) "User-centered policy evaluations of Section 508 of the Rehabilitation Act: Evaluating e-Government websites for accessibility", *Journal of Disability Policy Studies,* vol. 19, pp. 24-33.

Jaeger, P. T. & Bowman, C. A. (2005) Understanding disability: Inclusion, access, diversity, & civil rights, Westport, CT: Praeger.

Jaeger, P. T. & Thompson, K. M. (2003) "e-Government around the world: Lessons, challenges, and new directions", *Government Information Quarterly*, vol. 20, pp. 389-394.

Jaeger, P. T. & Thompson, K. M. (2004) "Social information behavior and the democratic process: Information poverty, normative behavior, and electronic government in the United States", *Library & Information Science Research*, vol. 26, pp. 94-107.

Lederer, A. L., Maupin, D. J., Sena, M. P. & Zhuang, Y. (2000) "The technology acceptance model and the World Wide Web", *Decision Support Systems*, vol. 29, pp. 269-282

Mahler, J. & Regan, P. M. (2002) "Learning to govern online: Federal agency Internet use", *American Review of Public Administration*, vol. 32, pp. 326-349.

Olson, J. R. & Boyer, K. K. (2003) "Factors influencing the utilization of Internet purchasing in small organizations", *Journal of Operations Management*, vol. 21, pp. 225-245.

Reddick, C. G. (2005) "Citizen interaction with e-Government: From the streets to servers?", *Government Information Quarterly*, vol. 22, pp. 338-357.

Robinson, L., Marshall, G. W. & Stamps, M. B. (2005) "Sales force use of technology: Antecedents to technology acceptance", *Journal of Business Research*, vol. 58, pp. 1623-1631.

Saade, R. & Bahli, B. (2005) "The impact of cognitive absorption on perceived usefulness and perceived ease of use in online learning: An extension of the technology acceptance model", *Information & Management*, vol. 42, pp. 317-327.

Section 508 of the Rehabilitation Act. 29 U.S.C. § 794d.

Singh, A. K. & Sahu, R. (2008). "Integrating Internet, telephones, and call centers for delivering better quality e-governance to all citizens", *Government Information Quarterly*, vol. 25, 477-490.

Stephanidis, C. & Savidis, A. (2001) "Universal access in the information society: Methods, tools, and interactive technologies", *Universal Access in the Information Society*, vol. 1, pp. 40-55.

Straub, D., Keil, M. & Brenner, W. (1997), "Testing the technology acceptance model across cultures: A three country study", *Information & Management*, vol. 33, pp. 1-11.

Streib, G. & Navarro, I. (2006), "Citizen demand for interactive e-Government: The case of Georgia consumer services", *American Review of Public Administration*, vol. 36, pp. 288-300.

Thompson, K. M., McClure, C. R. & Jaeger, P. T. (2003) "Evaluating federal websites: Improving e-Government for the people", in George, J. F. (ed.), *Computers in society: Privacy, ethics, and the Internet,* Upper Saddle River, NJ: Prentice Hall.

Vassilakis, C., Lepouras, G., Fraser, J., Haston, S. & Georgiadis, P. (2005) "Barriers to electronic service development", *E-Services Journal*, vol. 4, pp. 41–63.

Venkatesh, V., & Davis, F. D. (2000) "A theoretical extension of the technology acceptance model: Four longitudinal field studies", *Management Science*, vol. 46, pp. 186-204.

Venkatesh, V., Morris, M. G., Davis, G. B., & Davis, F. D. (2003) "User acceptance of information technology: Toward a unified view", *MIS Quarterly*, vol. 27, pp. 425-478.

White House (2003) e-Government Strategy: Implementing the President's Management Agenda for e-Government, Washington DC: Author.

Yu, J., Ha, I., Choi, M., & Rho, J. (2005) "Extending the TAM for a t-commerce", *Information & Management*, vol. 42, pp. 965-976.

Appendix A: Data Collection Approach

The study that inspired the discussion in this paper was conducted in 2005 and 2006 (Jaeger 2006; 2008). While the data collection techniques are not central to the concepts explored in the paper, the framework of the study provides context to this discussion. The study employed five data collection methods in the assessment of the implementation of Section 508 on e-Government websites: policy analysis, expert testing, user testing, automated testing, and a survey administered to federal webmasters that assessed their views on accessibility. The study examined major e-Government sites of the United States federal government and the sites of federal agencies with a mission related to service for persons with disabilities. These two types of sites were selected to compare the levels of attention accessibility standards received on prominent e-Government sites and on sites oriented toward persons with disabilities.

The study first engaged in the policy analysis to identify the range of federal laws, policy documents, instruments, and standards that related to the accessibility of government websites. The policy analysis was designed to provide context and serve as the basis for the development of testing protocols and questionnaires.

The expert testing was next conducted. Expert testing is the evaluation by persons knowledgeable about the design of websites based on an established protocol. The protocol was pre-tested before use, and experts were recruited from a population of web developers and researchers. The expert evaluators were persons who could identify the barriers to accessibility in design and understood the legal requirements for accessibility and how they should be properly implemented.

These questions were drawn from the specific Section 508 requirements and are necessary for achieving a broad understanding of the accessibility of the site. The testing was conducted to ensure as wide an analysis as possible. Sites were tested through multiple browsers and for compatibility with a range of technologies related to different types of disabilities, including narrators and screen readers, screen enlargement software, magnifiers, alternate color schemes, and alternate navigation devices, among others. Expert testing was conducted until no new issues were identified in subsequent tests.

Expert testing is particularly important because it is very unlikely that the evaluation of an e-Government site could be conducted so thoroughly as to include user tests that represented people who have all the different types and levels of disabilities that must be accounted for in designing for accessibility. Though the expert testing did not reach the same depth or granularity in identifying problems for any particular disability as a user with that disability would, expert testing did identify the major accessibility issues on each site.

User testing, the testing of a website by users under the guidance of a researcher, was conducted next and provided a great depth of information from the perspective of each user who was tested. The user tests were conducted with both guided and think-aloud protocols to get the broadest range of insights possible. The instruments were pre-tested before use, and subjects were recruited through disability organizations. Subjects were recruited to represent a wide range of types and levels of severities of disabilities, spanning quadriplegia to complete sight loss. Users with visual and mobility disabilities were targeted in this study because those groups among all types of disabilities face the most significant barriers to equal access to online content.

People with different levels of severity of the same kind of disability will often experience different accessibility issues on the same site. A person involved in user testing, then, can best provide information related to the experiences of people like themselves. As with the expert tests, user tests were conducted until no new information about the sites was identified in subsequent tests. The user tests took, on average, between one and two hours to complete.

The results of the automated testing were muted in comparison to the results of the expert and user testing. Not only did a range of commonly used automated testing programs reveal no additional insights beyond the expert testing and user testing, the automated programs found far fewer issues than most individual expert and user participants. While the automated programs were useful to corroborate the findings of the other forms of data collection, they did not contribute any independent data.

After the three types of testing had been completed, a questionnaire was sent to the webmasters of all of the sites being studied to gauge their perceptions of the accessibility of their websites and the emphasis given to website accessibility within their agencies. The questions for the survey were developed based on the findings from the four previous forms of data collection. The responses to the questionnaire revealed the agencies' perceptions of the accessibility of their websites, which often did not match the findings from the user testing and the expert testing.

Bridging the Digital Divide for e-Government inclusion: A United States Case Study

Janice C. Sipior and Burke T. Ward
Villanova University, USA
Originally published in EJEG (2005) Volume 3 Issue 3.

Like the two studies of youth engagement, this case study is also worth reading in conjunction with the preceding one. Janice Sipior and Burke Ward examine the related topic of the digital divide with a case based on computer illiterate people in a public housing community. The district studied, a housing development in Chester PA, is a deprived area with high levels of poverty and unemployment. The objective was to train people in the use of technology and the Internet in particular with a view to their having more inclusive access to e-government. The results were surprisingly positive with visiting rates to government website being higher than expected, in fact higher than the population as a whole. One reason for these results is, of course, the high public service needs of this demographic area. The participants were enthusiastic and there were many benefits. The problem, as always, is sustaining the programme once the funding expires, but the message about the need for public outreach is clear.

Abstract: This case study of computer-illiterate people in a public housing community was undertaken to explore the digital divide and e-Government inclusion and uses. Overall, the results indicate the importance of a community organizing strategy to secure internet access, coordinate education and training, and sustain internet use to initiate e-Government participation among the techno-disadvantaged. While first-time government website visitation by community participants was surprisingly high, the intent to continue use was lacking. Sustained use remains challenging due to external threats to the community initiative, including isolation from mainstream society, exploitive dependency by those ostensibly assisting the community, and a culture of failure. Public outreach, on the part of governmental and other organizations, is suggested to encourage e-Government inclusion among those previously excluded.

Keywords: e-Government, digital divide, country case study, internet access

1. Introduction

e-Government is the application of information and communication technologies (ICT) to government services. Within the United States (U.S.), the e-Government Act of 2002 was enacted to "create a law that will make it easier to get more government information and services online" (Hasson 2002). The realization of these goals requires that the digital divide be addressed. Indeed, in a study of e-Government use by citizens, the digital divide was found to be more pronounced among government website visitors than among internet users in general (Thomas and Streib 2003).

This paper explores the digital divide and e-Government inclusion in the U.S. through a case study of computer-illiterate people in a public housing community. This field study of a community organizing strategy was undertaken to reduce the divide by providing computer training to increase computer use and internet access among residents and to understand their inclusion in and uses of e-Government. The factors to be addressed in encouraging e-Government inclusion among the techno-disadvantaged are first considered. Next, the research methodology utilized for this case study is presented. Finally, the results and lessons learned reveal the importance of the community organizing strategy to secure internet access, coordinate education and training, and sustain internet use to enable e-Government inclusion.

2. e-Government inclusion and the digital divide

The most common application of e-Government within the U.S. is providing citizens with access to information via the internet, raising the issue of equal access (Marchionini et al. 2003). A necessary condition for equity in information access is that citizens have internet access. The divide between those with access to the internet and new ICT and those without, or in other words, the gap between the 'technology haves' and 'have-nots' is referred to as the digital divide (Holmes 2002, Novak and Hoffman 2000,

OECD 2001, Wilhelm and Thierer 2000). "The Digital Divide is arguably the single, largest, segregating force in today's world. If it is not made a national priority, a generation of children and families will mature without these tools that are proving to be the key to the future" (PR Newswire 2000). Indeed, the need to overcome the digital divide (Goodman and Brenner 2002) has been recognized by the G8 in their Digital Opportunity Taskforce (2001).

In a study addressing the adoption of e-Governance, public internet access was found to be the most important factor affecting the use of online government services (Prattipati 2003). For example, the 1996 U.S. national conventions of the Republican and Democratic parties were carried over the internet, giving opportunities for interaction. While the internet has the potential to create well-informed and empowered consumers, it will also help to change the passive relationship most people have with the government (Symonds 2000). However, people who did not have internet access could not participate in the "point-and-click" debate. In March 2000, Arizona registered voters with internet access were given an opportunity to vote online in the Democratic Party primary during the 96-hour period leading up to the opening of the polls (Wilhelm and Thierer 2000). Those without internet access were able to exercise their voting rights for just one day at the polling place. Exclusion from online voting, and other interactive opportunities, will weaken the voice of those who are techno-disadvantaged (Althoff 2004). These individuals are among the citizens likely to benefit most from government services (Lamb 2004). If the digital divide is not bridged, the powerful communication tools meant to enrich lives will serve as a social divider.

Empirical evidence suggests that simply providing access to ICT does not guarantee its use unless the concerns and abilities of users are addressed (Brookes 2004). This study reports on a community-based initiative to reduce the digital divide by surveying community needs, providing access to ICT, and training participants in computers and the internet, thereby increasing their capability to participate in and use e-Government. For a detailed discussion of narrowing the divide within this community, please see Sipior et al. (2004).

3. Methodology

e-Government inclusion and the digital divide emerged as a focus of concern in the 1990s and is thus a relatively new area of research in which few previous studies have been done. At an early stage of investigation, the research is exploratory, for which a single case study is appropriate (Benbasat et al. 1987 and Galliers 1992). The selection of the William Penn (WP) Housing Development, comprised of 158 households, is based on the community members as representative of the technologically disadvantaged. Few possessed skills or training in computer technology and the community had virtually no access to computer technology. The authors serve as volunteers within the community, which cultivated familiarity and trust necessary to collect data (Rubin and Rubin 1995). Any unintended influence of the authors is minimized as they were volunteers among several other volunteers who were not aware of the research objectives. Further, only two of the authors knew all research objectives.

Both positivist and interpretive data were collected. The positivist measures are based on survey data. The interpretive data includes contextual data; observation, including participant observation and volunteer fieldwork; community members' written and oral comments from informal interaction and feedback forms; documentary sources including internal community meeting minutes, memoranda, and reports; written and oral communications between the community and interested parties; published reports; and a class action lawsuit, providing a richer data set for broadened insight (Myers 2003; Silverman 1993). The hermeneutics approach (Larsen and Myers 1997; Myers, 2003) was employed to interpret the meaning of the data. Standards for the quality of conclusions drawn were incorporated, with the "justificatory" point of view supported by convergence among the multiple field workers involved (Miles and Huberman 1994) primary among them.

3.1. A United States case study

Applying the theoretical premises of the Assets-Based Community Development Model (Kretzmann and McKnight 1993), a community organizing strategy was initiated within the WP Housing Development. According to this model, an effective local organizing strategy is fundamental to successful community empowerment and community self-sufficiency. In applying this model, the WP Tenants Association initiated a community development plan, with assistance from volunteers including the authors; a Community Organizer, a position held by a professional community program planner; and Unity Center, Inc., a nonprofit corporation founded in 1987 to “bring people together who would normally not come together” to work on a common project. A community survey was undertaken in fall 1999. The results, with a response rate of 37.5%, revealed 60% of households have one or more members in need of employment. Job skills and/or specialized training, however, are present among the households surveyed, with 30% skilled or trained in construction and 24% in nursing and healthcare. While 20% expressed a strong interest in further education and/or training in construction and 28% in nursing, 46% indicated computer training. Indeed, only 12% reported job skills and/or specialised training in computer technology. Conspicuously, none had a computer in their home.

The WP Tenants Association Preliminary Development Plan (WPTA 1999) was formulated based on the results of the community survey. Among the priorities of the plan is access to technology and technological skills. As a result, a computer training program was launched in the fall of 2000 and continues through the present. This program provides on-site training to members of the community by university students. This study focuses on the first training session in the fall of 2000, at the completion of which a participant survey was administered.

3.1.1. *The case context: The William Penn housing development*

The WP housing development is located in Chester, Pennsylvania (PA), U.S., which occupies 4.8 square miles in Delaware County (Brief of Amicus Curiae 1998). This formerly industrial city is “one of the most distressed cities in the nation" (council of the city of Chester 1994). The low-income population of 39,000, which has the highest infant mortality rate in PA, is 65% African-American (Worsham 2000). By contrast, the remainder of Delaware County is 91% White (Brief of Amicus Curiae 1998).

In 1987, a class action suit, Clements v. City of Chester (1990), was filed by all residents of 1,732 Chester Housing Authority (CHA) public housing units claiming "substandard, intolerable and uninhabitable" housing including "dark hallways strewn with garbage, human waste, and the thrown-away paraphernalia of drug and alcohol activity; inadequate plumbing and sewage; unsafe electrical systems; leaking roofs; and doors without locks"

(Clements v. City of Chester 1990). As a result, Chester demolished substandard housing units in the early 1990's and built new housing. The WP Housing Development, completed in March 1999, includes reasonably attractive garden apartments and a multi-room community centre, surrounded by deteriorating houses, vacant lots, and high crime. The disturbing presence of social ills such as low educational performance, teenage pregnancy, vandalism, graffiti, noise, trash, drug use on the streets, violence, crime, drive-by shootings, murders, etc. fosters a culture of failure.

The authors discover that external threats obstruct progress within the community. Isolation from mainstream society not unlike that of an inner city, exploitive dependency fostered by those ostensibly trying to make improvements, and a culture of failure contribute to the lingering divide. Data in support of these external threats may be found in Sipior et al. (2004).

3.1.2. *The training program*

Plans for the WP Tenants Association Computer Training Program began in March 2000 with a proposal to Villanova University's Institute for Teaching and Learning. After overcoming dissent from local government, a training site at the Community Centre was secured. Local law firms donated 15 PCs. Students from local schools donated 14 refurbished PCs and made the on-site Computer Lab functional. An emergent community leader took the initiative to publicize the program and distribute fliers and sign-up forms. As word of mouth spread, newly interested individuals started showing up at weekly planning meetings, gaining ownership of the program. Motivation to voluntarily participate was provided by the promise of a refurbished PC to take home for those completing the Training Program. As word of this initiative spread, a second location, equipped with 15 computers, was developed at In the Name of Jesus Outreach Church, within two miles of the WP Housing Development. The program "kicked off" in September 2000 and concluded in December 2000. Participants successfully fulfilling program requirements completed a survey and received certificates and free refurbished PCs.

The training content is directed toward varying levels of computer experience. The topic of the internet is addressed in accordance with the objectives of the Development Plan (WPTA 1999) including Objective 3: Develop a community webpage and Objective 8: Develop a community network through internet connection. A community webpage was planned but deferred until Spring 2001 when web development software was to be installed. Objective 8 was deferred until PCs and internet connection are installed within homes in the community. The student trainers demonstrated their own personal websites for the purpose of advancing Objective 3.

4. Results

4.1. Demographic characteristics of the techno-disadvantaged Community

The key to bridging the divide is considered to be internet use (Keller 2001). When reported in conjunction with the most important demographic characteristics of the techno-disadvantaged (www.ntia.doc.gov 1999), the community participant characteristics are consistent with those on the disadvantaged side of the divide, as shown in Table 1.

Table 1: Internet use among community participants compared with previous findings characterizing the disadvantaged side of the divide

Demographic Characteristic	Community Participants (n = 31)	Comparable Statistic within the U.S.
Age	Mean is 43; in 35-44 age group, none use internet	In 35-44 age group, 39.8% use internet (www.ntia.doc.gov 1999)
Educational Attainment	Mode is high school diploma/ equivalency; 6.45% use internet	Of those with a high school diploma/ equivalency, 20.9% use internet (www.ntia.doc.gov,1999)
Race	100% African-American; 6.45% use internet	Among African-Americans, 19% use internet (www.ntia.doc.gov 1999)
Household Income (US$)	Mode is 15-25,000; 6.45% use internet	Average in PA: 43,742, U.S.: 42,148 (U.S. Census 2001); Of households with income <25,000, 19% use internet (U.S. Census 2001)
Household Type	Mode is married couple with children <18; 6.45% use internet	Among married couples with children <18, 37.6% use internet (www.ntia.doc.gov 1999)

Demographic Characteristic	Community Participants (n = 31)	Comparable Statistic within the U.S.
Geographic Location	Chester, PA USA population is 39,000; has neither DSL nor cable modem	Towns with population <10,000, <5% have DSL or cable modem; Cities with population >100,000, 56% have DSL; Cities with population >250,000, >65% have cable modem (U.S. Department of Commerce 2000)

4.1. Participants

Participant characteristics are presented in Table 2. Of the 60 community members who voluntarily began the program, 31 met the requirements set forth by the Technology Committee to receive a Participation Certificate. To qualify, the participant was required to attend at least 19 of the 22 classes.

Table 2: Characteristics of the community participants

Demographic Characteristic	Community Participants (n = 31)
Age	Range: 13-65 years of age Mean: 43
Sex	Male: 32.3% Female: 67.7%
Educational Attainment	Mode: 74.2% High school diploma
Race	African American: 100%
Employed	Overall: 58.1%
Household Income	Mode: US$15-25,000
Household Type	Mode: 38.7% Married with children

4.2. Internet access, computer skills, and e-Government inclusion

Keys to bridging the divide are home internet access (Keller 2001) and successful learning of computing skills (DiMaio et al., 2002 and Holmes 2002). The key for increasing use of government websites is public internet access at a nominal cost or no cost (Prattipati 2003). A case study of Singapore's success in providing e-Government reinforces the necessity for internet access at home and education programs to enhance computer literacy and awareness of e-Government (Wei and Ke, 2004).

The WP Tenants' Association Office in the community centre was equipped with five stand-alone 486s at the time the training program was planned, providing access to PCs by community members, but no internet connection. There were no public libraries in Chester, however, the Crozer Library, a private, non-profit corporation stated it would "soon offer computers with internet access" (www.chestercity.com 2000). Within the Chester/Upland school district, computer labs, with internet connections, were installed within the prior year, but use was not fully integrated within the curriculum. Neither cybercafés nor DSL or cable modem service are available within Chester. When the training program began, two dial-up modems competed for use of the only phone line in the Community Centre office. Internet access was obtained through Kmart's then free BlueLight.com. Thus, internet connectivity was limited, slow, and sometimes unavailable due to overwhelming demand for BlueLight.com.

To promote home internet access, participants fulfilling the requirements of the training program received free refurbished PCs to take home. The PCs provided may have lacked modems, and internet connectivity in homes remains unsupported. However, 7.1% of 158 households in the WP housing development received PCs, some with the potential for internet connectivity, compared to the previous none.

Participants were asked to rate their computer experience. As shown in Table 3, 24 (77.4%) rated themselves as beginners (described as no experience or games only) before the training program. After training, the majority no longer perceived themselves to be beginners, with only 6 (19.4%) rating themselves at this level.

Table 3: Community participants' self-assessment of computer experience

Computer Experience	Community Participants (n = 31)			
	Before Training		After Training	
	Frequency	Percent	Frequency	Percent
Beginner	24	77.4	6	19.4
Intermediate	2	6.5	5.14	45.2
Advanced	5	16.1	11	35.5

4.3. e-Government users

Equipped with access and computer skills, the community participants freely visited websites. Of the 31 participants, 19 (61.3%) reported to have visited a government website. Table 4 compares the characteristics of these participants with all 31 community participants.

Table 4: Comparison of community participant visitors to government websites with all community participants

Demographic Characteristic	Respondent Type			
	Community Participant Visitors to Government Websites (n = 19)		All Community Participants (n = 31)	
	Frequency	Percent	Frequency	Percent
Household Income (US$)				
Below 15,000	5	26.3%	11	35.5%
15-25,000	6	31.6%	9	29.0%
25-35,000	4	21.1%	6	19.4%
35-45,000	2	10.5%	3	9.7%
Over 45,000	1	5.3%	1	3.2%
Missing value	1	5.3%	1	3.2%
Age				
Under 18	3	15.8%	3	9.7%
18-29	5	26.3%	5	16.1%
30-44	4	21.1%	7	22.6%
45-64	7	36.8%	15	48.4%
65+	0	0%	1	3.2%
Educational Attainment				
No High School	1	5.3%	1	3.2%
Some High School	1	5.3%	2	6.5%
High School Equivalency	3	15.8%	5	16.1%
High School Diploma	14	73.7%	23	74.2%
Race:				
African-American	19	100%	31	100%
Household Type				
Single	4	21.1%	5	16.1%
Single with children	6	31.6%	9	29.0%
Divorced with children	1	5.3%	5	16.1%
Married with children	8	42.1%	12	38.7%
Geographic Location-				
Urban	19	100%	31	100%
No significant difference between groups.				

No significant difference was found between participants reporting government website visitation and no government website visitation. Contrasting government website users with general internet users, a study examining how citizens contact government websites reported government website users were more likely to have higher income levels, be more educated, and younger than general internet users (Thomas and Streib 2003). These users were also more likely to be white, but no difference was present for urban contrasted with rural residents. Internet use in general was found to increase with income and education, but decrease with advancing age. Further, use is higher among whites compared to non-whites and higher among urban dwellers than rural residents.

4.3.1. *Government website visitation*

The nearly two-thirds of participants reporting government website visitation is surprisingly high compared with the general population. For example, Thomas and Streib (2003) found 37.8% of 459 respondents reported visiting a website in the last 12 months. This same study examined reasons for visiting government websites, stating "Web contacts seem likely to be prompted by a relatively specific need, and they seem more likely to come from those who have greater stakes and greater interests in government" (Thomas and Streib 2003, p. 86).

As previously discussed, the residents of the WP Housing Development have been involved in a long-standing acrimonious relationship with local government. For example, the request to use space in their own community centre for the training program, unused except to store trash cans, was stiffly opposed and denied repeatedly by the CHA. Interestingly, these negative experiences motivated participants to visit the website for the city of Chester and the CHA. Participants, engaged as a group, were observed gathering around one PC to visit these websites. The visit was experienced as a group.

However, no participant indicated the intent to visit a government website again, indicating the visit was for one purpose, obtaining information, and occurred as a part of group interaction. Although the participants' experience with local government was negative, a previous study investigating citizen attitudes and federal e-Government use found no significant relationship between the two (West 2004). Specifically, views of trust in government, confidence in government, or belief that government is effective at solving problems and helping people were not significantly related to visiting federal government websites.

4.3.2. *Computer experience and government website awareness*

A significant relationship between computer experience and awareness of government websites was found. As shown in Table 5, Pearson Chi-Square is 15.353, significant at the .05 level. This significant relationship is consistent with findings from a previous study addressing attitude toward participation in e-Government (Charbaji and Mikdashi 2003). This previous study however, examined the unidirectional causal relationship of awareness preceding knowledge of the internet, but the population surveyed were all experienced users having used the internet for an average period of 2.5 years. The participants in this study represent those on the disadvantaged side of the divide. Thus, computer experience was first gained through the Training Program, providing participants with an understanding of the internet and websites. The unidirectional causal relationship of computer experience as a predictor of the number of government websites of which a participant is aware is significant, with a Somers' d value of .342, significant at the .05 level (see Table 5).

Table 5: Cross tabulation of computer experience with government website awareness

		Number of Websites Aware				Row
		0	1	2	3	Totals
	Beginner	n=2 p=.14	n=2 p=.5	n=2 p=.18	n=0 p=00	n=6 p=.19
Computer Experience	Intermediate	n=10 p=.71	n=2 p=.5	n=2 p=.18	n=0 p=00	n=14 p=.45
	Advanced	n=2 p=.14	n=0 p=00	n=7 p=.64	n=2 p=1	n=11 p=.35
	Total	n=14 p=.45	n=4 p=.13	n=11 p=.35	n=2 p=.07	n=31
Pearson Chi-Square = 15.353, significant at the .05 level with a low cell count						
Somers' d = .342 for Computer Experience as the dependent variable, significant at the .05 level						

4.3.3. *Computer experience and government website visitation*

Computer experience was found to be a significant predictor of government website visitation, as shown in Table 6 by the Somers' d value of .395, significant at the .01 level. This finding is consistent with previous studies. For example, Charbaji and Mikdashi (2003) found knowledge in using the internet to be a significant predictor of e-Government use.

Table 6: Cross tabulation of computer experience with government website visitation

		Visited Web site		
		Did not	Did	Row Totals
Computer Experience	Beginner	n=3 p=.25	n=3 p=.16	n=6 p=.19
	Intermediate	n=9 p=.75	n=5 p=.26	n=14 p=.45
	Advanced	n=0 p=00	n=11 p=.58	n=11 p=.35
	Total	n=12 p=.39	n=19 p=.61	n=31
Pearson Chi-Square = 11.130, significant at the .01 level with a low cell count				
Somers' d = .395 for Computer Experience as the dependent variable, significant at the .01 level				

4.3.4. *Computer experience and government website visitation*

Computer experience was found to be a significant predictor of government website visitation, as shown in Table 6 by the Somers' d value of .395, significant at the .01 level. This finding is consistent with previous studies. For example, Charbaji and Mikdashi (2003) found knowledge in using the internet to be a significant predictor of e-Government use.

4.3.5. *Government website awareness and visitation*

As shown in Table 7, government website visitation can be predicted from the number of websites of which the participant is aware, as indicated by Somers' d of .596, significant at the .01 level. This finding is consistent with previous studies. For example, Charbaji and Mikdashi (2003) found awareness leads to participation in e-Government. All participants who visited a government website were able to list at least one site when asked to name specific websites of which they are aware. Participants identified those of the City of Chester and the CHA. Only the two youngest participants, aged 13 and 16, named and visited a third website, the Southeastern Pennsylvania Transportation Authority (SEPTA), the regional public transit authority for Philadelphia and the surrounding areas.

Table 7: Cross tabulation of government website awareness with website visitation

		Visited Website		
		Did not	Did	Row Totals
Number of Websites Aware	0	n=11 p=.92	n=3 p=.16	n=14 p=.45
	1	n=1 p=.08	n=3 p=.16	n=4 p=.13
	2	n=0 p=00	n=11 p=.58	n=11 p=.35
	3	n=0 p=.00	n=2 p=.11	n=2 p=.06
	Total	n=12 p=.39	n=19 p=.61	n=31
Pearson Chi-Square = 17.904, significant at the .01 level with a low cell count				
Somers' d = .596 for Number of Websites Aware as the dependent variable, significant at the .01 level				

5. Lessons learned

This case study was intended to provide insight into e-Government inclusion of those on the disadvantaged side of the digital divide. Removal of barriers that exclude individuals from participating in the digital age is a prerequisite to e-Government inclusion. The application of the assets-based community development model (Kretzmann and McKnight 1993) as a community organizing strategy enables the identification of community needs. In this case, internet access and training in computing skills was necessary in order that actual computer use be realized. This computer experience led to government website awareness and visitation. The first visit may be encouraged by group activity devoted to a specific or compelling reason. This insight is consistent with the finding that e-Government be not only technically accessible, but usable and engaging (Donnelly and Merrick, 2003).

Continuation of internet use within the community is challenging. Only two PCs are equipped with modems at the community centre computer lab. The 31 PCs, awarded to those who successfully completed the training program, may have lacked modems and no formal technical support is provided. Internet access is attained through use of a free dial-up internet access service, which is not consistently available. Sustaining momentum in internet use requires motivated community members dedicated to continuing the community organizing strategy with the goal of community self-sufficiency.

Participants overwhelmingly expressed gratitude for the opportunity to participate in the training program, as such opportunities were perceived as lacking. Designed with and for the community, the program provided ownership and an environment conducive to learning. However, participants recognized the necessity to persevere in the struggle to overcome external threats to the community initiative, including isolation from mainstream society, a culture of failure, and exploitive dependency by those ostensibly trying to make improvements. By forming links and partnerships with those external to the community, such as neighborhood institutions, employers, and developers, the external threats may be reduced.

While first-time government website visitation was surprisingly high among the community participants, the intent to continue use was lacking. One-time use did not foster e-Government inclusiveness among the techno-disadvantaged. The community itself was able to begin building an environment enabling internet access and use through a community organizing strategy. The community reached out to form links and partnerships with external entities to work toward achieving its goals of attaining internet access and associated training. Sustained use remains a challenge due to external threats to the community. This suggests the necessity for public outreach, on the part of governmental and other organizations, to encourage e-Government inclusion among those previously excluded.

References

Althoff, Susanne (2004) "Point, Click, Elect Should Voting Be That Easy?" Boston Globe, Boston (MA), March 7, p. 26.

Benbasat, I., Goldstein, D.K., and Mead, M. (1987) "The Case Research Strategy in Studies of Information Systems," MIS Quarterly, Vol 11, No. 3, pp 369-386.

Brief of Amicus Curiae of Chamber of Commerce of the United States of America, National Black Chamber of Commerce, Inc., and Pennsylvania Chamber of Business and Industry in Support of Petitioners, (1998) Seif (No. 97-1620) available in Chester Residents Concerned For Quality Living v. Seif, 132 F.3d 925 C.A.3 (Pa.), WL457676.

Brookes, Robert, (2004) "Slipping Through the Net? A Study of the Effectiveness of Current UK Policy Regarding Public Access to Information Communications Technology," Proceedings of the 4th European Conference on E-Government, June, Trinity College Dublin, Ireland, pp. 91-98.

Charbaji, A. and T. Mikdashi (2003) "A Path Analytic Study of the Attitude Toward E-Government in Lebanon," Corporate Governance, Vol 3, No. 1, pp 76-82.

Clements v. City of Chester (1990), 1990 WL 92523, E.D.Pa.,1990, June 28, 1990.

City of Chester (2000) [online], http://www.chestercity.com.

Council of the City of Chester (1994) "Chester City Vision 2000, Comprehensive Plan & Economic Development Strategy."

Digital Opportunity Taskforce (2001) "Genoa Plan of Action," Digital Opportunities for All: Meeting the Challenge, May 11, [online], http://www.dotforce.org/reports.

DiMaio, A., Baum, C., and Keller, B. (2002) "Five Truths and Five Myths to Cross the Digital Divide," Gartner Research Note (TG-14-3578) February 1.

Donnelly, V. and Merrick, R. (2003) "Community Portals through Communitization," Proceedings of the ACM Conference on Universal Usability, Vancouver, British Columbia, Canada, 9-14.

Galliers, R.D. (1992) "Choosing Information Systems Research Approaches," in Robert D. Galliers (ed.) Information Systems Research: Issues, Methods, and Practical Guidelines, Alfred Waller Ltd., Henley-on-Thames, pp 144-162.

Goodman, M. D. and Brenner, S. W. (2002) "The Emerging Consensus on Criminal Conduct in Cyberspace," UCLA Journal of Law and Technology, Vol 3.

Hasson, J. (2004) "E-Gov Act signed into law," Federal Computer Week, 28 February 2004, [online], http://www.fcw.com/fcw/articles/2002/1216/web-egov-12-17-02.asp.

Holmes, T.E. (2002) "Crossing the Digital Divide," Black Enterprise, April, pp 51.

Keller, B. (2001) "Best Practices for Overcoming the Digital Divide," Gartner Research Note, (COM-13-3435) April 10.

Kretzmann, J. and McKnight, J.P. (1993) Building Communities from the Inside Out, ACTA Publications, Chicago.

Lamb, J. (2004) "Epublic: Access: A personal map of cyberspace," The Guardian, Manchester (UK), March 24, p 9.

Larsen, M.A., and Myers, M.D. (1997) "BPR Success or Failure? A Business Process Reengineering Project in the Financial Services Industry," Proceedings of the Eighteenth International Conference on Information Systems, pp 367-382.

Marchionini, G., Samet, H., and Brandt, L. (2003) "Digital Government," Communications of the ACM, Vol 46, No. 1, pp 24-27.

Miles, M.B. and Huberman, A.M. (1994) Qualitative Data Analysis, Sage Publications, Thousand Oaks.
Myers, M.D. (2003) "Qualitative Research in Information Systems," [online], MISQ Discovery, March 18, http://www.qual.auckland.ac.nz.
Novak, T. and D. Hoffman (2000). Bridging the Digital Divide: The Internet of Race on Computer Access and Internet Use, (http://elab.vanderbilt.edu/research/papers/html/manuscripts/race/science.html).
OECD (Organization for Economic Co-operation and Development) (2001) "Understanding the Digital Divide," [online], http://www.oecd.org/dataoecd/38/57/1888451.pdf.
PR Newswire (2000) "Congress Seeks to Bridge Gap between Tech Haves and Have Nots; Legislation Aimed at Inner Cities, Rural America, 13 New Co-Sponsors Join Bills Bridging Digital Divide Possible," September 12.
Prattipati, S. N. (2003) "Adoption of e-Governance: Differences between countries in the use of online government services," Journal of American Academy of Business, Vol 3, Issue 1/2, p 386.
Rubin, H. J. and Rubin, I.S. (1995) Qualitative Interviewing: The Art of Hearing Data, Sage Publications, London.
Seville European Council (2002) "eEurope 2005: An information society for all, Executive summary," [online], http://europa.eu.int/information_society/eeurope/2002/news_library/documents/eeurope2005/execsum_en.pdf, June 2002, Last update: 25/09/2003.
Silverman, D. (1993) Interpreting Qualitative Date: Methods for Analyzing Talk, Text, and Interaction, Sage Publications, London.
Sipior, J.C., Ward, B.T., Volonino, L., Marzec, J.Z. (2004) "A Community Initiative that Diminished the Digital Divide," Communications of the AIS, Vol 13, Article 5, January, pp 29-56.
Symonds, M. (2000) "Government and the Internet: Digital Democracy," The Economist, June 24, p. not available.
Thomas, J.C. and Streib, G. (2003) "The New Face of Government: Citizen-Initiated Contacts in the Era of E-Government," Journal of Public Administration Research and Theory, Vol 13, No. 1, pp 83-102.
U.S. Census (2001) [online], http://www.census.gov.
U.S. Department of Commerce (1999) "Falling Through the Net: Defining the Digital Divide," November, [online], http://www.ntia.doc.gov/ntiahome/digitaldivide
U.S. Department of Commerce (2000) "National Telecommunications and Information Administration and United States Department of Agriculture – Rural Utility Service, Advanced Telecommunications in Rural America: The Challenge of Bringing Broadband Service to All Americans," April, [online], http://www.ntia.doc.gov/reports/ruralbb42600.pdf
Wei , K.K. and Ke, W. (2004) "Successful e-Government in Singapore," Communications of the ACM, Vol 47, No. 6, pp 95-99.

West, D.M. (2004) "E-Government and the Transformation of Service Delivery and Citizen Attitudes," Public Administration Review, Vol 64, No. 1, Jan/Feb, pp 15-27.

Wilhelm, A.G. and Thierer, A.D. (2000) "Should Americans Be Concerned about the Digital Divide," Insight on the News, Vol 16, No. 33. September 4, p. not available.

William Penn Tenants Association (WPTA) (1999) "Preliminary Development Plan," December.

Worsham, J.B.L. (2000) "Disparate Impact Lawsuits Under Title VI, Section 602: Can A Legal Tool Build Environmental Justice?" Boston College Environmental Affairs Law Review Vol 27, No. 631.

Adoption of e-government Initiatives in Developing Countries: Exploring Citizen Issues in Tanzania

Jim Yonazi, Henk Sol and Albert Boonstra
University of Groningen, The Netherlands
Originally published in EJEG (2010) Volume 8 Issue 2.

This case is a study at the level of national strategy. Jim Yonazi, Henk Sol and Albert Boonstra present a case study of e-government adoption in Tanzania and highlight some of the specific challenges faced by that country. There have, the authors note, been only a small number of studies of e-government in Tanzania to date. There is a need for many more. In this study, they look at three organisations, the National Examinations Council, the Tanzanian Revenue Authority and the Ministry of Finance and Economic Affairs and identify five key factors which may explain take-up namely organizational preparedness, citizen preparedness, services intrinsic issues, access infrastructure and organizational context. This study is of value at several levels, not least because it adopts an alternative to the TAM approach discussed by Jaeger and Matteson.

Abstract: Adoption plays an important role in the success of e-government initiatives. Low adoption, particularly by citizens, indicates inadequate utilization and rejection of the initiatives by the intended users. This may lead to failure of e-government initiatives. This is particularly important in the context of developing countries such as Tanzania where e-government is a newly imported innovation. It is therefore imperative to understand and proactively consider issues underlying citizen adoption of e-government initiatives in that context. This study is aimed at identifying issues underlying adoption of e-government initiatives in Tanzania, a typical developing country. The results are important for designing, deploying, and evaluating the initiatives in the country. In this paper, we present research results concerning issues influencing adoption of e-government initiatives by citizens in Tanzania. Using the case study approach as our strategy, we investigated the adoption of three government organisations. We found that the adoption of e-government initiatives in Tanzania is determined by (1) perceived organisational preparedness (2) citizen preparedness (3) service intrinsic issues, (4) access limitations, and (5) organisational context. We perceive that it is possible to achieve a higher degree of citizen adoption of e-government initiatives in Tanzania. However, the government need appropriate strategies to overcome challenges posed by the issues identified in this study.

Keywords: e-government, Tanzania, adoption, Africa, developing countries

1. Introduction

Adoption is an important aspect for the success of e-government initiatives in developing countries. High adoption of the initiatives increases the chance that e-government will facilitate social and economic benefits to citizens (Margetts, 2006). However, designing citizen adoptable e-government initiatives is still a challenge to many developing countries' governments. This is because successful implementation of adoptable e-government initiatives in that context requires complex customisation between technology and implementation context in developing countries (Heeks, 2006). In addition, implementation of adoptable e-government initiatives requires structural, procedural, cultural, and attitudinal change in the governments (Scholl, 2006). Such changes are difficult and resource intensive. Accordingly, government in developing countries are still experimenting between automation and adjustments of government processes, and delivery of citizen adoptable initiatives (ibid). Consequently, e-government initiatives are implemented with less emphasis on citizen adoption possibilities.

Existing theories provide useful insights concerning citizen adoption of e-government initiatives. However, they also emphasize and predict different and varied determinants of e-government adoption, mainly from the developed countries perspective. For instance, Jeyaraj, Rottman & Lacity (2006) and Sabherwal, Jeyaraj, & Chowa (2006) identify 45 and 121 different empirical adoption studies respectively. In addition Kamal (2006) presents a list of 40 issues possible to influence e-government adoption. Consequently, governments and e-government practitioners in developing countries are left on a trial-and-error situation on how to approach e-government adoption. This may lead to uninformed prioritisation, and contextualisation when designing and implementing e-government initiatives. Such a situation may result in e-government initiatives which are less likely to be adopted by citizens, hence failure of the initiatives.

2. Background: E-government in Tanzania

Tanzania is an example of a typical developing country (World Bank, 2009). E-government implementation in Tanzania resembles that of many other developing countries. In 2008 Tanzania had an e-readiness index of 0.2929 (UN, 2008). Various e-government initiatives have been implemented in the country. They include the establishment of the Government Network Centre intended to house the central government ICT node. Other reported initiatives include training of 3000+ government officials, purchasing and installing ICT equipments, networks, and software, implementation of internal government systems (Sawe, 2007). In addition, individual government organizations have been implementing initiatives based on their organizational priorities and budgets.

Adoption of e-government initiatives is equally important to Tanzania. However, limited studies have been identified to have empirically studied e-government adoption in Tanzania. The closest studies are those of Kaaya, (2004) and Mgaya (1999), and Yonazi, et al. (2008). While Kaaya (ibid) investigated the implementation of e-government in East Africa, Mgaya (ibid) examined the adoption of Group Support Systems in the government. Yonazi, et al. (ibid) explored general adoption issues. None of the studies cited established reasons underlying citizens' decisions towards the adoption of specific e–Government in Tanzania. As a result the understanding of the adoption situation and the actual issues influencing the uptake of specific e-government initiatives in the country is still limited.

The preceding discussion highlights an important deficiency in theory and practice. Empirical studies on e-government and e-government adoption in Tanzania are still rare. As a result the literature does not provide information concerning adoption issues relevant to Tanzania. This suggests that the current initiatives have been implemented with inadequate understanding of issues that determine their adoption. This situation needs to be addressed. Otherwise, e-government initiatives may fail and cause severe loss of tax payers' and sponsors' scarce resources. In this study we aimed at investigating issues influencing the adoption of e-government initiatives in Tanzania. We focused on initiatives that may involve the exchange of information between citizens and the government of Tanzania, i.e. citizen-focused initiatives.

3. Method

3.1. Strategy

We focused on establishing the issues underlying citizens' adoption of specific e-government initiatives in Tanzania. This would allow us to understand the situation and issues related to the adoption of e-government initiatives in Tanzania. To achieve this, we studied the adoption of e-government initiatives at a government institution level. This is where e-government initiatives are designed, deployed, adopted and evaluated. Such an environment comprised of the implementers (government institutions) and expected adaptors (citizens) of e-government initiatives provided us with an appropriate application environment for this study. Accordingly, we found that the case study approach was relevant to facilitate our study and we approached our investigation inductively (Yin, 2003). This approach is relevant when answering the 'how' and 'why' questions. It is also useful when investigators have little control over events, and when the focus is on contemporary phenomena within some real-life context (ibid). This description fits well with the nature and purpose of our study in this phase for three main reasons: 1) we wanted to understand how the current adoption situation of e-Government initiatives by citizens is in Tanzania, 2) we aimed at establishing why the situation is the way it is, and 2) our study concerned a new innovation (e-Government) in the public sector. Accordingly, we had a limited control on various issue influencing variables (e.g. government activities, respondents, and attitude towards e-Government). Therefore, we found that the case study approach was relevant to facilitate our study.

3.2. Case selection

The choice of case organizations was based on the objective of the study. We wanted to establish issues underlying citizens' adoption of e-government services in Tanzania. However, Tanzania is a unitary republic comprising Tanzania mainland and Zanzibar. Thus, it was necessary that we choose central government organisations because they cover both sides of the union (Tanzania Mainland and Zanzibar). We especially focused on organisations with experience of providing some services to citizens by means of a website. Three organisations (Table 1) granted access to us. We investigated factors influencing their adoption by citizens in Tanzania.

Table 1: Case study organisations

S/N	Organization	e-government initiative
1	National Examinations Council of Tanzania (NECTA)	Online provision of secondary school and teachers colleges examination results
2	Tanzania Revenue Authority (TRA)	Online provision of tax related information
3	Ministry of Finance and Economic Affairs (MoFEA)	Online provision of finance related information and reports

3.2.1. *NECTA*

NECTA is a government body established in 1973 by the Parliament Act No 21 of 1973 (URT, 1973). The organization is responsible for formulating, conducting and regulating examinations in Tanzania. NECTA deals with all examinations, from primary and secondary schools to other professional examinations, including teacher college examinations. We observed that the NECTA website received a seasonal high utilization degree (Table 2).

Table 2: NECTA Usage Statistics

Month	Monthly totals					
	Sites	Kbytes	Visits	Pages	Files	Hits
Aug-08	3224	4016353	12638	85150	219632	369507
Jul-08	4870	5337949	20288	119423	347169	558349
Jun-08	5746	6280011	21655	142491	357186	588527
May-08	12,744	55,850,399	191,683	1,865,029	3,281,508	5,320,417
Apr-08	8929	7381280	28315	176047	420194	742332
Mar-08	4190	3498524	8640	62316	139284	234788
Totals		82,364,516	283,219	2,450,456	4,764,973	7,813,920

Source: NECTA, 17 August, 2008 (Generated by Webalizer Version 2.01)

This utilization takes place only during the announcement of examination results. The website experiences a low utilization degree in other periods, for example during exam registration and results-slip seeking.

3.2.2. *TRA*

TRA is a central government revenue body established in 1995. The organization is responsible for assessing and collecting specified revenue, and administering and enforcing the tax related to government revenue (URT, 2006). The degree of utilisation of the TRA website was established by analysing the web counter figures, and the discussion with the management and other stakeholders. In April 2008, the web counter (installed in November 2007) had registered about 60,000 visits. On 1st, 22nd, and 24th July, we recorded the web counter at 97,825, 100,124, and 102,653 respectively. We hence interpreted this situation as indicating low adoption.

3.2.3. *MoFEA*

The degree of utilization of the website was established by analysing the web-hits of the top most visited WebPages (Table 3). This information was also discussed with the management and the other stakeholders during interviews and FGDs respectively (Appendix 11.B). Table 3 shows that the landing page (about the Ministry) was the most visited webpage since the launching of the website in 2006. It had recorded 13,556 hits by 11th Sept, 2008. Both management and user respondents perceived that such figures indicate a low degree of utilisation of the website for a period of 2 years.

Table 3: MoFEA - 10 Most Accessed Webpages (2006-2008)

S/N	Title Page	Page impression
	About the Ministry	13556
	Regular News	11133
	Human Resource Management	10680
	Budget	8914
	Millennium Challenge Account - Tanzania	8245
	Advertisements	6874
	Revenue & Taxation Policy	6037
	Structure of MoFEA	5230
	Central-Local Government Finances	4715
	Government pensioners	4714

Source: MoFEA, 11th September, 2008 (Generated by Webalizer Version 2.01)

3.3. Data collection instruments

We needed information that could inform us of potential issues to explain adoption of the selected e-government initiatives. Accordingly, we sought information from the case organisations and their stakeholders. Specific information sources were officers and customers of the organisations, and other documentary evidence. Managers and customers provided us with experiences, opinions, and actions that pointed to adoption issues. Documentary cases informed us of recorded evidence. Table 4 provides a summary of the tools used per each case.

Table 4: Summary of data collection tools used per case

Technique	NECTA	TRA	MoFEA	Total
Interviews	16	11	7	34
Focus Group Discussions	8	5	7	20
Observation reports	2	2	1	5
Internal workshop	1	-	-	1
Web statistics report	1	1	1	3
Internal documents Analysed	5	5	5	15
Newspapers analysed	26	-	-	26
Stakeholders workshops	-	-	-	3

4. Results

Data were analysed qualitatively (Straus & Corbin, 1990). During open coding we generated an initial code list to highlight key issues. However, whenever we encountered a fresh idea, a new code was assigned to it. This coding practise was useful because it allowed us to enrich our initial understanding through revelation of new insights from the cases. Axial and focused coding involved scrutinizing the codes and categories to establish their relationship with the adoption of e-Government. Memos were then written to explain the resulting categories and the relationship with the adoption phenomenon. Whenever a concept was encountered and needed clarification, a follow-up interview, mainly over the phone, was initiated and clarification sought.

We identified five potential key issues to explain citizen adoption the three e-government initiatives in Tanzania. They are organisational preparedness, citizen preparedness, services intrinsic issues, access infrastructure, and organisational context (Table 5). We present each of the issues and their supporting evidences from coding in Appendix 1. We denote the codes in a form of X.Y where X stand for the first latter of the organisation and Y for code number. E.g. N2 means code number 2 from NECTA code list.

Table 5: Adoption issues from cases

Issue	Subcategories	Codes
Organisational preparedness	Organisational wide buy-in	N9-13; T13-16; M9-10
	Adequacy of internal processing machinery	N14-16; T17-19; M11
Citizens preparedness	Need for ICT skills	N3-4; T4-5; M4-5
	Financial affordance	N1, T1-2, M2
	Service awareness	N2; T3; M4
	Preference for face to face	N5; T6; M7-8
	Age	M3
Services intrinsic issues	Information characteristics	N17-23; T21-25; M13-17
	Website characteristics	N26-29; T31-34; M21-22
	General service characteristics	N24-25; T26-30; M18-20
	Fit in the Union	N30; T20; M23
Adequacy of Access Infrastructure	Adequacy of ICT Networks	N6; T7-8; M1
	Availability of ICT equipment	N7; T9-10
Organisational context	Limit of responsibility	N8; T11; M12
	Nature of the organisation	N9; T12

4.1. Organisational preparedness

Organisational preparedness relates to the extent to which a government organisation appears to be prepared to serve citizens in a digital fashion. This issue explains citizens' perceptions regarding the extent to which a government organisation appears to be prepared for e-government. It is the result of the citizens' evaluation two key aspects: (1) visible actions and attitudes of people in a respective organisation, and (2) adequacy of internal machinery towards electronic working environment. We provide a cross case analysis of this issue in table 6.

Table 6: Organizational Preparedness across Cases

Subcategory	Similarities	Differences
Organizational buy-in	All the organizations demonstrated considerable internal oriented buy-in of top management	• NECTA's buy-in is centred at the CEO level, but informal and less embraced by low level management • TRA has established a formal administrative buy-in, however less supportive to website based services • MoFEA has a formal internal oriented buy-in, though not embraced organizational wide
Adequacy of internal machinery	Processed, are dominated by the manual paper-based file system and ICT policies are mainly internally oriented Systems are standalone	• NECTA has no written policies • TRA has ICT policies, strategies, and emphasis on internal electronic processing • MoFEA has no ICT policies, but embraces internal electronic practices

We noticed some differences on organisational-buy on and adequacies of internal machinery. However, as shown in table 6 all the organisations indicated similarity in inadequacies in their organisational preparedness towards e-government services provision across cases. Inadequate preparedness is indicated by deficiencies in either management actions and/or internal processing machinery. Adequate preparedness requires strength in both aspects. Citizens' evaluation of the organisational preparedness determines their perceptions on the extent to which the organisation is prepared to serve them electronically. Citizens' perception on inadequate organisational preparedness will result in low adoption of respective e-government initiatives. Adequate preparedness will promote high a degree of adoption of the initiatives.

4.2. Citizen preparedness

Citizen preparedness relates to the extent to which citizens are confident to seek and utilise government electronic services. Citizen preparedness is determined by (1) adequacy of ICT skills (2) financial affordance (3) awareness of existing e-government services, (4) preference for face-to-face communication, and (5) the age of a user. We observed that citizens need to have an adequate level of ICT skills, awareness of existing e-government services, and financial affordance to adopt e-government. In addition, they also need to overcome the limitations of age and cultural preference of for face to face contact in order to be able to communicate digitally with the government. Similarities and differences regarding citizen preparedness are presented in table 7.

Table 7: Citizens' Preparedness

Subcategory	Similarities	Differences
Financial Affordance	Low income is the main obstacle in all of the three cases	• NECTA serves mostly family dependent young students who depend on their guardians to fund their internet access costs • TRA and MoFEA users rely on office facilities and internet cafés. This helps them to avoid financial constraints in accessing websites
Need for ICT skills	Need for ICT, especially computer skills was important across the cases	• NECTA provided mainly the viewing of examination results, this required moderate ICT skills • Searching and downloading information from TRA and MOFEA required more confidence in using ICTs
Awareness of existing services	Apart from general information, other specific services are still unknown	• NECTA website is well known country wide • TRA website is known, but mainly in Dar es Salaam • MoFEA website is less popular especially with ordinary citizens
Preference for face-to-face	Face-to-face communication was observed as preferred in all the cases	-

Specific differences were on the possibility for each target user to mitigate the constraints related to financial costs, and ICT skills levels required to use the websites. While students are required to pay to access NECTA's website, users of TRA and MoFEA websites can access the websites through office facilities. Further, users of NECTA website are young students with reasonable ICT skills and awareness of the electronic services. TRA and MoFEA users are adults with limited ICT skills and awareness of electronic services of the government. However, both users are comfortable with face to face contact with the government.

Citizen preparedness can be used to explain the current level of e-government adoption in Tanzania. Inadequate citizen preparedness is a result of low financial affordance, low ICT skills, high unawareness, and high preference for face-to-face communication. When there is inadequate preparedness, adoption will also be low. This category reveals the importance of various user centred issues that may influence citizens to adopt e-government.

4.3. Perceived services intrinsic issues

From case studies we learned that important services quality elements in Tanzania are (1) information quality, (2) website quality, and (3) generic service quality aspects. Information and website quality relate to content and system quality. Respectively, generic service issues include timely responsiveness, usefulness, and convenience of using government electronic services. Citizens will adopt e-government initiatives which meet and exceed their expectations. They need to perceive that contents, systems, and generic properties (e.g. responsiveness) satisfy their expectations. Otherwise they will opt to seek government services physically. This will result in low adoption of e-government initiatives.

Table 8 provides observations regarding the services issues category across cases.

Table 8: Service Intrinsic Issues

Sub-category	Similarities	Differences
Information characteristics	Information incompleteness Information complexity due to use of English Information obsolescence (outdated) Information usefulness	NECTA provides seasonal information
Website characteristics	Complexity, design, reliability	MoFEA website is searchable
General service characteristics	Poor response to user inquiries The benefit of the nature of the internet (Usefulness/convenience)	-

We observed that the key differences were the seasonality of information on the NECTA website and searchability of the MoFEA website. Otherwise inadequacies of the information, websites, and other general characteristics mentioned above were common across the cases.

The service intrinsic issues category suggests that the deployment of e-government services will require a careful consideration of various general and contextual service related factors. These factors concern properties of the content (e.g. information), and channels through which the content is communicated (container). General issues such as response and the contextual fitting are also important. We observe that low adoption will be contributed to by the low value of information communicated through low value channel.

4.4. Access issues

Access issues refer to ways through which citizens get access to e-government initiatives. Results showed that adequacy of ICT infrastructure and availability equipment for accessing e-government services are necessary. Adequacy of ICT infrastructure concerns the availability and coverage of telecommunication and supporting infrastructure such as electricity and roads. Availability of ICT equipment explains the availability of equipment, especially computers, for accessing e-government. We present the key similarities and differences in table 9.

Table 9: Access Issues

Sub-category	Similarities	Differences
ICT Infrastructure inadequacy	All cases are affected by the current status of inadequate ICT networks of the country	NECTA users rely heavily on cybercafés, while TRA and MoFEA users rely on their organizational facilities
Availability of computers	Computers are available in mainly urban areas, and the majority of the users do not have computer. this is not also a case issue	

Access issues may not necessarily be an organisational level issue. They reflect the infrastructural situation of the country. The inadequate access situation in the country results in low e-government adoption. This will be contributed by the inadequacy of ICT networks and supporting infrastructure, and the unavailability of access to appropriate access equipment. For high adoption the infrastructure situation will need to be improved. Alternatively, mitigation strategies for alternative connectivity (mobile phones, TV, and radio) can be more appropriate to tackle the situation. Otherwise fewer citizens will adopt e-government initiatives.

Inadequacy of access infrastructure plays an important role in the adoption of e-government. Citizens need to have means of accessing electronic services intended for them. With improved access citizens will be encouraged to seek and utilise the electronic services. On the other hand, inadequate access to electronic services will discourage citizens from usingthe services. This may result in to low adoption of e-government initiatives.

4.5. Organisation context

Organisation context relates to the business environment of a government organisation. This issue comprises two categories namely the nature of the organisation and its business, and organisational autonomy. Nature of the organisation suggests that different organisations are perceived differently by the citizens and this influences their adoption of the e-government initiatives. For instance, a website by the army will attract fewer adopters as compared to NECTA website. This is because fewer citizens are attracted to the activities of TRA (Table 10). Contrarily, for NECTA, business activities are generic and are voluntarily sought by many people. Citizens are likely to seek and utilise initiatives by NECTA as compared to the army website. Likewise, initiatives by the Zanzibar Government will attract people differently as compared to those by the Tanzania Government (fit in the Union). Government organisations need to understand that what they are and do influences citizen adoption of their electronic initiatives.

Table 10: Organisation context

Sub-category	Similarities	Differences
Nature of the organization and business	All organisations have their statutory autonomy limitation	NECTA website attracts more people because examination results are mandatory
Organizational autonomy	Computers are available in mainly urban areas, and the majority of the users do not have a computer. This is not also a case issue	

Organisational autonomy was a subtle issue during our investigation. However it emerged as an explanation of the structural limitation on various government organisations. Each government organisation has its own statutory mandate, budget, and limit of authority. Hence, it can only deal with its e-government initiatives that are under its jurisdiction. It is therefore possible to strategize on some aspects but limited on others. For instance, an organisation can be responsible for its organisational preparedness and intrinsic issues of its e-government initiatives. However, it may not be possible for an organisation to deal with citizen preparedness and infrastructural situation of the country. Such issues will require joint efforts of the central government. Likewise an organisation is responsible for the quality of its services (e.g. completeness), but limited on what it can do to improve the ICT skills the citizens.

Organisational context may have an important role in the adoption of e-government. From their statutory nature and the services they offer, government organisations traditionally attract citizens differently. This can be the case in the electronic environment. E-government initiatives by government organisations which attract many citizens in the traditional way, will also receive higher adoption. Likewise, organisations which will successfully overcome their limits of its autonomy may provide services which are more likely to meet user expectations. This may promote adoptions amongst the citizens of Tanzania.

5. Discussion

The results of this study provide us with issues concerning adoption of e-government initiatives at an individual level. In this section we provide our reflection of the results and their implication for the existing body of knowledge. This helps us to highlight key theoretical similarities and differences which emerged in the course of this study.

We found in the literature various factors pointing to the importance of organisational preparedness on the adoption of e-government (Ebrahim & Irani, 2005; Lam, 2005; Moon & Noris, 2005; Seifert, 2003; Titah & Barki, 2006; Tseng *et al*, 2008; Welch & Pandy, 2007, Webber, 2008). We acknowledge the value of these contributions to e-government implementers. Our results differ from them in one important way. Citizens do not have a checklist of factors to help them decide to adopt or reject an e-government initiative. Instead, their adoption decisions are influenced by the extent to which a government organisation appears to be prepared to serve them in electronic fashion. Specifically they evaluate organisational wide buy-in in the actions of senior as well as junior staff of an organisation, and the adequacy of the processing machinery.

Issues related to citizen preparedness issues are also supported by the literature. They include the importance of financial affordance (Seifert & McLoughlin, 2007), ICT skills (Kumar et al, 2007), awareness of existing service (Choudrie & Dwivedi, 2005), face-to-face communication preference (Hart-Teeter, 2003; Mofleh & Wanous, 2008), and age (Thomas & Streib, 2003; Venkantesh et al, 2003). These issues have different importance in different contexts (e.g. Carter & Weerakkody, 2008). Accordingly, researchers present the issues in varied and discrete ways. In this study we provide an overarching category; citizen preparedness. We observe that it is more useful to understand the significance of the preparedness of their citizens. This will help to seek and address specific issues that determine the preparedness in specific contexts.

e-government adoption issues related to service have been widely discussed in the literature and support our findings. Typical examples are usefulness, complexity, dependability, completeness, trustworthiness, up-to-datedness, completeness (Al-Adawi, Yousafzai, & Pallister, 2005; Davis, 1989; Gilbert, Belestrini, Littleboy, 2004; Gupta, et al, 2008; Huang, D'Ambra, Bhalla, 2002; Wangpipatwong, Chutimaskul, Papasratorn, 2005; Warkentin et al, 2002). However, in this study we identified and categorised in relation to the content, container, and generic issues. The content issues refer to the information being offered in electronic form, while the container issues were those related to the system of delivery (website). Generic service characteristics encompass those factors which relate to the mode of delivery; the internet (e.g. usefulness/convenience and responsiveness).

The categorisation of service issues presented above is not new. This approach is similar to that used by Dragulanescu (2002), Parasuraman et al (1991), and Rotrchanakitunuai (2008). However, these theories present service issues in two dimensions only; content and container. Our findings further the existing propositions by suggesting generic issues (e.g. usefulness/convenience and responsiveness). We draw specific attention to contextual importance on the use of Kiswahili to add value to contents of e-government initiatives in Tanzania. These are important contributions in enhancing our understanding of the issues around the services offered in various e-government initiatives.

Findings on the importance of access and the adoption of e-government is also theoretically supported (Reddick, 2008, UN, 2008). This issue is typical to developing countries contexts and Africa in particular (Kalu, 2007, Schuppan, 2008). Although this finding was expected, we were able to categorise specific access issues that contribute to access limitation. We found that inadequacy of ICT and supporting infrastructure, and unavailability of ICT equipments contribute to the low adoption of e-government initiatives. This observation is similar to that of Fuchs and Horak (2008); however our findings differentiate infrastructure limitations from access equipment limitations. In the case of Tanzania, the general country ICT infrastructure is poor. Regardless, organisations should not be hindered from implementing e-government initiatives for citizens. Alternative channels such as mobile phones, TVs, and radios are widely available. E-government initiatives can hence be designed to be delivered and accessed using such equipments. This contribution helps to mitigate general ICT infrastructure challenges and to separate them from constraints.

Organisation context is a new revelation in the e-government debate. That is, the natures of government organisations and their business have an impact on the adoption of its e-government initiatives. Citizens may be attracted differently to use e-government initiatives offered by government organisations with different natures. The main attraction elements are the nature and the business the organisations dealt with. This thinking is yet to be established in the technology and e-government adoption literature. We relate this issue to the extant concept of organisational image (Christensen & Askegaard, 2001, The Economist, 2008). Corporate image influences the customer perceptions concerning a business organisation and its services/products (Gray & Balmer, 1998). Likewise, this is relevant to government organisations and their electronic initiatives. Corporate images may influence citizens' perceptions and adoption decisions to provide e-government initiatives. This finding was also an important contribution from this study.

The influence of organisational autonomy on citizen adoption of e-government initiatives was a new discovery. Currently theoretical propositions related to this issue are still rare. The closest findings we found are those by Gil-Garcia & Pardo, 2005, and EOCD (2003, p.48). This may be because it is not directly related to the wiliness to adopt innovation. However, as we observed, each organisation has a limit of responsibility in relation to its electronic services. This issue is useful for explaining organisation and central government responsibilities in relation to the factors identified in this study. It is hence an important contribution in this study.

6. Conclusion

The objective of this study was to establish potential issues in the adoption of e-government by citizens in Tanzania. We identified five issues; government preparedness, citizen preparedness, services intrinsic issues, access limitations, and organisational context. The findings have implications for e-government adoption research, stakeholders, and for the developing countries. They contribute to the existing general and subject-specific adoption theories by extending and expounding constructs used to explain e-government adoption. This benefits e-government stakeholders in their efforts to implement e-government. The findings may be applied in other developing countries. Therefore, we can suggest that the utilisation of the highlighted issues may benefit other countries provided that contextual issues are considered.

Our results face some important limitations. Firstly, the factors may have causal effects towards each other. In this study we did not investigate that aspect. Secondly, issues such as national administration style may have an impact on citizen adoption. Thirdly, because this study was conducted only in Tanzania, care must be taken in utilizing its conclusions in other contexts. However, they still provide an important starting point as far as citizen adoption of e-government is concerned. They provide initial understanding for designing appropriate approaches for overcoming any resulting and associated e-government adoption challenges in the country.

References

Al-Adawi, Z., Yousafzai, S., Pallister, J. 2005, 'Conceptual Model of Citizens' Adoption of E-government', The Second International Conference on Innovations in Information Technology, Cardiff University, UK.

Carter, L., Weerakkody, V., 2008, 'E-government adoption: A cultural comparison', Journal of Information Systems Front, Vol.10, pp. 473-382

Choudrie, J., Dwivedi, Y., 2005, 'A survey of Citizens' awareness and Adoption of E-government Initiatives, The 'Government Gateway': A United Kingdom Perspective', e-government Workshop '05, Brunel University, UK

Christensen, L. T., Askegaard, S. 2001 'Corporate identity and corporate image revisited: A semiotic perspective', European Journal of Marketing, Vol. 35, No.3 / 4, pp. 292-315

Davis, D. F. 1989, 'Perceived Usefulness, Perceived Ease of Use, and User Acceptance of Information Technology', MIS Quarterly, Vol. 13, No 3, pp. 319-340

Dimitrova D.V., Chen, Y., 2006, 'Profiling the Adopters of E-government Information Services: The Influence of Psychological Characteristics, Civic Mindedness, and Information Channels', Social Science Computer Review, Vol. 24, pp. 172-188

Dragulanescu, N. 2002, 'Website Quality Evaluations: Criteria and Tools', The International Information & Library Review, Vol.34, Issue 3, pp. 247-254

Fuchs, C., Horak, E., 2008, 'Africa and the digital divide', Telematics and Informatics, Vol. 25, pp. 99-116

Gilbert, D., Balestrine, P., Littleboy, D., 2004, 'Barriers and Benefits in the adoption of e-government', International Journal of Public Sector Management, Vol.17, No. 4, pp. 286-301

Gil-Garcia, J.R, Pardo, T.A, 2005, 'E-government success factors: Mapping practical tools to theoretical foundations', Government Information Quarterly, Vol. 22, pp. 187-216

Gray, E. R., Balmer, J. M. T, 1998, 'Managing corporate Image and Corporate Reputation', Long Range Planning, Vol. 31, no. 5, pp.695-702

Gupta B., Dasgupta, S., Gupta, A., 2008, 'Adoption of ICT in a government organization in a developing country: An empirical study', The Journal of Strategic Information Systems, Vol.17, Issue 2

Heeks, R., 2006, Implementing and managing e-government: An international Text, SAGE Publications, London

Huang, W., D'Ambra, J., Bhalla, V., 2002. 'An empirical investigation of the adoption of e-government in Australian citizens: some unexpected research findings.' Journal of Computer Information Systems, Vol. 43, Issue 1, pp 15–22.

Jeyaraj, A., Rottman, J. W., Lacity, M. C., 2006, 'A review of the predictors, linkages, and biases and IT innovation adoption research', Journal of Information Technology, Vol. 21, No. 1, pp. 1–23

Kaaya, J. 2004, 'Implementing e-government Services in East Africa: Assessing Status through Content Analysis of government websites', EJEG, Vol.2, Issue.1

Kalu, K. N., 2007, 'Capacity Building and IT Diffusion: A Comparative Assessment of E-government Environment in Africa' , Social Science Computer Review, Vol.25 No.3, pp 358–371

Kamal, M.M., 2006, 'IT innovation adoption in the government sector: identifying the critical success factors', Journal of Enterprise Information Management, Vol. 19, No. 2

Kumar V., Murkerji B., Butt, I., Persaud A., 2007, 'Factors for Successful e-government adoption: a conceptual Framework', The Electronic Journal of E-government, Vol. 5, Issue 1, PP 63 – 76

Lam, W. 2005, 'Barriers to e-government integration', Journal of Enterprise Information Management, Vol. 18 No.5, pp.511-30

Margetts, H., 2006, 'E-government in Britain—A Decade On', Parliamentary Affairs Vol. 59 No. 2, 250–265

Mgaya, R.B.S 1999, 'Adoption and Diffusion of Group support Systems in Tanzania', PhD Thesis, Delft University of Technology, The Netherlands. Retrieved September 14, 2006, from Connecting-Africa

Mofleh, S.M., Wanous, M., 2008, 'Understanding Factors Influencing Citizens' Adoption of e-government Services in the Developing World: Jordan as a Case Study', retrieved on: 12, March, 2009, from: www.dcc.ufla.br/infocomp/artigos/v7.2/art01.pdf

Moon, M., Norris, D. (2005), 'Does managerial orientation matter? The adoption of reinventing government and e-government at the municipal level', Information Systems Journal, Vol. 15 pp.43-60

Reddick, G.C. 2004, 'Empirical models of E-government Growth in Local Governments', E-Service Journal, Vol. 3. No. 2, pp. 59-84p.63

Sabherwal, R., Jeyaraj, A., Chowa, C., 2006, 'Information System Success: Individual and Organizational Determinants', Management Science, Vol. 52, No. 12, pp. 1849–1864

Sawe, D. 2007, Serikali Mtandao; madhumuni, matatizo, mafanikio, na changamoto, POPSM

Schuppan, T., 2008 'e-government in developing countries: Experiences from sub-Saharan Africa, Government', Information Quarterly, doi:10.1016/j.giq.2008.01.006

Seifert, J.W., McLoughlin, G.J, 2007, 'State E-government Strategies: Identifying Best Practices and Applications', CRS report for Congress, Retrieved on 12th Nov, 2008, from http://www.fas.org/sgp/crs/secrecy/RL34104.pdf

Seifert, W.J. 2003, 'A primer on E-government: Sectors, Stages, Opportunities, and Challenges of Online Governance: Report for Congress', The Library of Congress Retrieved 12 October, 2006 from http://www.fas.org/sgp/crs/RL31057.pdf

The Economist, 2008, The electronic bureaucrat: a special reports on technology and government, The Economist Intelligence unit

Titah, R. and Barki, H. 2006, 'E-government Adoption and Acceptance: A Literature Review,' International Journal of Electronic Government Research, Vol. 2, Issue 3, p.p. 23-57

Thomas, C.J, Streib, G., 2003, 'The new face of Government: Citizen-Initiated contacts in the Era of E-government', Journal of Public Administration and Theory, Vol. 13, No.1 pp. 83-102

Tseng, P.T.Y, Yen , D.C., Hung Y., Wang, N.C.F, 2008, 'To explore managerial issues and their implications on e-government deployment in the public sector: Lessons from Taiwan's Bureau of Foreign Trade', Government Information Quarterly, Vol. 25, pp. 734–756

UN 2008, E-government Survey 2008: From E-government to Connected Governance, United Nations, New York

UN, 2005, Global E-government Readiness Report 2005: From E-government to E-Inclusion, United Nations, New York

UN, 2004, Global E-government Readiness Report 2004: Towards access for Opportunity, United Nations, New York

Wangpipatwong, S., Chutimaskul, W., Papasratorn, B 2005, 'Factors Influencing the Adoption of Thai e-government Websites: information Quality and Systems Quality Approach', Proceedings of the Fourth International Conference on eBusiness, pp. 19-20, Bankok, Thailand

Webber, A., 2005, 'Making e-government Web Sites Usable', Forester, Accessed on 24th November 2008, From BNET

Welch, E.W., Pandy, S., 2007, 'Multiple Measures of Website Effectiveness and their Association with Service Quality in Health and Human Service Agencies', Proceedings of the 40th Hawaii International Conference on System Sciences, accessed on 10th October, 2008, From: http://www.hicss.hawaii.edu/hicss_40/decisionbp/04_07_03.pdf

World Bank, 2009, 'Country Classification', World Bank, Retrieved, November 12th, 2009,From: http://web.worldbank.org/WBSITE/EXTERNAL/DATASTATISTICS/0,,contentMDK:20420458~menuPK:64133156~pagePK:64133150~piPK:64133175~theSitePK:239419,00.html

Yin, RK 2003, Case study research: design and methods, 3rd ED, Sage, Thousand Oaks, CA, USA

Yonazi, J., Sol, H.G., and Boonstra, A., 2008, 'Developing a Framework for Assessing Adaptability of Citizen-Focused e-government Initiatives in developing Countries: the Case of Tanzania; Exploratory Phase Results', 8th European Conference on e-government, Lausanne

Appendix 1: Coding process

Table 1: National examinations Council of Tanzania - coding summary

Code No.	Open coding	Axial Coding	Focused Coding
	Affording to pay-for	Affording to pay-for	Citizens preparedness
	Awareness of the existence of the service	Awareness of the existing services	
	Interest on using ICT	Need for ICT knowledge	
	Need for ICT skills		
	Face-to-face preference	Preference for face-to-face	
	Infrastructure - Inadequacy	Access infrastructure limitations	Inadequacy of access Infrastructure
	Infrastructure - Optimisation of available technology	Lack of computers	
	Impact of external entities	Limit of responsibility	Limit of responsibility
	Nature of the organisation	Nature of the organisation	Nature of the organisation
	Administrative buy-in	Buy in	Perceived organisational preparedness
	Lack of enforcing strategy		
	Need for Mindset change		
	Need for coordinating mechanism		
	Policy inadequacy	Need for supportive policies, procedures and processes	
	Practises, procedures, processes inadequacy		
	Internal status		
	Information incompleteness	Information characteristics	Perceived Service intrinsic issues
	Information complexity		
	Information out datedness		
	Information unreliability		
	Expert - Outdated information		
	Expert - Missing service		
	Usefulness	Information characteristics	Perceived Service intrinsic issues
	Poor Responsiveness	General service issues	
	Privacy concern		
	Website complexity	Website characteristics	
	Website design		
	Website reliability		

Code No.	Open coding	Axial Coding	Focused Coding
	Expert - Poor system design		
	Service - Fit in the union	Fit in the union	

Table 2: Tanzania Revenue Authority - coding summary

Code No	Open coding	Axial Coding	Focused Coding
	Afford to pay for	Affording to pay-for	Citizens Preparedness
	Infrastructure - Cost		
	Awareness of the existence of the service	Awareness of existing services	
	Interest in using ICT	Need for ICT knowledge and skills	
	Need for ICT skills		
	Face-to-face preference	Preference for face-to-face	
	Infrastructure - Inadequacy	Infrastructure Inadequacy	Inadequacy of access Infrastructure
	Infrastructure - Point of access		
	Infrastructure - Optimisation of available technology	Lack of computers	
	Preferred mode of obtaining services		
	Impact of external entities	Impact of external Entities	Limit of responsibility
	Nature/type of the organisation	Nature of business	Nature of business
	Citizen usage by sanctions	Buy in	Perceived Organisational Preparedness
	Administrative buy-in		
	Need for mindset change		
	Need for sanctioning		
	Practices, procedures, processes inadequacy	Need for change in business practices and processe	
	Policy inadequacy		
	Coordinating Mechanism		
	Service - Fit in the union	Union Service issue	Perceived Service intrinsic issues
	Information Completeness	Information characteristics	
	Information complexity		
	information out-datedness		
	information Reliability		
	Expert - Missing service		
	Source of Funding (Service Reliability)	Service issues	

Code No	Open coding	Axial Coding	Focused Coding
	Convenience		
	Responsiveness		
	Trust on technology used		
	Usefulness		
	Expert - Poor website design	Website characteristics	
	Website complexity		
	Poor website design		
	Website reliability		

Table 3: Ministry of Finance and Economic Affaires - code summary

Code No.	Open coding	Axial Coding	Focused Coding
	Infrastructure - Access limitation	Access Limitation	Access infrastructure limitations
	Affording to pay	Affording to pay-for	Citizens preparedness
	Age	Age	
	Awareness of what is available	Awareness of existing services	
	Interest on ICT	Need for ICT knowledge	
	Need for ICT skills		
	Trust on the system (Technology)	Preference for face-to-face	
	Preferring face-to-face		
	Government Buy in	Buy in	Government preparedness
	Need for sanctioning/incentivising		
	Government Practise and policies	Need for supportive Practices and policies	
	Limit of responsibility	Limit of responsibility	Limit of responsibility
	Information reliability	Information characteristics	Perceived service intrinsic issues
	Information completeness		
	Information complexity		
	Poor up-to-datedness		
	Need for Usefulness		
	Use for Convenience	Service issues	
	Usefulness of the internet		
	Poor Responsiveness to enquiries		
	Poor website design	Website characteris-	

Code No.	Open coding	Axial Coding	Focused Coding
	Website reliability	tics	
	Union factor	Union factor	

Public Service Reform through e-Government: a Case Study of 'e-Tax' in Japan

Akemi Takeoka Chatfield
University of Wollongong, New south Wales, Australia
Originally published in EJEG (2009) Volume 7 Issue 2.

Possibly because of language barriers there seems to be relatively little in the e-government literature about what is happening in Japan. Akemi Chatfield uses the case of the electronic taxation system in Japan to explore the relationship between e-government and public service reform on the one hand and government performance on the other. Like everywhere else in the world, Japan's tax system seems to get progressively more complicated to administer with time and the e-Tax system was a significant part of the reform programme. The system has been highly successful and Chatfield concludes that it has delivered major benefits and has had a transformative effect on Japan's National Taxation Agency. However, reflecting on the study she says that two lessons learned from the research were that there is a need both to focus on sophisticated e-government and to give up our belief in the magical power of e-government.

Abstract: There is a growing interest in the debate on whether or not e-government has the transformational impact on government performance, governance, and public service, as we addressed this very issue at the 2007 ECEG. However, e-government research results on the transformational impact are mixed. This may be an apt reflection of either the early stages of e-government development or the newness of e-government research field or both. Our research goal as scholars of e-government must be to penetrate appearances to ascertain whatever lessons and meanings might lie beneath. This paper is an initial attempt toward achieving this goal. The main objective of this paper is to examine the relationship between public service reform through e-government and actual government performance. We achieve this objective through a multi-method approach, including a case study of Japan's National Tax Agency (NTA)`s sophisticated e-government initiative: an integrated "e-Tax" system networking the NTA with local tax offices throughout Japan. The "E-Tax" provides a citizen-centric, online income and other tax returns filing and payment services for individuals and corporations. A preliminary case analysis provides evidence in support of the transformational impact of e-Tax on NTA performance. This paper makes an important contribution to the growing e-government research literature on the transformational impact of e-government particularly on service process reform.

Keywords: transformational impact of e-government, public service reform, electronic tax filing, case study, National Tax Agency, Japan

1. Introduction

E-government refers to the use of information and communication technologies, particularly the Internet, to deliver government information and services (ANOA 2006). National governments worldwide are engaged in public service reform initiatives and e-government initiatives. The two initiatives may run in parallel in some governments with very little overlap or coordination. Alternatively, in others e-government initiatives are means for implementing public service reform policy goals. Japan`s "E-Government Establishment Plan" (CIO Council 2003) is an example. There is a growing interest in the debate on whether or not e-government has the transformational impact on government performance, governance, and public services, as we addressed this very issue at the 2007 ECEG. Here the term "transformational" is used to convey radical change in strategic direction, in contrast to incremental change in day-to-day operational routines. The radical and strategic nature of organizational transformation has been referred to as "the third kind of game change" (Flamholtz and Randle 1998) in change management and "the second-order organizational transformation" (Scholl 2005) in e-government. According to Flamholtz et al., transformational change requires a complete change in strategic direction. The organization fundamentally changes the basic concept of its core business. Similarly, Scholl (2005) defines the second-order organizational transformation as "a discontinuous, radical organizational change involving a paradigmatic shift" by drawing on the work of Levy and Merry (1986). The new concepts of "transformational government" (UK HM Government 2007; Irani et al. 2007) may signal the emergence of this discontinuous, radical transformational change intent of public administrations to move, from bureaucracies and the traditional government-centric public service "silos" that are often ineffective and inefficient in creating new value (Bannister 2001), towards citizen-centric public services and policy outcomes through the transformational impact of e-government to meet the demands of continually changing, globalized society.

While the radical and strategic kind of organizational transformation holds the promise of the highest-level return (Flamholtz and Randle 1998), achieving organizational transformation of bureaucracy through e-government is highly risky and complex because of internal stakeholder buy-in and commitment required from policy makers, management, and public servants. In the case of tax administration reform through e-government, the level of risk and complexity further increases because of the imperative of gaining external stakeholder trust in government and ensuring voluntary adoption of the Internet channel and effective use of new software tools before the public administration can achieve the potential transformational impact of e-government and realize the desired policy outcomes. Given the high-level risk and complexity involved in realizing public service reform through e-government, therefore, it is not surprising to find that e-government research results on the transformational impact are mixed (Scholl 2005). However, this may be an apt reflection of either the early stages of e-government development or the newness of e-government research field or both. Our research goal as scholars of e-government must be to penetrate appearances to ascertain whatever lessons and meanings might lie beneath. This paper is an initial attempt towards achieving this goal. The main objective of this paper is to examine the relationship between public service reform through e-government and actual government performance. Our research strategy for achieving this objective includes a case study of Japan's National Tax Agency (NTA) and its core e-government initiative: "e-Tax" – an online income tax returns filing and payment services for individuals and corporations. Like other nations' e-tax filing systems, Japan's "e-Tax" is an add-on self-service option through the Internet channel. This new channel choice is made available to citizens and corporations, not as a substitute, but as a complement to extant ways of fulfilling national tax law compliance. By offering this channel choice, NTA intended to transform the bureaucratic tax public administration into a modern, citizen-centric "service" organization, regain citizen trust, and achieve the policy outcomes – better tax law compliance in the globalized industrial nation of ageing population (NTA 2007). Since "e-Tax" adoption is voluntary and also requires considerable switching costs (e.g. obtaining digital signature for taxpayer authentification and learning new software tools), citizen adoption of "e-Tax" can be viewed as evidence that citizens perceive "e-Tax" channel choice as superior, with respect to extracting value from NTA, to the traditional (e.g. paper-based tax filing and face-to-face and phone consultation) tax services. A preliminary case analysis provides evidence in support of the transformational impact of "e-Tax" on NTA performance and public services. This paper makes an important contribution to the growing e-government research literature on the transformational impact of e-government particularly on service process reform.

The remainder of this paper is organized as follows. Section 2 presents a literature review of e-government research on the transformational impact of e-government. Section 3 describes the case study background on Japan's National Tax Agency (NTA) and tax administration reforms. Section 4 discusses the agency's tax service reform through "e-Tax". Section 5 discusses transformational impacts of "e-Tax" on agency performance and public service delivery. Section 6 presents the conclusion on the transformational impact of e-government and future research directions.

1.1. Transformational impact of e-government

While the concepts of public administration reform are not new at all in government research and practice (e.g., Light 2006), the new ideas such as public service quality and government responsiveness to the public (Teicher et al. 2002) and IT-enabled public service reform are relatively new and emerging in government policy and multi-disciplinary research.

1.2. Mixed research findings on the transformational impact of e-government

Against the explicit transformational intent articulated in the US "E-Government Strategy" (Executive office of the President of the United States 2002) and the UK "Transformational Government enabled by Technology" (Cabinet Office 2005; UK HM Government 2007), extant research findings on the transformational impact of e-government are mixed. Scholl (2005, p. 1) concludes: "While one group of e-Gov researchers emphasizes the transformational impact of e-Gov on the business of government, others have squarely questioned this assertion."

On the one hand, positive research findings support the transformational impact of e-government. Sophisticated e-government services such as IRS's eFiling and Ireland`s Revenue Online Service initiatives produced the positive impacts on improving public service quality (Bird and Oldman 2000; O`Donnell et al. 2003) and restoring public trust (Moon 2003). Similarly, advanced functionalities of e-government such as transaction, transparency, and interactivity directly impacted perceived public satisfaction with e-government service and indirectly impacted public trust (Welch et al. 2004). In his review of the literature on the transformational impact of e-government, Scholl (2005, p. 1) concluded: "e-Gov, at least in the short term, has the capacity to transform the business of government in mode rather than in nature." On the other hand, research results failed to find evidence for the transformational impact of e-government. West (2004, p. 24) concludes that "evidence from this research is consistent with incremental rather than transformational change". Based on the two local e-government surveys in the U.S., Norris and Moon (2005) also reported very few transformational impacts at the local government level. Despite their seemingly negative conclusions, however, the authors suggest future conditions under which the transformational impact of e-government may be plausible. For example, West concludes (p. 24): "Few government Web sites have progressed to the fully integrated and executable online service delivery or interactive democracy stages. ... For government agencies to realize the transformational power of the Internet, officials need to rely on models that emphasize integration, functionality and democracy enhancement." Similarly, Norris and Moon (2005, p. 64) conclude that "the movement toward integrated and transactional e-government is progressing much more slowly" in comparison to the progress made by local governments so far in providing less sophisticated and largely informational e-government. Their conclusion on the slow progress of sophisticated e-government still remains valid in light of 2007 global e-government survey findings. In the survey of 1,687 government websites in 198 different nations, only 28 percent of government websites provide transactional capabilities, which did not change much from the previous year (West 2007).

One plausible reason for the mixed findings is the general lack of sophisticated e-government developments for new and different ways to provide improved public services that make a difference to the public and hence create value from e-government investments. This suggests the urgent need for e-government research on exploring transformational impact from sophisticated e-government development initiatives that offer advanced capabilities such as transaction, transparency, and interactivity.

2. Research questions

According to West (2004), public buy-in of the transformational impact of e-government requires evidence of:

- Major improvements in government performance
- Information technology (IT) use in government is responsible for the improvement.
- This research aims to address the transformational impact of e-government by exploring links between public service reform through e-government and actual government performance. In this research paper we raise two questions:
- What are major transformational improvements in government performance?
- To what extent is e-government responsible for the transformational change?
- To address these questions we adopt a multi-method approach which is necessary to understand the complexity of the social and political processes (Scholl 2005): a case study of Japan's tax administration service reform through e-government, a web site analysis, and a content analysis of government policy statements and central Government meeting minutes (in Japanese) which were collected through Japan`s e-government portal: "www.e-gov.go.jp".

3. National Tax Agency and tax administration reforms

The central Government's push for e-government has seen many e-government initiatives being launched by the Japanese Government Ministries and Agencies. This section describes Japan's National Tax Agency (NTA) and its historical tax service reforms. The next section 4 discusses the NTA's e-government initiative, "e-Tax".

3.1. Background

As part of the post-war structural reform of government, NTA was founded in 1949 as the Ministry of Finance's operating agency for centralized management and control of national tax administration. A 2003 NTA planning document outlines standards and guidelines on NTA's tax administrative tasks and performance evaluation (NTA 2004). According to this document, the NTA needs to create "favourable environments for taxpayers" that promote effective and efficient tax administration. The NTA performance depends on creating the favourable tax environments which are defined by the following organizational capabilities to:

- Provide taxpayers with accurate information of the laws and administrative procedures related to filing self-assessment tax returns and paying taxes;
- Answer promptly and consistently taxpayers' inquiries;
- Obtain broad cooperation and participation of the public in fulfilling their tax compliance.

The organizational structure of NTA consisted of the head office, 11 regional taxation bureaus and 497 local tax offices at the inception. Over the years, this structure remains unchanged, except a slight increase of local tax offices to 518 (NTA 2007). However, the number of the NTA employees has been sharply reduced from Fiscal 2004 to Fiscal 2006, which is due to the central Government's 2001 reform policy including government downsizing. Figure 1 shows this downsizing trend of NTA.

3.2. Historical tax service reforms

At the inception, the NTA was required to introduce a radical tax administration reform to control the rapid inflation in the after-war Japan. The adoption of a US style self-assessment system, however, created an unexpected level of confusion among small and medium-sized enterprises which lacked sufficient knowledge of accounting and taxation. In consequence, about 70 per cent of taxpayers were subjected to correction or determination for non-filing or under-filing of income tax returns (Usui 2002). The bureaucratic and inefficient responses in handling the public confusion and administrative problems further contributed to taxpayers' distrust of the tax administration agency.

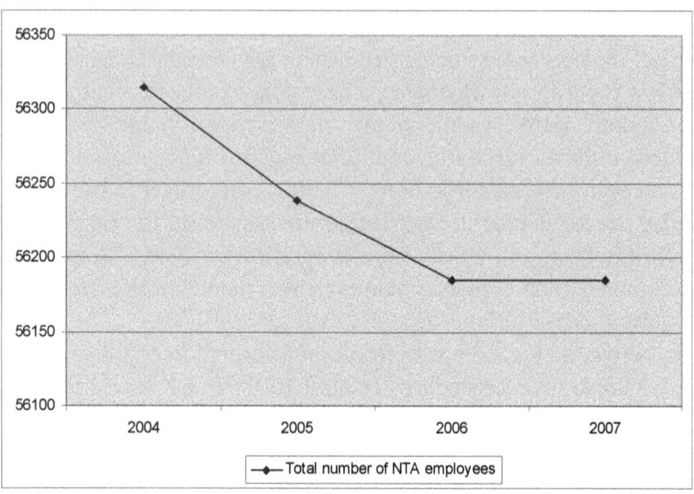

Figure 1: Recent trend for NTA downsizing

The NTA decided to introduce a new "tax consultation" method, which remains in use until recently (NTA 2007). This new method was intended to provide a platform for the consultation services necessary for taxpayers to file their returns voluntarily and correctly. The typical procedures based on the new method involve the following steps: 1) Tax officers request business income earners to visit a NTA office at an appointed date and time; 2) Tax officers answer taxpayers' questions about accounting procedure or tax laws. The latter visit the office with their accounting books and records to calculate their income; 3) If taxpayers ask, tax officers instruct them on how to fill in the return form or fill in the form on their behalf (Usui 2002). The idea behind this new tax consultation method was to eliminate government influence and taxpayer dependence on the NTA by encouraging taxpayer self-service in filing income tax returns. While the new tax consultation method was intended to increase self-service, it required taxpayers to visit the NTA local offices for consultation, often multiple visits, to file their national income tax returns. Because the new tax consultation method is time-consuming and taxpayers are required to wait in a long queue, taxpayer compliance costs are considerable, particularly for business owners of small and medium size enterprises which dominate the Japanese private sector economy. In consequence, as the number of income tax returns filings and other tax forms filings increased with the economic growth over the years, the NTA tax administration efficiency was increasingly challenged.

3.3. Increasing tax administration workload

In Fiscal 2007, the NTA collected ¥53.5 trillion in national tax revenue, which represents 64.5% of Japan's ¥82.9 trillion national revenue, (NTA 2007). This contrasts to ¥43.8 trillion in national tax revenue in Fiscal 2002 (NTA 2002). With the increased national tax revenue collection, the number of income tax returns filed by individuals and corporations increased. The total number of returns continues to rise from 11 million in 1978, nearly 18 million at the beginning of the 1990s, 20.4 million in 2000, and 24.49 million in 2007 (Usui 2002; Okada 2002; NTA 2007). This increasing tax administration workload problem was made worse with the recent NTA downsizing trend discussed earlier in Section 3.1.

The problem of the increasing tax administration workload was particularly serious in suburban tax offices adjacent to large cities. With the growing number of taxpayers visiting local tax offices for consultation, taxpayers frequently had to wait for hours to receive the services. With the increasing number of income tax returns filed in the first half of the 1990s, there was considerable concern among senior administrators about "an explosion of taxpayer complaints concerning this congestion". In consequence, addressing this central problem became the most critical issue of income tax administration (Usui 2002, p. 18). This concern led to a comprehensive review of administrative reform to tax consultation. The initial solution was to replace the individual "face-to-face" method with the "group consultation" method for tax consultation. Most recently, however, the concern led to e-government development: an integrated online self-service tax return filings and payment through the Internet channel. Hence, "e-Tax" was launched in 2004 nationwide.

4. e-Tax

The NTA's transactional website through "e-Tax" is a prime example of the Japanese public service reform efforts through e-government. Its software development outsourcing cost government ¥50 billion (NTA 2007). "E-Tax" is intended to radically improve tax administration efficiency in both back office tax record management and front-line tax consultation and to significantly reduce the public's tax compliance costs: the dual benefits for both internal (NTA tax administrators and front-line tax consultants) and external stakeholders (taxpayers). Jiro Makino, the NTA Comissioner, presents the case for e-government-enabled tax service reform in his 2007 report to taxpayers (NTA 2007, p. 29): "In order to provide more convenient services for the public and manage administrative operations in more simplified, efficient, advanced and transparent manners by utilizing IT in the civil services and reviewing administrative operations and systems, the "E-Government Establishment Plan" was determined in July 2003. Since then, the Japanese Government as a whole has been working on IT-based civil service reforms to provide better and more convenient civil services."

4.1. NTA's transactional website

The central Government operates the whole-of-government web portal (www.e-gov.go.jp) as the primary, convenient, one-stop entry point to government online information and services to the public.

According to the UN 2008 survey of global national e-governments, Japan ranks 11th in global "e-readiness" among a total of 192 member nations (United Nations 2008). This recent global rank signals a marked improvement in the Japanese Government's IT use in providing sophisticated e-government services across many Ministries and Agencies.

Taxpayers can access the NTA home page (Figure 2) from the central Government web portal with one mouse click (or one page down from the portal). On the left-hand side of Figure 2 there is a column of main menus including "e-Tax" (the last menu choice and highlighted in a different shade). In the middle of the home page, there is a list of several tax news and topics. On the right-hand side, the public can access the NTA performance audit reports, annual reports, public comments, agency information and statistics as well as national tax laws and new e-government laws.

Figure 2: NTA home page (in Japanese)

The public can access the "e-Tax" page (Figure 3) which is one page down from the NTA home page (Figure 2). Through "e-Tax" the public can access online transactional functions: registering "e-Tax" use, preparing individual and corporate income tax returns online, obtaining map-based property valuation online through a geographical information system (GIS), and paying all types of taxes online through direct links to taxpayers' online banks. The NTA's transactional website with advanced "e-Tax" functions is meant that taxpayers can fulfil their national tax obligations anywhere and anytime at their convenience without visiting and waiting in a long queue at a NTA local office. For those who do not have their own computer, the NTA provides PCs and touch screens at local tax offices.

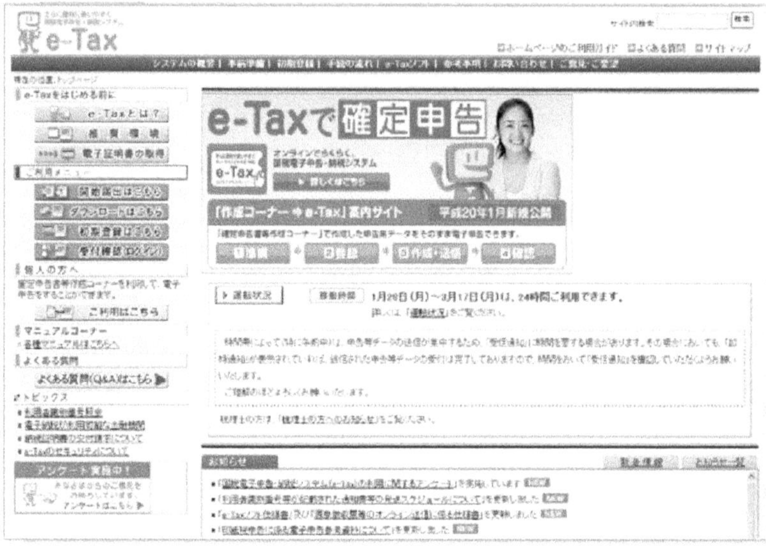

Figure 3: "e-Tax" page (in Japanese)

4.2. Online "e-Tax" returns filing and payment workflow

National tax data contain sensitive personal and financial information. Any security breach will have negative impacts on the credibility of tax administration and public information privacy rights. So the NTA requires taxpayers to comply the NTA security standards, including the purchase of a taxpayer authentification system (cost about ¥3,000) and digital signature (see "prior procedures" in Figure 4 below). In consequence, taxpayers without sufficient computer literacy and Internet efficacy find it intimidating to start using "e-Tax". Moreover, there is a not-so-trivial learning curve in getting used to the use of "e-Tax" software. Hence, switching costs – costs incurred a taxpayer from switching from the traditional ways of fulfilling tax laws compliance to this new Internet-enabled tax filing and payment method – are considerably high for many taxpayers. In fact, despite the central Government push for "e-Tax" adoption and diffusion, only 15 of the 144 Diet members (policy makers) used "e-Tax" in their personal income tax returns filing and payment (The Japan Times 2007). Figure 5 shows the online e-Tax returns filing workflow among the "e-Tax" user, NTA employees, and Financial Institutions over the Internet.

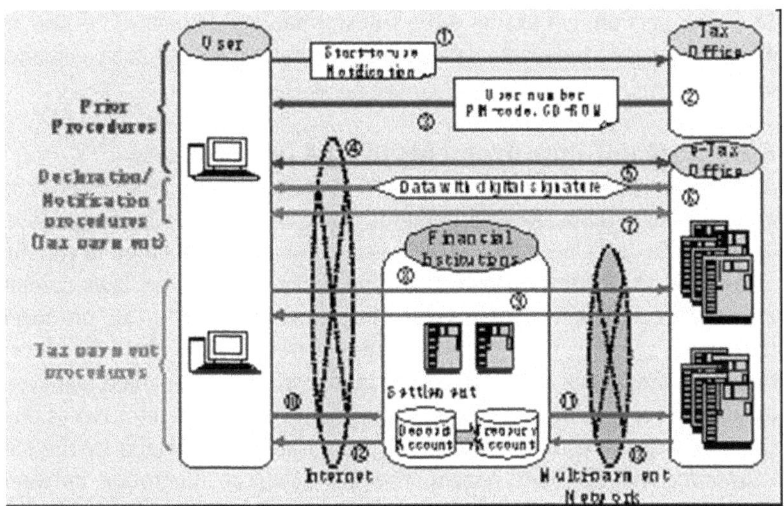

Figure 4: e-Tax workflow adopted from NTA (2005)

The data transferred through "e-Tax" with digital signature are processed and managed by the NTA Comprehensive Information Management System (known as KSK system). This internal tax record processing system was introduced in some local offices in 1995, evolved into a vertically and horizontally integrated enterprise record management system, and was fully operational nationwide in 2001. The KSK system links all Regional Taxation Bureaus, Okinawa Regional Taxation Office and the NTA head office. It enables authorized front-line tax consultants to view taxpayers' income tax returns and tax payment records online during tax consultation sessions as well as for the purpose of tax audit.

5. Transformational impacts of "e-Tax"

As discussed earlier in Section 2.2, the case for the transformational impact of e-government requires evidence of:

- Major improvements in government performance
- IT use in government is responsible for the improvement (West, 2004).

So in this section, we examine the transformational impact of "e-Tax" by evaluating case study data to determine whether or not such evidence exists.

5.1. Major improvements in NTA performance

As discussed earlier in this paper, the NTA's performance depends on "creating the favourable tax environments". The NTA tried to achieve this by launching "e-Tax". With the "e-Tax" system use, the NTA aimed to simplify extant tax administration processes and make national tax laws compliance more convenient. The successful implementation of "e-Tax" produced two major benefits: (1) reduced tax administration costs and (2) reduced taxpayer compliance costs. Firstly, the launch of "e-Tax" enabled taxpayers to submit income tax returns and tax payment through the Internet as digital data, which are then transferred, processed and managed by the KSK knowledge management system. The technological integration between the web-based "e-Tax" system and the centralized internal information system enabled to network the NTA tax officers, front-line tax consultants, and taxpayers to share information through digital records rather than paper-based income and other tax forms. In consequence, the NTA could get things done more efficiently with less time. It is noteworthy that the increased pace of the NTA performance was realized in the challenging operational environment. The NTA could keep up with the increased workload with the radically downsized staff. The NTA workload increased over the years. The total number of tax returns filed rapidly increased from 7.3 million income tax returns in 1975 to 23.5 million in 2007. On the other hand, the total number of local tax office employees was downsized from 44,171 in 2004 to 43,870 in 2007. Secondly, the NTA's operational efficiency gains benefitted taxpayers: they received quick response to their tax questions and more consistent tax consultation services across all the local tax offices distributed throughout Japan. The "e-Tax" channel option enabled to reduce the local tax office congestion problem and address the NTA`s central concern about the taxpayer dissatisfaction with the NTA tax services. This is a significant organizational transformation, given the public distrust of the NTA (Section 3.2) with respect to the bureaucracy and inefficiency in responding and engaging citizens (Section 3.3).

5.2. "E-Tax" is responsible for the improvements

Senior managers considered it difficult to achieve the major improvements in performance; namely efficiency gains in tax administration and a paradigmatic shift to the new citizen-centric tax services, without the launch of advanced transactional "e-Tax", particularly under the adverse operational environment they faced. Besides the favourable perception of the NTA senior managers, internal stakeholders of the "e-Tax" initiative, is there other positive or negative evidence for us to conclude that "e-Tax" is or is not responsible for the major improvements in the NTA performance?

The NTA Commissioner, Jiro Makino, was considerably concerned with providing taxpayers with a more convenient tax law compliance environment (NTA 2007). By offering the "e-Tax" channel choice, the NTA intended to transform the bureaucratic tax public administration into a modern, citizen-centric "service" organization, regain citizen trust, and achieve the policy outcomes – better tax law compliance in the globalized industrial nation of ageing population (NTA 2007). Since "e-Tax" adoption is voluntary and also requires considerable switching costs (e.g. obtaining digital signature for taxpayer authentification and learning new software tools), citizen adoption of "e-Tax" can be viewed as evidence that citizens perceive the "e-Tax" channel choice and online self-service option as superior, with respect to extracting value from the NTA tax services, to the traditional tax services (e.g. paper-based tax filing and face-to-face and phone consultation). Therefore, we argue that the increased level of "e-Tax" adoption can be considered as positive evidence for the NTA performance improvement in achieving better tax laws compliance online through e-Tax. Furthermore, unlike the US, the UK, Ireland, and Australia, the NTA did not provide "e-Tax" users with any other incentives than convenience: neither fast track processing nor quick tax refund (Ministry of Finance, 2007). Hence, the voluntary citizen adoption of the "e-Tax" option is used in this paper to assess the role of e-government in achieving the transformational change in public administration performance. Figure 5 shows a trend in the "e-Tax" adoption data from 2003 to 2007, showing the number of income tax returns filed by "e-Tax" users. "E-Tax" was piloted in Nagoya city in 2004 and rolled out nationwide only three months of piloting. It was operational on the NTA home page since 2004. According to CIO and IT project teams, the initial "e-Tax" software system went through many continuous revisions and changes to reflect the user feedback and suggestions. The use of quality circles encouraged active engagement of the internal IT project teams as well as some power users. In 2006, less than two years since the launch of "e-Tax", the number of tax returns filed through "e-Tax" was 1,057,153. In 2007, after three years since the launch, the number of "e-Tax" filings reached over 1.6 million. This initial stage of rapid diffusion compares favourably against the reported poor take-up of e-tax systems in advanced e-government nations such as the UK (Kablenet 2007). However, the NTA needs to promote take-up of "e-Tax" more effectively given the number of NTA website access has been steadily increasing, reaching almost 11 million visitors during the tax period (Figure 6) and far exceeds the number of "e-Tax" return filers (Figure 5).

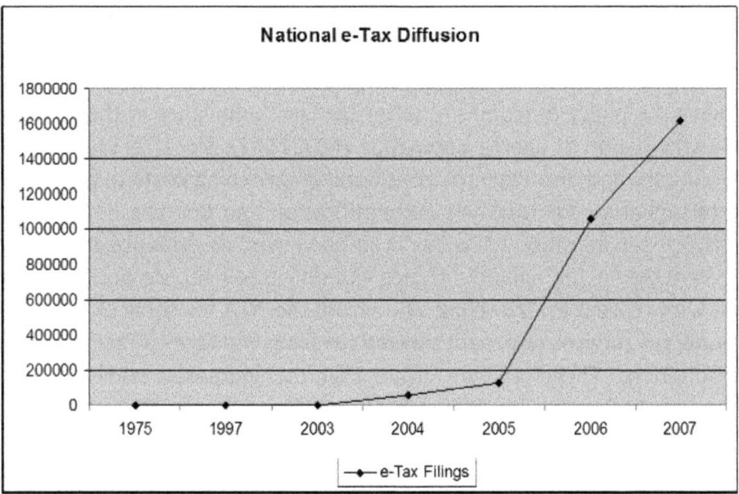

Figure 5: National e-Tax diffusion

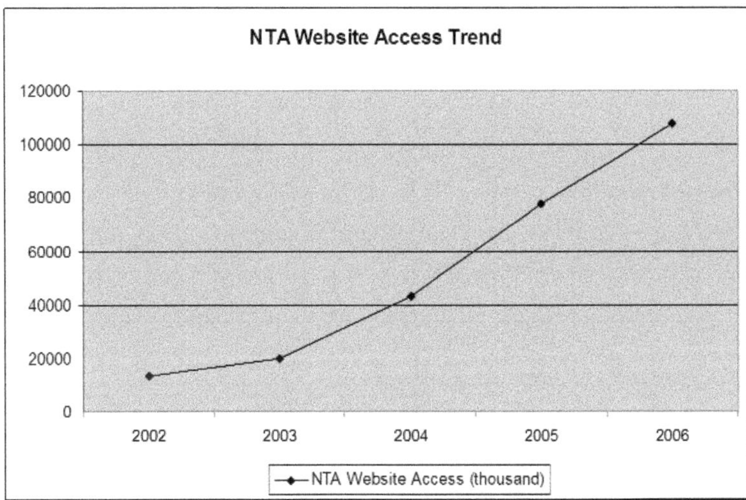

Figure 6: NTA website access trend

Finally, to assess the overall transformational impact of e-government we examine time series of the number of final tax returns filed by individuals. Figure 7 below shows the number of final individual income tax returns and individual income tax plus consumption tax filed by individuals from 1967 to 2006. The longitudinal data do not separate income tax filed using "e-Tax" but instead include all means of tax filing available to the public: "e-Tax" through the NTA website, touch screens installed in local branch offices, telephones, mobile phone devices, and paper forms. The two line graphs in Figure 7 show some overall increases in both individual income tax and consumption tax filings (wide line) and individual income tax filings (narrow line) from 1967 to 2004. However, after 2004 when e-Tax was first launched through the NTA website, a very sharp increase is observed in the number of final tax returns filed by individuals in 2004. This is true for individual income tax as well as for individual tax plus consumption tax. These sharp increases after 2004 provide evidence that the NTA's e-government initiative through "e-Tax" had transformational impacts on organizational performance and improved taxpayer compliance in filing income tax returns and other tax obligations. In other words, "e-Tax" had a significant impact on the agency's public service reform goal of "creating a favourable national tax administration environment" that makes tax filing and tax payment more convenient to the public.

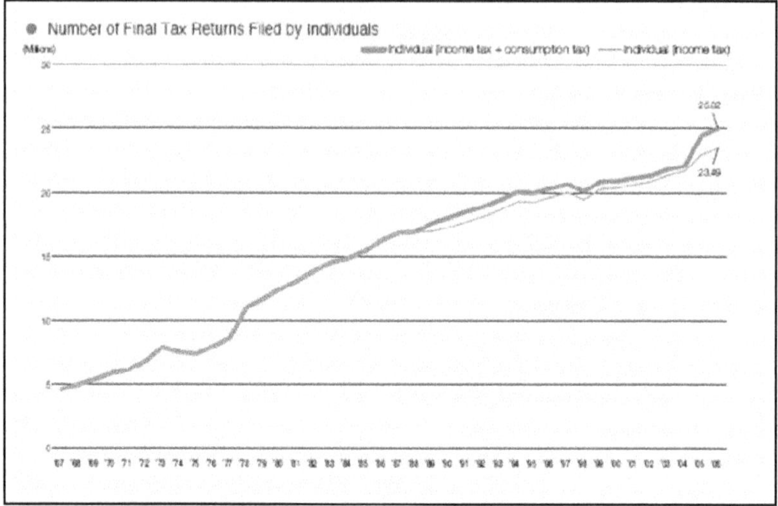

Figure 7: A trend of final tax returns by individuals

6. Discussion and conclusion

This paper examined the transformational impact of e-government by exploring links between public service reform through e-government and actual government performance using the case study of "e-Tax" initiative launched in 2004 by Japan's National Tax Agency. Though cautionary, this study concludes that "e-Tax" had the two major transformational impacts on the government agency performance. The NTA through "e-Tax" reduced tax administration costs internally and reduced tax laws compliance costs by providing the new, convenient, faster, and improved public services. We argue that it is difficult to achieve the observed major improvements in NTA performance without the successful implementation of the integrated, sophisticated "e-Tax" system and the high-level, voluntary citizen adoption of the "e-Tax" system.

In light of the findings of this study, we conclude that due to the relative newness of e-government research field we have paid insufficient attention to two necessary conditions that may explain the mixed findings on the transformational impact of e-government. The two conditions are: the need to focus more on sophisticated e-government and the need to give up our belief in the magical power of e-government.

6.1. Sophisticated e-government

Firstly, sophisticated e-government development is necessary for the transformational impact of e-government to occur. In other words, government will not transform public service quality and responsiveness with the current provision of informational government websites. In discussing the transformational power of e-government, West (2004, p. 24) concludes that "evidence from this research is consistent with incremental rather than transformational change". However, the author also concludes (p. 24): "Few government Web sites have progressed to the fully integrated and executable online service delivery or interactive democracy stages. ... For government agencies to realize the transformational power of the Internet, officials need to rely on models that emphasize integration, functionality and democracy enhancement." Based on the two local e-government surveys in the U.S., Norris and Moon (2005) report very few transformational impacts of e-government at the local government level. However, they also conclude that "the movement toward integrated and transactional e-government is progressing much more slowly" (p. 64) in comparison to the progress made by local governments so far in providing less sophisticated and largely informational e-government. In this case study, we described the integrated, sophisticated "e-Tax" system which was designed as software tools for transforming the traditional national tax agency facing the challenging operational environment into a provider of citizen-centric tax administration services. The integrated, sophisticated e-government system enabled the transformation of the NTA as a networked information sharing organization linking all the front-line tax con sultants and back office staff.

6.2. Giving up our belief in the magical power of e-government

Secondly, sophisticated e-government provision by itself is not sufficient to effect public service reform through the use of e-government. The transformational impact of e-government requires mobilizing internal resources particularly people to implement changes through e-government initiatives. Particularly, transformational change in contrast to incremental change requires effective leadership (Rainey and Thompson 2006). In the case of public service reform through e-government, what matters is top management team's strategic intent to transform public services as well as strategic communication of that intent throughout the government organization. In the corporate strategy literature, strategic intent of a senior executive or top management team conveys a clear sense of new future direction to achieve success (Hamel and Prahalad 1989). What is implied here is that strategic intent is a key antecedent of empowering people who actually implement strategy at the grassroots level in the organization. A long-term, integrated, strategic approach to communicating with key stakeholders is another antecedent of empowering people to successfully implement strategic change in the organization (Argenti et al. 2005). Extant e-government research methodology is often limited to an analysis of government websites. However, government's strategic intent to transform public service and strategic communication of strategic intent need an examination beyond the website and indeed require an in-depth analysis of public policies, official government meeting minutes, and leadership behaviours that may shed light on organizational operations, management, and performance. In this paper we adopted a multi-method approach which is necessary to understand the complexity of the social and political processes (Scholl 2005).

This second observation is consistent with the conclusion made by Lynne Markus and Robert Benjamin (1997). In their seminal paper, "The Magic Bullet Theory in IT-enabled Transformation", they explored the difficult reality of realizing IT-enabled transformation within the organization. In their conclusion they underscored the imperative of giving up our blind trust in the magical power of IT in order to successfully implement transformational change. They also conclude: "The hard reality of IT-enabled transformation is that change is everyone's job (p. 55)."

There are some limitations to this research which assessed the transformational impact of e-government on government performance and its public service reform. In this study, we have not addressed the transformational impact of e-government on taxpayers. For example, public satisfaction with "e-Tax" was not explicitly investigated, although the increasing "e-Tax" take-up from 2004 to 2007 can be considered as evidence of public approval for the NTA's public service reform efforts through e-government. Future research is needed to address this limitation through a survey of "e-Tax" users and non-users.

References

Argenti, P., Howell, R. and Beck, K. (2005) "The strategic communication imperative", MIT Sloan Management Review, Vol. 46, No. 3, pp. 83-39.

Australian National Audit Office (ANAO). (2006) Measuring the Efficiency and Effectiveness of E-Government. Audit Report No. 26 2004-2005, Canberra.

Bannister, F. (2001) "Dismantling the silos: Extracting new value from IT investments in public administration", Information Systems Journal, Vol. 11, pp. 65-84.

Bird, R. and Oldman, O. (2000) Improving Taxpayer Service and Facilitating Compliance in Singapore, The World Bank PREM Notes, Public Sector, December, No. 48, pp. 1-4.

Cabinet Office (2005) Transformational Government-Enabled by Technology Strategy Document.

CIO Council. (2003) E-Government Development Plan, [online] http://www.e-gov.go.jp/doc/030717CIO.html (accessed May 13 2004).

Executive Office of the President of the United States. (2002) Implementing the President's Management Agenda for E-Government: E-Government Strategy, [online], http://www.whitehouse.gov /omb/inforeg/egovstrategy.pdf (accessed June 20, 2003)

Flamholtz, E. and Randle, Y. (1998) Changing the Game: Organizational Transformations of the First, Second, and Third Kinds, Oxford University Press, London.

Hamel, G. and Prahalad, C. (1989) "Strategic intent", Harvard Business Review, May-June, pp. 63-76.

Irani, Z., Sahraoui, S., Ozkan, S., Ghoneim, A. and Elliman, T. (2007) "T-Government for benefit realisation", Proceedings of European and Mediterranean Conference on Information Systems 2007 (EMCIS 2007), June 24-26 2007, Polytechnic University of Valencia, Spain www.emcis.org, pp. 1-11.

Kablenet. (2007) "Poor take-up of e-Tax system", 4th December, 2007, [online], http://www.theregister.co.uk/2007/12/04/poor_etax_takeup/print.html. (accessed December 28, 2007)

Levy, A. and Merry, U. (1986) Organizational Transformation: Approaches, Strategies, Theories, Praeger, New York.

Light, P. (2006) "The tides of reform revisited: Patterns in making government work", Public Administrative Review, Vol. 66, No. 1, pp. 6-19.

Ministry of Finance. (2007) Denshiseifu no jitsugen – kokuzei no denshi shinkoku nado (Realizing e-government – NTA's e-Tax and other initiatives), June 2007.

Moon, M. (2003) "Can IT help government to restore public trust? Declining public trust and potential prospects of IT in the public sector", Proceedings of the 36th Hawaii International Conference on System Sciences (HICSS'03).

National Tax Agency (NTA). (2002) National Tax Agency Report, [online], http://www.nta.gov.jp. (accessed May 7, 2007).

National Tax Agency (NTA). (2004) National Tax Agency Report, [online], http://www.nta.gov.jp. (accessed May 7, 2007).

National Tax Agency (NTA). (2007) National Tax Agency Report, [online], http://www.nta.gov.jp. (accessed December 29, 2007).

Norris, D. and Moon, M. (2005) "Advancing e-government at the grassroots: Tortoise or hare?", Public Administration Review, Vol. 65, No. 1, pp. 64-75.

O`Donnell, O., Boyle, R., and Timonen, V. (2003) "Transformational aspects of e-government in Ireland: Issues to be addressed", Electronic Journal of E-Government, http:www.ejeg.com.

Okada, Y. (2002) The Japanese Tax Administration National Tax Agency, Tax and Integration, [online], http://www.iadb.org/INT/Trade/1_english/2_WhatWeDo/Documents/_d_TaxDocs/2002-2003/f_The%20Japanese%20Tax%20Administration.pdf (accessed December 28, 2007)

Rainey, H. and Thompson, J. (2006) "Leadership and the transformation of a major institution: Charles Rossotti and the Internal Revenue Service", Public Administration Review, Vol. 66, No. 4, pp. 596-604.

Scholl, H. (2005) "Organizational transformation through e-government: Myth or reality?", Proceedings of EGOV 2005, pp. 1-11.

Teicher, J., Hughes, O. and Dow, N. (2002) "E-government: A new route to public sector quality", Management Service Quality, Vol. 12, No. 6, pp. 384-393.

The Japan Times. (2007) "Lawmakers shun 50 Billion yen e-Tax system", May 10, 2007, [online], http://www.search.japantimes.co.jp/print/nn20070510a6.html (accessed October 30, 2007).

UK HM Government. (2007) Transformational Government Enabled by Technology, [online], http://www.cio.gov.uk/documents/pdf/transgov/transgov-strategy.pdf (accessed December 28, 2007).

United Nations (2008) UN E-Government Survey 2008 From E-Government to Connected Governance, [online], http://unpan1.un.org/intradoc/groups/public/documents/UN/UNPAN028607.pfd (accessed January 20, 2008).

Usui, N. (2002) Penetration of the Self-Assessment System for Income Tax: Half-a-Century's Experience in Post-war Japan, Tax and Integration, [online], http://www.iadb.org/INT/Trade/1_english/2_WhatWeDo/Documents/d_TaxDocs/2002-2003/h_Self% 20 Assessment%20in%20Japan.pdf (accessed December 28, 2007).

Welch, E., Hinnant, C. and Moon, M. (2004) "Linking citizen satisfaction with e-government and trust in government", Journal of Public Administration Research and Theory, Vol. 15, No. 3, pp. 371-391.

West, D. (2004) "E-government and the transformation of service delivery and citizen attitudes", Public Administration Review, Vol. 64, No. 1, pp. 15-27.

West, D. (2007) Global E-Government, 2007, Taubman Center for Public Policy, Brown University, [online], http://www.InsidePolitics.org/egovtdata.html (accessed October 25, 2007).

www.ingramcontent.com/pod-product-compliance
Ingram Content Group UK Ltd.
Pitfield, Milton Keynes, MK11 3LW, UK
UKHW021052270726
13967UKWH00012B/577